GW01086134

Blood and Honor:
THE HISTORY OF THE 12th SS PANZER DIVISION "HITLER YOUTH," 1943-1945

by
Craig W.H. Luther, Ph.D.

1st EDITION

COPYRIGHT 1987
by
CRAIG W.H. LUTHER

ISBN No. 0-912138-38-6

Printed in the United States of America

Designed
by
Roger James Bender

Type Set
by
Perez Productions

All rights reserved. This book, or parts thereof, may not be reproduced in any form without permission of the author or publisher.

R. JAMES BENDER PUBLISHING
P.O. Box 23456, San Jose, Calif. 95153 (408) 225-5777

TABLE OF CONTENTS

To the memory of my beloved grandfather
William Henry Hedegaard
A brave and stalwart Dane who, in 1918, fought with the 89th U.S. Infantry
Division at St. Mihiel and earned a Purple Heart

ABOUT THE AUTHOR

Born in December 1950, Craig W.H. Luther received his B.A. from Claremont McKenna College in 1974 and his M.A. from San Jose State University in 1976. Following a year of research in West Germany on a Fulbright Scholarship (1979-80), he began work on his Ph.D. in Modern European History at the University of California at Santa Barbara–completing the degree in June 1987.

Mr. Luther's publications include several articles on German military history in the British Army Quarterly and Defence Journal and the Balkan Studies Journal.

Since May 1984, Mr. Luther has been employed with the United States Air Force as a civilian historian.

ACKNOWLEDGEMENTS

This manuscript is the culmination of a long labor of love that began in the fall of 1977. There were, however, many times during the past decade when the spirit flagged, when I began to question if I would ever complete this project. Thus, I share with those of you who have been close to me over the years a special feeling of triumph and accomplishment.

To acknowledge the contribution of everyone who has assisted me with this manuscript would hardly be possible. Yet there are certain individuals and institutions without whose graciously given support I could never have completed my work; they deserve special acknowledgement.

Let me thank first professors Joachim Remak, Dmitri Djordjevic, and Lawrence Badash at the University of California Santa Barbara. For their support and careful reading of the manuscript I am grateful. Another scholar who provided critically needed support is Professor Dr. Hans-Adolf Jacobsen of Bonn University, and I thank him sincerely for helping me with research grants to West Germany in 1979-80 and again in 1983. Other individuals worthy of mention are San Jose State Professor Dieter Schulz and Dr. Timothy P. Mulligan. Dr. Schulz gave many hours of his time to help me transcribe a particularly troublesome German document, scribbled almost illegibly in old German script; Dr. Mulligan, employed at the National Archives' Military Archives Division, responded to my many queries in timely fashion, helping me to locate much needed documentation.

Perhaps the most significant contribution to my work was made by the many veterans of the 12th SS Panzer Division "Hitlerjugend," who completed my questionnaires and who graciously consented to interviews in their homes, at Bad Hersfeld, or upon the Normandy battlefields. The insights gleaned from such encounters provide the text with a human dimension that, hopefully, will make my account of the division's history a more compelling one. Specifically, I want to thank Mr. Hubert Meyer, himself author of an impressive work on the Hitler Youth Division, for reading the manuscript and offering many valuable suggestions. Also deserving acknowledgement for their special support are Mr. Heinz Berner, Mr. Hans Siegel, and the late Dr. Willi Kändler. I thank them and all of the veterans of the 12th SS who assisted my efforts. I trust they are aware that I have tried to tell their story as dispassionately and objectively as possible.

Not to be overlooked are the efforts on my behalf by veterans of the 3rd Canadian Infantry Division. These men, via questionnaires, also furnished many insights into the fighting in Normandy in 1944; in addition, they offered useful impressions concerning the fighting qualities of the Hitler Youth

Division–their opponent during much of the Normandy campaign. Although I did not use as much of the material these men provided as I had hoped to use, I am grateful nonetheless for their assistance. Special thanks are due Mr. Dixon Raymond, Mr. Alex Adair, Mr. John Shearer, and Mr. R.R. Dixon.

For believing in me and my project I warmly acknowledge the Fulbright Commission and the German Academic Exchange Service. Without the grants these institutions gave me in 1979-80 and 1983, respectively, I could never have completed this history. My only hope is that these and other academic exchange programs will be expanded in the future, for the opportunities they afford the scholar are priceless.

Finally, I would like to express my appreciation to those institutions whose pertinent documentary holdings formed the basis of my study:

Bundesarchiv-Militärarchiv (Freiburg)
Militärgeschichtliches Forschungsamt (Freiburg)
Berlin Documentation Center (West Berlin)
United States National Archives (Washington, D.C.)
Public Archives of Canada (Ottawa)
Public Record Office (London)

Craig W.H. Luther
Carmichael, California

PUBLISHER'S ACKNOWLEDGEMENTS

The photographic coverage of the 12th SS Hitler Youth Division would have been but a fraction of what is held between the covers of this book without the enthusiastic assistance of many individuals and institutions. The division photographer, Wilfried Woscidlo, warrants our special thanks for making his vast photographic files available for the production of this work. Jost W. Schneider, whose Waffen SS-related photo collection is among the finest in the world, also unselfishly supplied numerous photos for use to choose from. As has been the case in the past, many of our friends also searched their files for photographic support and are listed below with sincere appreciation and thanks.

Institutions:
  Bundesarchiv (Koblenz)
  ECPA
  Imperial War Museum
  The U.S. Army

Individuals:

J.R. Angolia	Tom Pooler
J. Keith Baker	Daniel Rose
Klaus Bartels	Hugh Page Taylor
W. Kretzschmar	Charles W. Zvarich

FOREWORD

Our interest in the history of the Second World War continues unabated. The accounts of that conflict fill publishers' lists, bookstore shelves, library ranges, and private collections. They provide fascination, entertainment, and learning to generations born long after that conflict. Strange.

The historical struggle over interpreting and describing that critical human event has followed several directions, often separated by time and purpose. For the moment the military history field is dominated by the recyclers and stylists. The first group are the masters of current technology. These writers read widely but neither understand nor pursue research. They peruse the standard histories and memoirs while reworking them with the aid of computers and word processors. Their bibliographies include the same titles, their descriptions utilize the same word programs, their organizations demonstrate the same formats. The sole difference is the merchandising through advertising and sensationalism. They depend on emotion, immediacy, and fortune. Their paper is often as cheap as their content.

A second group of current military observers would be the stylists. These are frustrated individuals who cannot find a niche in publishing as novelist, analyst, historian, etc. These people must seek notoriety through descriptive excellence, sudden revelations, or artificial creativity. They lack the professional understanding or the careful training required for creative, important work and put profit above contribution, immediacy above continuity, and form above substance. Their paper has little worth beyond that of the recyclers.

For serious concerns these groups pose major concerns. To do serious research costs time, energy, and treasure. As well the committed scholar often provides the substance for the more superficial colleagues who misuse the material in pursuit of fame and fortune. While one may view this uneven alliance of worker and exploiter sadly, the reality provides a sad proof.

When one adds the awesome SS image to this combustive mixture, the result can be explosive. The SS stands as a preconceived symbol of the past and its members must continuously struggle with that mythology. Few current writers have studied the reality or the circumstances of the SS in the Second World War. The recyclers and stylists prefer generalities and uncertainties to investigation, to comprehension, to reality. They prefer generalization and stereotyping about such symbols.

In this sense Dr. Luther's study provides a refreshing original contribution. He has labored through the source materials, the collected memories of friend and foe, and has carefully evaluated the product. As a result he contributes a balanced, fair evaluation which demonstrates both judgement and understanding. His account describes the immediacy, the appeal, the reality, the horror of human conflict. Young individuals caught up in struggle and emotion must make immediate decisions which history will judge by other standards. They act within that framework and spend their subsequent years with the verdict. Too often we neglect that reality of life.

Dr. Luther's account describes war and the price paid by young men who gave their lives to and for a purpose. One may argue about the validity of that decision and direction but one cannot dispute their commitment, their involvement, or their price. The text provides an enviably researched, carefully considered, and professionally structured account of a division of young men who believed, served, and died for their country.

Let us respect those who did their best within their understanding and circumstances. The Chinese employ a marvelous observation about life: "If you wish to know another man's problems, walk two leagues in his shoes." Dr. Luther has walked those leagues with care and with judgement. We, and history, benefit from his research, awareness and purpose.

Charles Burdick
Los Gatos, California

The late Dr. Willi Kändler, Hubert Meyer and Dr. Luther, south of Caen, in June 1983.

Wenn's etwas gibt, gewalt'ger als das Schicksal,
So ist's der Mut, der's unerschüttert trägt.
(Geibel)

Woscidlo

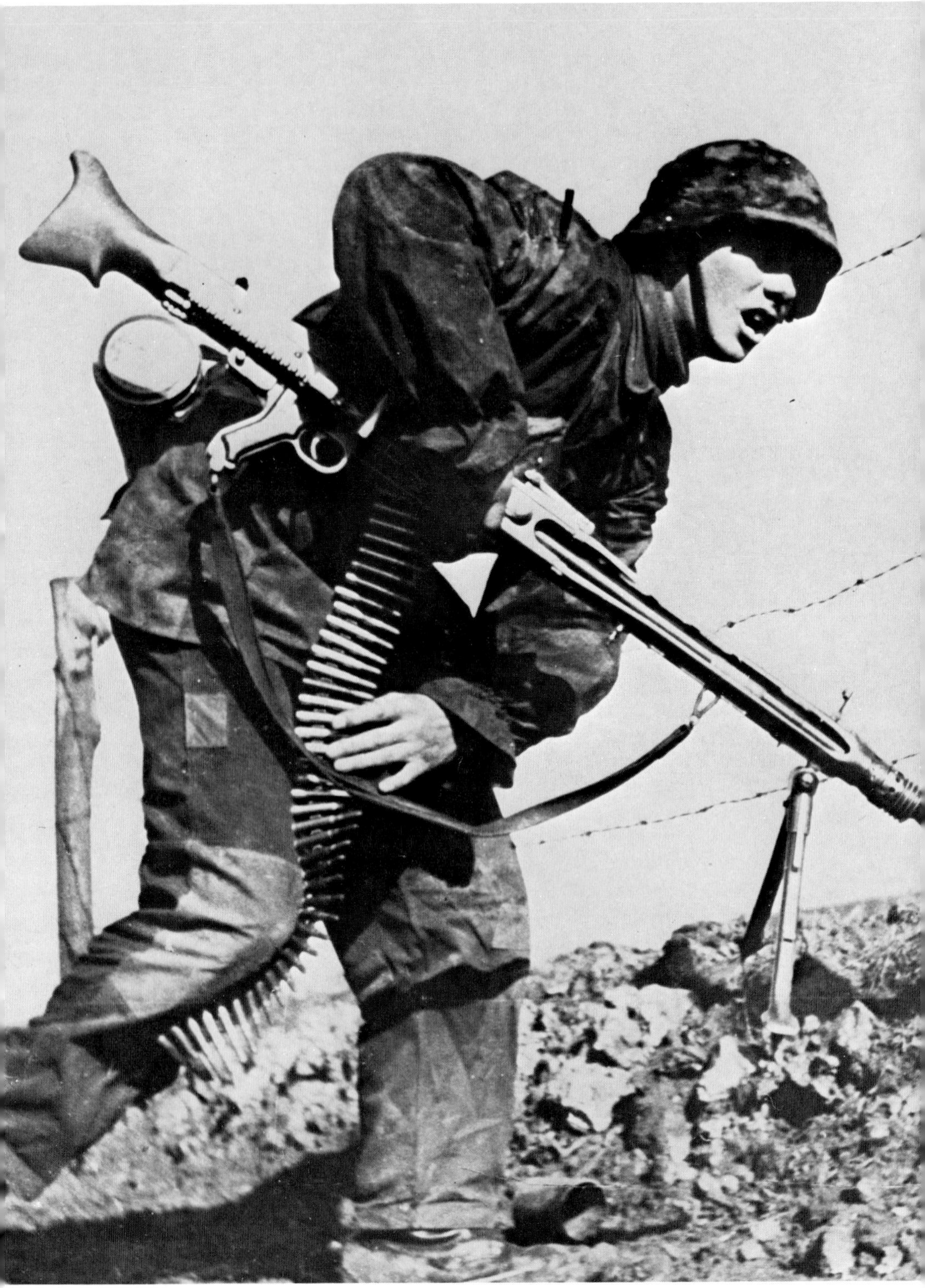

Chapter 1
THE HITLER YOUTH AND TOTAL WAR

We are a generation without roots and without depth. Our depth is the abyss.

(Wolfgang Borchert)

What horror this war brings forth! There was the German youth, light-hearted, filled with faith and hope. And then the war comes and drives them from the sun of their heavenly life and into the glowing cauldron of hell . . . And then the young men storm forward across cratered fields and through a hail of bullets, hardly recognizing or fearing their sound. And then suddenly they fall and are silent, as if it had never been otherwise. Oh God, is this your love?

(Jürgen Mogk)

On February 3, 1943, the Wehrmacht High Command (Oberkommando der Wehrmacht, or OKW) issued a special communiqué over the German radio: "The battle of Stalingrad has ended. True to their oath to fight to the last breath, the Sixth Army . . . has been overcome by the superiority of the enemy and by the unfavorable circumstances confronting our forces." The communiqué was preceded by the roll of muffled drums, and followed by the solemn tones of the second movement of Beethoven's Fifth Symphony. Adolf Hitler proclaimed four days of national mourning.

While the Third Reich officially mourned, 91,000 of its soldiers, half-starved and frostbitten, many of them wounded, trudged wearily through the ice and snow towards the railroad cars that would transport them to the prisoner-of-war camps of Siberia. These beaten soldiers, only 5,000 of whom would ever see Germany again, were the survivors of Field Marshal Friedrich Paulus' Sixth Army, once the most powerful force the Wehrmacht had ever sent into battle. Only months before, in the summer of 1942, the Sixth Army had spearheaded the German offensive in southern Russia. Confident of victory, their fighting qualities honed in the Blitzkrieg campaigns of 1939-41, Paulus' divisions had plunged eastward across the barren tableland of the Russian steppe, elements of one corps reaching the Volga above Stalingrad on August 23rd. Yet then Soviet resistance stiffened and the German offensive lost momentum. In November the Russians counterattacked and encircled the Sixth Army in the ruins of Stalingrad. The German front in southern Russia had collapsed.

Other disasters also plagued the Reich by the beginning of 1943. In North Africa, the remnants of Erwin Rommel's famed Africa Corps were tumbling westward in defeat towards Tunisia, outnumbered eight to one by the pursuing enemy. In the skies above Germany, the Allied strategic air forces had stepped up their attacks. American heavy bombers struck Wilhelmshaven in broad daylight on January 27th; three days later British bombers pounded Berlin at noon. As if to consummate this catalogue of disasters, the Anglo-Americans declared at Casablanca on January 24, 1943, that they would accept no end to the European war short of the Reich's unconditional surrender.

The tide of war had turned dramatically against Germany. Hitler's response to this sudden shift in fortune was to initiate the program he had hitherto scrupulously avoided--the total mobilization of Germany for war. Every able-bodied person was to be harnessed to the war machine, and new divisions raised to replace those that had melted away in the snows of western Russia. Under the direction of Albert Speer, the production of armaments and munitions was to be rapidly expanded. To underscore the commitment of the National Socialist leadership to this new and foreboding course, Propaganda Minister Joseph Goebbels delivered a defiant proclamation of total war in a speech at the Sportpalast in Berlin. Now there could be no compromise, no turning back. Germany would fight on to victory or annihilation.

On February 16, 1943, just two days before Goebbels' fiery speech, representatives of Germany's only youth organization, the Hitler Youth, and of Heinrich Himmler's SS had gathered at Hitler Youth headquarters in Berlin for a special planning conference. Among those present were the leader of Germany's youth, Reichsjugendführer Artur Axmann, and the Chief of the Waffen SS[1] Recruiting Office (Ergänzungsamt der Waffen-SS) SS-Gruppenführer Gottlob Berger. Anxious to make a special contribution to the expanding war effort, the conferees agreed to accept 17-year-old volunteers (class of 1926) from the Hitler Youth for the creation of a new Waffen SS division.[2] These boys, they reasoned, would provide a living symbol of the commitment of German youth to the Reich's total war effort.[3] In this manner, the decision to establish a special Hitler Youth division emerged from the crisis that confronted Germany in early 1943, and was an immediate consequence of the mobilization for total war.

*　　*　　*

Many an eligible youngster would greet the decision to form a Hitler Youth division with enthusiasm. Years of ideological indoctrination, coupled with the purposeful manipulation of youthful idealism within the Hitler Youth organization, had convinced them that no sacrifice for Germany could be too great. Their role models were the fallen heroes of the First World War, among

---

[1]The armed, or military branch of the SS. For a comparative table of ranks, U.S. Army and Waffen SS, see Appendix 2.

[2]Class of 1926 (Jahrgang 1926) simply signifies that the boys were born in that year. T-175/108/2631249-51. Berger to Himmler, Geheim! Betr.: Aufstellung der Division Hitler-Jugend. 18.2.43.

[3]See also Panzermeyer, Grenadiere (München-Lochhausen: Schild Verlag, 1956), p 204 (Hereafter cited Meyer, K., Grenadiere).

them the university students and grammar school pupils who, in November 1914, had advanced resolutely into the withering fire of the British machine guns at Langemarck with the Deutschland Lied on their lips. More directly, the boys looked up to their fathers, older brothers and relatives serving in the Wehrmacht or the Waffen SS. Many of these men had already been killed or wounded at the battlefront, but this only strengthened the youngsters' resolve to do their part in the terrible struggle that now engulfed Germany.

The class of 1926 had entered the Jungvolk, the junior organization of the Hitler Youth (ages 10 through 14), in 1936. The Hitler Youth leadership had declared 1936 the "Year of the German Jungvolk" and had launched an ambitious campaign to recruit the entire eligible age group.[4] At this time membership in the Hitler Youth was still technically voluntary, though pressure of various kinds was brought to bear upon those youths who still evinced little enthusiasm for the organization. The recruitment drive reached its high point in the weeks preceding the Führer's 47th birthday, and ended with the induction of some 800,000 ten-year-olds, about 95 percent of the class of 1926, into the ranks of the Jungvolk.[5] On April 20, 1936, the Hitler Youth officially celebrated the success of its efforts in a solemn ceremony at the Marienburg--the ancient castle of the Teutonic Order. There, in the Gothic main hall, lit by flickering candles and torchlight, the new members of the Jungvolk swore the oath that would be repeated every April 20th, the Führer's birthday:

> I promise
> In the Hitler Youth
> To do my duty
> At all times
> In love and faithfulness
> To help the Führer
> So help me god.

From that moment on the lives of these boys would be largely dominated by an organization that would expand into virtually every corner of their existence, for like the Third Reich in general, the goals of the Hitlerjugend (HJ) were intrinsically totalitarian: to mobilize and to discipline an entire generation of German youth in the spirit of National Socialism; to loosen their ties to the Church, the family, and the past; to inculcate the ideal that the State was everything and the individual nothing. Unlike the Wandervogel,[6] the independent German youth movement that had preceded World War One, the purpose

---

[4]A useful interpretive overview of the Hitler Youth, and of the German youth movement as a whole, is offered by Peter Stachura's work, *The German Youth Movement 1900-1945: An Interpretive and Documentary History* (New York: St. Martin's Press, 1981); Also of value, albeit somewhat erratic in presentation, is H.W. Koch's *The Hitler Youth. Origins and Development 1922-45* (London: MacDonald and Jane's, 1975).

[5]Dr. Arno Klönne, *Hitlerjugend. Die Jugend und ihre Organisation im Dritten Reich* (Hannover: Norddeutsche Verlagsanstalt, 1956), pp 16-17.

[6]The progressive political radicalization of the German youth movement from World War One on paralleled the growing politicization of large segments of German society as a whole. According to Stachura, the HJ was a "unique phenomenon in the

of the HJ was thus overtly political; its principal responsibility was to establish a system that would indoctrinate German youth in the teachings of National Socialism and equip them physically and ideologically for the great challenges of the future.

In the mid-1930s the task of accomplishing these goals fell to Baldur von Schirach. In 1931 von Schirach had become the youth leader of the National Socialist Party; following Hitler's seizure of power in 1933, he had assumed the post of Youth Leader of the German Reich (Reichsjugendführer). By 1936, at age 29, he was recognized as one of Nazi Germany's leading officials, reporting directly to the Führer himself. Von Schirach's arrogance, stilted style of public speaking and weakness for adolescent ideas made him unpopular with other party members, yet by the end of 1936 his tireless efforts had helped to bring about a more than ten-fold expansion of the HJ from early 1933 (from 55,000 to 5,437,601).[7]

Baldur von Schirach

The Reich Youth Leader was passionately devoted to Adolf Hitler, and set about the task of steeping his young charges in National Socialist ideology with an ardor that bordered on fanaticism. He brought Hitler's teachings to bear by infusing all HJ activities with a political purpose. Racist instruction, the concept of German supremacy, and the virtue of obedience and loyalty to Führer and Fatherland were assiduously cultivated. To mold the desired political soldiers, the HJ emphasized the need for self-sacrifice through such slogans as

German youth movement," and had "no substantive connections with either the pre-1914 Wandervogel or contemporary Weimar groups." Rather, it "represented a complete break in the youth tradition of Germany, in the same way as the NSDAP was a new kind of political party . . . In the last analysis, the HJ's totalitarianism demanded that it prove its uniqueness by destroying the youth movement altogether." Stachura, *The German Youth Movement,* p 117.

[7]Ibid., pp 128, 131.

"The Flag means more than Death," and "We are born to die for Germany." The latter slogan, in fact, could be found above the entrance to every Hitler Youth training camp. "Complementing this emphasis," writes Peter Stachura, "was the extravagant promotion of the Führer cult, for which von Schirach with his profusion of aesthetically poor poems and songs was primarily responsible. The depiction of Hitler as the God-given saviour of Germany was de rigueur in HJ publications and propaganda exercises."[8] Von Schirach would often speak of Hitler in mystical or quasi-religious terms, or invoke the terminology of Christianity to describe the Führer and his "mission" to the Hitler Youth. The following speech is representative of the Reich Youth Leader's fulsome style, and captures the naive idealism and reverence for Adolf Hitler that permeated the HJ of the pre-war years:[9]

> This Sunday morning ceremony doesn't aim at presenting arguments . . . but at imbuing life and men with courage and strength to fulfill their greater and lesser tasks through unqualified faith in the divine power and the ideology of the Führer and his movement . . . The service of Germany appears to us to be . . . the service of God; the banner of the Third Reich appears to us to be His banner; and the Führer of the people is the savior whom He sent to rescue us from the calamity and peril into which we were actually plunged by the most pious parties of the defunct Weimar Republic.

Ideological training also included instruction in German history and in the life of the Führer--both topics twisted, of course, to serve the politicization process. Focal points of historical discussion included the foundation of modern Germany in 1871, the First World War, the "humiliation" of Germany by the Versailles peace treaty, and the hated Weimar Republic. The Reich's avowed enemies, such as the Jews and the Communists, the nefarious role they played in world history and the threat they posed to Germany were also clearly depicted. The life of the Führer was presented as an heroic adventure; the more embarrassing episodes in Hitler's life distorted or neglected entirely. Hitler Youth leaders led the boys in discussions of Mein Kampf, yet when one considers that even educated adults found it difficult to wade through the book's turgid prose and rambling ideas, it is doubtful the youngsters extracted much of substance from such exercises.

The Hitler Youth leaders shouldered the day-to-day responsibility for organizing and conducting the myriad activities of the HJ. In filling its leadership positions the HJ attempted scrupulously to adhere to Goethe's maxim that "youth must be lead by youth." Although not always successful in achieving this goal, the overall age level of the movement's leaders was low. In 1938, for example, the average age of a HJ Bannführer (a middle rank) was 25; lower ranking leaders were commonly just a few years older than their charges. Therefore, there was "no generation gap, which had been the source

---

[8]Ibid., pp 138-39.
[9]Eugene Davidson, *The Trial of the Germans* (New York: Macmillan, 1966), p 287.

of so much tension in the early Weimar youth movement. The war, especially from 1942-43 onwards, even accelerated the trend towards youthful leaders, as military call-up took its toll of those already in office."[10]

At the core of National Socialist philosophy was the conviction that war was an ennobling and a spirtually renewing act, a natural and desirable state of affairs. Consequently, HJ indoctrination conveyed a highly romanticized picture of modern mechanized war and its gruesome effects. In the summer camps of the HJ, youngsters listened intently while veterans of the World War's front lines (Frontkämpfer) rendered enthusiastic accounts of their experiences in Germany's "undefeated" army. Such stories did not miss their mark, for in the 1930s the history of the Great War still exercised an almost hypnotic influence upon large segments of German youth.

Just as the war had fundamentally altered German society as a whole, so too had it transformed the nature of the German youth movement. During the Weimar Republic nationalistic youth groups had introduced overtly military games into their activities, the boys often taking to the peaceful German countryside armed with wooden machine guns and cardboard tanks. Such Kriegsspiele became popular in the HJ as well. In the 1930s and throughout the early war years the weekly newsreels (Wochenschauen) also served to reinforce romantic and unduly aesthetic notions about modern warfare. "Through the newsreels," remembers one former Hitler Youth,[11]

> we saw the victorious German olympic team of 1936 . . . We saw the cheering Austrians, the proud marching soldiers of the Condor Legion after the end of the Spanish campaign, as well as all heroic deeds on land, in the water and in the air. Naturally, the newsreel narratives were not lacking in propaganda, which had a subtle effect upon one's psyche and especially upon us youths, who had not yet developed a critical faculty for such things, and who were led to false conclusions. It was driven home to us that "to die for the Fatherland was an honorable act."

The process of socialization that helped to forge the attitudes of so many young Germans is clearly recollected by an Austrian who joined the Hitler Youth in 1938:[12]

> The period following 1930 exercised an enormous (ungeheueren) impression upon me . . . The World War remained a recent memory and the veterans were still in their best years. Still fresh was the remembrance of our lost empire, and of our lost self-confidence. War books appeared in the marketplace; much was written about the heroism of the fighting soldiers, and of how the war was

---

[10]See Appendix 1 for a table of Hitler Youth leadership ranks. Stachura, *The German Youth Movement*, p 131.

[11]Gurowski, Günther. "Fragebogen zur Geschichte der 12. SS Panzerdivision 'H.J.' im Normandie Feldzug" (Hereafter all questionnaires completed for the author by former Hitler Youth Division members cited simply as Fragebogen).

[12]Morawetz, Alois. "Bericht über meine Zeit in der SS Panzerdivision 'Hitlerjugend' von März 1943 bis zum Beginn der Invasion im Juni 1944."

lost behind the front. Self-discipline, loyalty and obedience were the declared values. One of the first films that I saw was the film of the Nibelungen, and we read the legends of the knights. In the schools the history of ancient civilization and of the middle ages was taught in line with the above values. We carved wooden swords, made gayly colored shields and played (war-like games). Former German naval officers visited us in school, bringing with them scale models of armored cruisers and U-boats, which they explained to us . . . When in 1938 the Anschluss with Germany came we joined the Hitler Youth . . . No political preparation or pressure of any kind was required to get us to join, for the intervening years had already conditioned us. (In the Hitler Youth) the training in toughness (Härte), in comradeship, in an awareness of duty and in a willingness to sacrifice for our people fell on well-prepared ground.

By 1939, the HJ had largely completed the task of rendering the great majority of German youth subservient to the demands of National Socialism.[13] A large percentage of this majority, moreover, evinced a real enthusiasm for the monolithic youth organization. That this was so should hardly be surprising, for National Socialism fancied itself a movement (Bewegung) of young people, a claim supported by the sociological and generational composition of its membership. The Nazi regime was lavish in its praise of and attention to youth, and early on had made it clear that young people would play a privileged part in the building of the 1000 year Reich. At the Nürnberg party rally in September 1933 Hitler had confirmed youth's special place in the new Germany with language calculated to quicken the heart of many an eager young idealist. With a HJ contingent assembled before him he had said: "You are the Germany of the future . . . on you are now set all our hopes, our people's confidence, and our faith . . . My youths, you are the living guarantors of Germany, you are the living Germany of the future . . . upon you depends the continued existence of our people . . ."[14]

*   *   *

Despite the emphasis placed by HJ propaganda on molding the future soldiers of the Reich, a phrase no doubt often meant metaphorically, the prewar years did not bring a comprehensive militarization of the Hitler Youth. Von Schirach, in fact, actively resisted the imposition of formal military training within his organization. As one observer noted, the Reich Youth Leader preferred "poetry to steel helmets and guns." His goal was to shape young minds and hearts in total obedience to the Führer—soldiering would come later. However, a definite trend towards strict conformism and militarism is

[13]Nevertheless, as late as the spring of 1939 a minority of over one million youths were still not members. To remedy the situation, von Schirach finally felt compelled to abandon all pretense that his HJ was a voluntary organization. The promulgation of two executive orders (Durchführungsverordnungen) on March 25, 1939, made membership in the Hitler Youth legally compulsory for all young people between the ages of 10 and 18.

[14]Stachura, *The German Youth Movement*, p 122.

clearly discernable from about 1936 on, paralleling the transition of the Reich to a more aggressive and expansionist foreign policy. In the broadest sense, physical conditioning and competitive sports, both central to the program of the HJ, served an important pre-military function. Activities such as hiking, swimming, fencing and boxing ceased to be pleasurable ends in themselves and became another form of service to Germany. Hitler knew only too well what he wanted. His ideal was to forge a generation of youth "slim and strong, swift as greyhounds, tough as leather, and hard as Krupp steel"--a generation of future soldiers. As one HJ leader candidly admitted, "every youngster (Pimpf) who diligently does sport knows this: service in the field grey uniform of the soldier comes most easily to the youth trained and steeled through sport. He will bring the greatest accomplishments to his people, and earn the greatest honors."[15]

The HJ established small arms training at an early date and it became increasingly popular in the late 1930s. Under the tutelage of specially trained Hitler Youths (HJ Schiesswarte), the youngsters practiced with air guns and small-bore rifles. In 1938 alone some 1,250,000 youths received small arms instruction in the Jungvolk or in the HJ proper.[16] Other activities served to inculcate pre-military skills of a more general nature. Instructive in this context

Hitler Youth members during rifle training.

[15]Werner Klose, *Generation im Gleichschritt* (Hamburg: Gerhard Stalling Verlag, 1964), p 121.
[16]Ibid., pp 120-21.

is a kind of field exercise (Geländedienst), which also makes clear just how demanding some HJ activities could be. The exercise required the boys to cover large distances cross country and to demonstrate skills such as map and compass reading, the proper use of camouflage and ground cover, and the determination of target distance and designation. To fulfill partial requirements for the Hitler Youth Merit Badge in Silver (HJ-Leistungsabzeichen in Silber), for example, a 16-year-old would have to march 12 miles laden with a 15 pound pack in no less than four and no more than five hours' time.[17]

Hitler Youth Merit Badge in silver.

Formal cooperation between the Wehrmacht and the Hitler Youth for the purpose of pre-military training became more significant after 1936. The Army established a liaison group with the HJ in 1937, and, for a brief period, then Lieutenant-Colonel Erwin Rommel played a leading role in the group. Agreements between von Schirach and General Ludwig Beck, Chief of the Army General Staff, in 1938, and between the Youth Leader and Field Marshal Wilhelm Keitel, Chief of the Wehrmacht High Command (OKW), in 1939, strengthened the partnership. The ties between the HJ and Himmler's SS also became more intimate as the Second World War drew closer, creating a firm basis for an expansion of the relationship during the war, most significantly with the Waffen SS.[18]

Of greatest value to the military were the special formations (Sondereinheiten) of the HJ--a fact openly acknowledged by the Wehrmacht. These formations included special HJ naval, motor, and flying units, which by 1938 boasted roughly 50,000, 90,000, and 74,000 members, respectively.[19]

The basic purpose of the Hitler Youth Flying Corps (Flieger-HJ) was to provide rudimentary instruction in the theory and practice of aviation. Clad in Luftwaffe-blue uniforms with light blue piping and the armband of the HJ, younger members of the flying corps built model airplanes, while the older boys learned to fly gliders and attempted to earn their "wings"--the A, B, and C certificates in gliding. Cooperation with the Luftwaffe was close, and the youngsters often spent exciting moments aloft as passengers in bomber aircraft or two-seated fighters. In the Marine-HJ, the boys could participate in sailing or in river navigation exercises, or perhaps partake in an exciting Baltic

---

[17]Ibid., pp 119-20.
[18]Stachura, *The German Youth Movement*, pp 142-43.
[19]Klönne, *Hitlerjugend*, p 19.

maneuver aboard one of the two sailing vessels used by the German Navy to train its naval cadets--the "Gorch Fock" and the "Horst Wessel." The Motor-HJ furnished its members the opportunity to drive motorcycles, to gain mechanical knowledge, and to learn the international and German traffic codes. An internal memorandum of the Reichsjugendführung (RJF) clearly shows that membership in the Motor-HJ was considered preparatory training for the motorized formations of the Wehrmacht.[20]

*   *   *

The outbreak of war in 1939 found Germany's youth well prepared. Immersed in a spirit of self-sacrifice and animated by the primitive activism so intrinsic to the National Socialist movement, the boys and girls of the Hitler Youth made an immediate and ever-expanding contribution to the war effort. HJ leaders normally enlisted in the elite units of the Army, such as the regiment Grossdeutschland, with which von Schirach himself served for a brief period in 1940. The crack regiments of the Waffen SS were also popular with the Hitler Youth.

For those too young to join the armed forces, service for the Fatherland began innocently enough, and was even conducted in a certain romantic spirit during the early years of the war before it impinged too directly on their daily lives. The Hitler Youth had even begun to play their part in the week immediately preceding the outbreak of war with Poland, for it was they who delivered the thousands of call-up papers throughout Germany. Almost at once all physically able sixth-formers (16-year-olds) were drafted for service on the farms to help bring in the harvest.[21] For most of these boys, this was the end of school life forever, for service on the farms would be followed by the obligatory stint in the Labor Service, and, thereafter, by induction into the armed forces.

In general, the youths busied themselves with innumerable little tasks. One concerted HJ action in the initial weeks of the war was carried out in association with the blackout: to make it easier to cross streets in darkness, HJ members painted the curbs at each street corner white. The curb painting was repeated annually and was quite popular as well, being one of the very few activites for which the youngsters were actually paid. When the government called for the collection of materials such as scrap metal, iron, brass, copper, paper, wood, and clothing, the Hitler Youth met the challenge. Young middle echelon Jungvolk leaders (Fähnleinführer) organized the collection campaigns with military precision, distributing their boys into small groups according to districts, streets, and blocks of houses. In the past, the HJ had often gathered scrap metal to support Hermann Göring's Four Year Plan, but now Germany was at war, and the youths responded with indefatigable energy and enthusiasm:[22]

---

[20]Koch, *The Hitler Youth,* pp 229-31.

[21]In 1942, for example, approximately 600,000 boys and 1,400,000 girls were active in this area. The value of such service should not be underestimated, for it freed thousands of others for service in the Wehrmacht. Klönne, *Hitlerjugend,* p 21.

[22]Quoted in Koch, *The Hitler Youth,* pp 233-34. See also Klose, *Generation im Gleichschritt,* p 240.

H . . . is collecting bottles. I see him before me as he is running from door to door begging patiently for his bottles. And then the moment when it came to take them to the collection centre. In his uniform, on the back a satchel stuffed with bottles, in the left hand a basket full of them, balanced only by a massive net in the right hand, also full of bottles. And all that beneath a face looking as though through him and his bottles the war would be won.

In addition, the boys acted as couriers for Wehrmacht and party agencies, and saw duty as temporary firemen, postmen, road workers, and auxiliary personnel for the police and the railroad. The girls also performed valuable services, taking care of children in state kindergartens, or working as clerks, typists, and telephonists. Groups from the League of German Girls within the HJ (Bund deutscher Mädchen, or BDM) also served as Red Cross auxiliaries, and could often be found at the field hospitals entertaining and caring for the wounded. Others waited patiently on the platforms of railway stations, ready to ply soldiers in transit with food and drink. For the youngsters of the Hitler Youth total mobilization for war had come considerably earlier than for the rest of the civilian population.

Beginning in October 1939, pre-military training for 16 to 18-year-olds intensified, and, as the war progressed, was increasingly supervised by former HJ leaders with front experience. The training was given additional impetus through Hitler's decree of March 1942, which established HJ Military Instruction Camps (Wehrertüchtigungslager, or WEL). Conducted by Army and Waffen SS personnel with combat experience, these camps provided short courses in intensive basic infantry training for boys 16½ and older; by the end of 1943, there were 226 such camps in existence. The inspector of the WELs was HJ-Oberbannführer Gerhard Hein, who had been wounded at the front and decorated with the Knight's Cross and Oak Leaves.[23]

HJ-Oberbannführer Gerhard Hein with HJ recruits from the 12th SS Division.

[23]Hans-Christian Brandenburg, *Die Geschichte der Hitlerjugend. Wege und Irrwege einer Generation* (Köln: Verlag Wissenschaft und Politik, 1968), p 230; Stachura, *The German Youth Movement*, p 164.

As the war began to turn against the Reich the Hitler Youth suddenly found themselves on the firing line. From January 1943 on, grammar school pupils 15 and older manned anti-aircraft and searchlight batteries and served as dispatch riders. The boys wore Luftwaffe uniforms with the HJ armband, but were classified as Wehrmacht auxiliaries (Wehrmachtsgefolge), not soldiers. They were paid 50 Pfennig per day. After an air raid, they helped to extinguish fires or to dig out air raid shelters buried beneath the rubble.[24] For the Hitler Youth, it had been a gradual, albeit inexorable, shift from the periphery to the center of the storm:[25]

> In a suburb of Berlin I saw a row of dead Flakhelfer lying side by side. An air raid had just ended. The flak position in which these schoolboys served had received several direct hits. I entered a barrack room in which the survivors had gathered. They sat along the wall on the floor turning their white faces distorted by terror towards me. Many cried.
>
> In another room lay the wounded. One of them, a boy with a soft round child's face, tried to come to attention when an officer in whose company I was asked him whether he suffered any pain: 'Yes, but this is not important. Germany must be victorious.'

Even to the unsophisticated intellects of the young Hitler Youth, however, it was apparent that final victory would demand even greater sacrifice. And for that National Socialism had prepared them well. Many boys waited anxiously for the opportunity to serve in the armed forces. "As the war continued," recalls a former Hitler Youth,[26]

> more and more news came concerning acquaintances who were either killed in battle or had suffered serious wounds. But we also got news of individuals who had been decorated because of extraordinary accomplishments at the front. Gradually, it became clear that the war would not be won in the twinkling of an eye. With that came the thought that we might also be sent to the front. At first it was a new feeling, but it wasn't long until an impatience had gripped me to join up as soon as possible. Since talk of death and destruction was everywhere--in the interim the bombing attacks on our large cities had caused many civilian deaths--it made little impression to think that I might also not come home. My inborn readiness to take the risk made me all the more unconcerned.

In the summer of 1944, he and thousands of youngsters like him would serve at the front with the Hitler Youth Division in the cataclysmic environment of modern total war:[27]

---

[24]Brandenburg, *Die Geschichte der Hitlerjugend,* p 231; Klose, *Generation im Gleichschritt,* p 253.

[25]Quoted in Koch, *The Hitler Youth,* pp 240-41.

[26]Gurowski, Fragebogen.

[27]SS Leitheft 10 (October 1944). "Der schwere Kampf der SS-Panzer Division 'Hitler Jugend,'" pp 9-10.

Thousands of aircraft, rolling barrages of the batteries, massed tank attacks hammered them with bombs and shells. The earth heaved thunderously. An inferno was unleashed. But faith was the strongest support of courage. Smeared with blood; covered with dust, gasping and fighting, doggedly dug into the earth, these youths brought the Anglo-Americans to a halt.

* * * * *

Chapter 2

ORIGINS AND RECRUITMENT OF THE HITLER YOUTH DIVISION

> Today the Reich Youth Leader has released you from the Hitler Youth and presented you to the *Waffen SS*. Now, in your new *Waffen SS* uniforms, you will go home on a fourteen-day furlough (stormy applause!). After a few months in SS barracks you will enter a great formation, an SS Panzer grenadier division. You will then train some more, lose many drops of sweat in order to save drops of blood and finally will march alongside of its sister division, the *Leibstandarte* SS Adolf Hitler. You will carry the name that the Führer gave you: SS Panzer Grenadier Division 'Hitler-Jugend.'
>
> (Heinrich Himmler)

Artur Axmann, who replaced von Schirach as Reichsjugendführer in August 1940, has generally received credit for the idea to establish a Waffen SS division composed of Hitler Youths, and, at first, even Himmler seems to have had this impression. However, the idea more likely originated with SS-Gruppenführer Gottlob Berger, the energetic and unscrupulous Chief of the Waffen SS Recruiting Office.[1] Berger, supported by the Chief of Staff of the Reichsjugendführung, Helmut Möckel, appears to have taken the initial steps that led to the formation of the division. Yet in the mood of crisis created by the Stalingrad debacle the idea to mobilize Hitler Youths in a separate military unit might have occurred to any number of agencies or individuals. The Army, in fact, made a belated effort to do this, and even Göring appears to have toyed briefly with such a project.[2] But given the ever growing power and prestige of the SS, and the declining political influence of the Wehrmacht, it is doubtful that any competitor could have wrestled the project away from Himmler's organization.

---

[1] In July 1943, Berger received a note from Himmler's chef de cabinet, Dr. Rudolf Brandt, asserting that the idea to establish the division had come from Axmann. Berger, in a reply to Brandt, objected strongly, insisting that the idea to set up a HJ division was his, and that the chief supporter (Hauptverfechter) of his plan had been Stabsführer Möckel of the RJF. T-175/108/2631226-27. Berger to Brandt, Betr.: Division "Hitlerjugend," geheime Kommandosache, 3.7.1943.

[2] General Rudolf Schmundt, Hitler's senior military advisor, had proposed the establishment of a HJ division under the auspices of the Army. When Himmler got

Gottlob Berger, Chief of the Waffen SS Recruiting Office.

Reichsjugendführer Artur Axmann.

On February 9, 1943, Berger and Möckel conducted the first known discussion concerning the formation of a Hitler Youth Division; to avoid premature opposition to their intent they talked in secret. Meeting at Berger's office in Berlin, they agreed that the new division should consist of 17-year-olds from the class of 1926. To prepare the boys for military service, they were first to receive six weeks of pre-military training at the HJ Military Instruction Camps (WELs), followed by four weeks in the Labor Service (Reichsarbeitsdienst). Training would conclude with sixteen weeks of intensive military drill under SS auspices. To provide the youths with proper nourishment during the six month training period, the special rations of the Luftwaffe would be requested.

Berger, perhaps carried away by the excitement of the moment, nominated himself for division commander–a proposal politely rebuffed by Himmler a week later.[3] Concerning the formation of the divisional officer corps, Möckel

---

wind of this he responded with a curt missive to Schmundt: "From the Führer I heard that you have proposed to set up a Hitler Youth division within the Army. Surely it has escaped you that I already made such a proposal to Hitler at the beginning of February. As proof of this I send you a copy of a letter that I wrote to Reich Youth Leader Axmann following my report to the Führer on February 13, 1943." T-175/108/2631233. Himmler to Generalmajor Schmundt, Führer-Hauptquartier, 22.3.1943.

[3]According to Berger, this was the "first and only time" in his life he had ever nominated himself for anything. Himmler's rebuff was diplomatic: "Dear Berger! . . . Concerning your wish to be appointed division commander, well, I can certainly understand that. But dear Berger, you know that I need you in another capacity. I believe that a time will come again for all of us in this difficult war. Please do not become impatient with me." T-175/108/2631245. Himmler to Berger, Geheim, 16.2.1943.

optimistically offered to provide veteran HJ leaders, who, though now serving at home, possessed front experience as company and battalion commanders. Upper echelon command positions (i.e., regimental commanders and division commander) could be filled by the Waffen SS.[4]

The next day the Reichsführer SS, Heinrich Himmler, conferred with Hitler at the latter's Wolf's Lair (Wolfschanze) headquarters deep in the East Prussian forest. Himmler informed the Führer of the nascent efforts to form a division of Hitler Youths that would possess the quality of the super-elite 1st SS Leibstandarte SS "Adolf Hitler" Panzer Grenadier Division (or LAH); he also expressed Axmann's wish that the division be designated in a manner that would clearly indicate its origin and solidarity with the HJ. Hitler responded with enthusiasm and authorized Axmann to commence recruitment at once. Although the Führer liked Himmler's proposal to name the unit "Hitlerjugend," he deferred a final decision on this matter. Circumstances permitting, however, he would waive the Labor Service requirement for HJ division volunteers.[5]

On February 16th, representatives of the SS and of the Hitler Youth met at HJ headquarters in Berlin for the first divisional planning conference. Present at the meeting from the Hitler Youth were Axmann, Möckel and Dr. Ernst Schlünder; representing the Waffen SS Recruiting Office were Berger, SS-Brigadeführer Jürs, and his deputy, SS-Sturmbannführer Brill. These six men would largely determine the fate of the 20,000 teenagers who eventually found themselves upon the battlefields of Normandy in June 1944 as soldiers in the Hitler Youth Division. Tragically, only days before the conference, on February 12th, Berger had lost a son fighting with the Leibstandarte in southern Russia.

The conferees agreed to accept volunteers from the class of 1926 with a minimum height of 1.70 meters as infantry recruits; in special cases, the height requirement could be reduced to 1.68 meters for signal units, tank crews, and motorcycle troops. The only additional requirements were that the recruits be physically fit (kriegsverwendungsfähig), and, whenever possible, possess the HJ Merit Badge. The Reichsjugendführung promised to place 30,000 youths who had been carefully examined by HJ doctors at the disposal of the Waffen SS. In cooperation with the HJ Regional Directorates, the boys would then be mustered by SS Acceptance Commissions (Annahmekommission der Ergänzungsstellen) between March 15th and April 1, 1943, and examined once again. Those accepted would be inducted into the 39 WELs still staffed by the SS for the six week preliminary training course. Thereafter, they would go directly to the division. In cases where a boy had yet to reach his seventeenth birthday, a special Führer decree or negotiations with the OKW would be needed to secure the youngster's release for induction.

---

[4]T-175/108/2631262-63. Aktenvermerk: Berger. 9.2.1943; Gerhard Rempel, *The Misguided Generation: Hitler Youth and SS: 1933-1945* (University of Wisconsin: unpublished doctoral dissertation, 1971), pp 607-8.
[5]T-175/108/2631254. Himmler to Axmann. Geheim, 13.2.1943.

The RJF was confident that it could furnish a significant percentage of the divisional officer corps, provided that Hitler could be persuaded to transfer required personnel from Army or Air Force reserve status to active duty in the Waffen SS. The divisional organization tables called for 840 officers and some 4,000 NCOs; the HJ representatives hoped to supply some 400 and 2,500, respectively--all Hitler Youth leaders.[6] Providing the requisite numbers of officers and NCOs, however, would become the most difficult problem facing the organizers of the divison; ultimately, the division would have to seek its own solutions during the training period, albeit with limited success.

On February 17th, Axmann outlined the negotiations to establish a HJ division at a regularly scheduled conference of HJ regional leaders in Berlin. To his audience it was apparent that the Reich Youth Leader envisaged the new division as an elite formation--a "Guard of the Führer," alongside the Leibstandarte, "fully motorized, equipped with the heaviest weapons and led mostly by Hitler Youth leaders." Concerning recruitment of the unit, "eagerness for action" and "enthusiasm" should be the decisive factors. In addition, recruiters were to accept only those youths who were "physically fit," "spiritually alive," and who had demonstrated "exemplary records in the Hitler Youth." Preference was also to be given to holders of the HJ Achievement and Marksmanship medals. Parental consent for enlistment was unnecessary. Recruitment was to begin at once, and to be pursued with "full vigor;" the regional HJ leaders were "personally responsible" for the success of the campaign. Preliminary training in the Military Instruction Camps of the HJ would commence on April 4, 1943.[7]

With furious recruitment underway, Berger convened a second major planning conference on the afternoon of March 8th. Also in attendance was the Chief of the SS Personnel Main Office, SS-Obergruppenführer Maximilian von Herff, as well as Brill, Möckel and Schlünder. Berger's exclusion of SS-Obergruppenführer Hans Jüttner, the head of the Waffen SS Operational Headquarters (SS-Führungshauptamt),[8] from the meeting was a deliberate oversight, which Jüttner would resent and Berger later regret.[9]

Berger unveiled his plan for pre-military training and the subsequent transfer of qualified volunteers to the HJ Division. His timetable called for staggered training periods, beginning in April and continuing until August 15, 1943. On April 4th, 2,000 HJ leaders from the class of 1925 (18-year-olds), who had been released by a special Führer decree from compulsory Labor Service,

---

[6]T-175/108/2631249-51. Berger to Himmler, Geheim! Betr.: Aufstellung der Division Hitler-Jugend, 18.2.1943.

[7]Rempel, *The Misguided Generation,* pp 612-13.

[8]The SS Führungshauptamt had been established in August 1940. Its principal responsibilities included the training and organization of Waffen SS field formations. Dr. K.G. Klietmann, *Die Waffen-SS - eine Dokumentation* (Osnabrück: Verlag "Der Freiwillige," 1965), p 45.

[9]Apparently Berger was convinced that Jüttner would not look favorably upon his idea to create a HJ division. As events were to demonstrate, Berger was not far off the mark. T-175/108/2631226. Berger to Brandt. Betr.: Division "Hitler-Jugend," geheime Kommandosache, 3.7.1943.

Illustrated are three recruitment postcards designed to entice Hitler Youth members to the Waffen SS.

were to assemble in 20 WELs, where the Waffen SS was to train them. These youngsters, mostly with superior records in the Hitler Youth, would receive four weeks of instruction as training assistants (Hilfsausbilder). Thereafter, they would transfer to other camps to assist the regular SS trainers conducting the courses for the rank and file Hitler Youth Division recruits. Finally, the 2,000 HJ leaders would go to Waffen SS NCO schools for training as noncommissioned officers (Unterführer) for the division.

On May 1, 1943, the first 6,000 recruits from the class of 1926 would be inducted into the WELs staffed by SS personnel. Some 2,000 additional 17-year-olds were to assemble in a camp at St. Veith, in Oberkrain, Austria, for special training. The RJF was optimistic that the SS camp personnel, supported by the 2,000 HJ training assistants, would suffice to train the initial 8,000 recruits. Training was to continue for six weeks, until June 15th. On July 1st, the youths would enter the Waffen SS. These boys, earmarked for the technical units of the division, were then to receive an additional six weeks of preliminary training.

On July 1st, the process would be repeated, with 6,000 recruits again inducted into the WELs and 2,000 more into the special training camp at St. Veith. The 2,000 HJ training assistants who had meanwhile left for the Waffen SS NCO schools would be replaced by SS personnel. Preliminary training was to conclude on August 15th, and, by September 1, 1943, 16,000 teenagers from the class of 1926 and 2,000 HJ leaders still in the NCO schools were to be ready for the HJ division.

Concerning commissioned officers, von Herff agreed to seek Himmler's permission to transfer 60 SS-Obersturmführer and SS-Untersturmführer (first and second lieutenants) from other Waffen SS formations to the Hitler Youth Division. In addition, it was hoped that 600 HJ leaders now serving as NCOs and other ranks in active SS field units could be transferred to the division and dispatched to an officer training course. Those who failed the course could still see duty as NCOs. In any case, the Reichsjugendführung planned to specially nominate all 660 of these youths for assignment to the HJ Division.[10]

The conference left several other issues unresolved, including the need to secure technical officers for the division. Completely ignored was the larger question of release from the Labor Service of the 16,000 recruits from the class of 1926.[11] Moreover, the decision to send 2,000 HJ leaders to NCO schools still left the division short half of its complement of noncommissioned officers.[12]

---

[10]By early 1943, however, the rapid expansion of the Waffen SS coupled with limited training facilities and heavy losses at the front had created a serious shortage of experienced SS officers and NCOs. For a thoughtful discussion of this problem see Bernd Wegner's *Hitlers Politische Soldaten: Die Waffen-SS 1933-1945* (Paderborn: Ferdinand Schoningh, 1982), pp 284-85.

[11]Information concerning the March 8, 1943 conference is gleaned from T-175/108/2631235-38. Aktenvermerk Berger, SS-Hauptamt, Berlin. 9.3.1943.

[12]The shortfall was even greater than anticipated, for actual recruitment efforts would fall far short of the initial target figure of 2,000 HJ leaders for the NCO schools of the Waffen SS. How Berger specifically planned to drum up an additional 2,000 NCOs is unclear, although the direct intervention of the Führer (Führerbefehl) was considered necessary in any case. Ibid.

The plan that emerged from the conference would undergo certain revisions; in part, it would not be put into effect at all. Angered by his exclusion from the conference, Jüttner quickly squashed the proposed solution to the divisional officer corps. In a letter to Berger on March 10th, Jüttner made his position clear. All HJ leaders serving in the Waffen SS, he stated, were automatically officer candidates; as such, they represented a substantial portion of the reserve officer pool for existing SS field units. New formations besides the Hitler Youth Division, such as the 9th and 10th SS Divisions, also had considerable manpower needs that could not be neglected. "These factors," Jüttner concluded, "prevent a solution in the recommended fashion. As before it will be necessary to find at least half the required officers in some other way." The SS-Führungshauptamt, "in view of the newly forming units could make no essential contribution."[13]

*　　*　　*

Set in motion in mid-February the recruitment of the division was to be conducted secretly, for authorities feared that public awareness of the plan might arouse fears of a second Langemarck, where boundless enthusiasm combined with inadequate training had led to a slaughter of innocents. A special spring recruitment campaign for the Waffen SS in general had already been arranged, and authorities were hopeful it would net some 35,000 HJ recruits nationally. The decision to establish a HJ Division, however, added some 20,000 to 30,000 recruits to the overall figures. The HJ regions received instructions to produce their Hitler Youth Division contingents by March 15th. Consequently, with mustering by the SS Recruiting Stations scheduled from March 15th to the 30th, a mere 26 days were alloted to recruit the entire division.

The recruitment process encountered immediate obstacles, thus supplementary recruitment efforts would continue well into the summer.[14] The RJF, for example, experienced difficulty recruiting boys in vocational schools, who would not normally complete vocational training until the fall. In late March, therefore, Axmann concluded an agreement with the German Business Chamber (Reichswirtschaftskammer) that enabled the youths to take an early examination in April, clearing the way for their induction into the second series of WEL training courses beginning on July 1st. The recruitment of non-vocational students who had yet to complete their course work was even more complicated; only through tough negotiations with the Ministry of Education (Reichserziehungsministerium) were Axmann and Berger, by May

[13]T-175/108/2631241-42. SS-Führungshauptamt an das SS Hauptamt, Geheime Kommandosache. Betr.: Aufstellung der SS-Division "Hitler-Jugend." 10.3.1943; Rempel, *The Misguided Generation*, pp 617-19.

[14]The RJF would order a supplementary recruitment campaign (Nachwerbung) for May 1943. Although initially only youths from the first half of the class of 1926 (i.e., those born January to June 1926) had been eligible for enlistment in the HJ Division, in late July the HJ regional offices were permitted to recruit from the second half of the class; those so recruited were dispatched to Waffen SS boot camps without the benefit of WEL preliminary training. In addition, boys returning home on furlough following completion of WEL training courses had instructions to persuade friends to join the division. Rempel, *The Misguided Generation*, pp 637-39.

1943, able to find a satisfactory solution to this problem. Parents and guardians who got wind of the recruitment effort could also pose a stumbling block, for their protective instincts often compelled them to discourage boys from enlisting in the division.

The requirements for induction into the Waffen SS, still highly selective even at this stage in the war, posed an additional challenge, as did the anti-SS attitude relatively prevalent in southern Germany. In this context, the frustration experienced by Gefolgschaftsführer Wald of HJ District Dillingen (Swabia) during the supplementary recruitment drive in May was probably typical:[15]

> The class of 1926 contains 386 boys in District Dillingen. Of these, 185 boys were born before June 30, 1926. During my first recruiting effort I already spoke to each of the 386 boys personally and managed to persuade 31 boys to volunteer for the HJ Division. That was an unheard of number considering the ideological situation in Dillingen! The fact that only six out of 31 were judged 'suitable' is due to the fact that most of them were under 1.68 meters tall.
>
> Now once more I have called the 1926 class together (for the third time in two-and-a-half months!) with the aid of the mayor and talked to each boy individually. The result, despite use of every possible means, is fully negative. Only one boy volunteered.
>
> It must be clear that a rural district like ours, with a total of 185 eligible boys, cannot produce a contingent of 30 suitable recruits. In District Dillingen the obvious reason is the ideological situation, of which we became fully aware during the last three SS recruiting campaigns.

Securing requisite numbers of noncommissioned officers turned out to be as difficult as the recruitment of the rank and file. Early in March, Hitler released Waffen SS officer candidates from the Labor Service, but this had little demonstrable effect on HJ leaders' readiness to volunteer. On March 9th, Axmann instructed all regional leaders to recruit at least 10 percent of their eligible unit leaders of the class of 1925 for the divisional NCO corps, but the HJ districts expected to furnish the recruits already suffered from severe manpower shortages. HJ Region Swabia, for example, was expected to provide 26 NCO candidates and to send them to WEL Kuchberg near Geislingen, Wurttemberg for pre-military training; yet the response to the call for volunteers was a disappointment and initially only 13 youths were dispatched to WEL Kuchberg. Most of the eligible boys in this region preferred to serve in the Labor Service, refused to surrender their officer candidate status with the Army and the Luftwaffe, or desired to finish their formal education first. In general, the recruitment results in Swabia "reflected the inadequate national results."[16]

---

[15]Ibid., pp 637-38.
[16]Altogether, Swabia would dispatch a contingent of 17 to WEL Kuchberg, 11 of whom were actually accepted as NCO candidates for the division. Ibid., pp 613-14; 624-27; 633-35.

To circumvent recruitment obstacles it is hardly surprising that authorities sometimes resorted to coercion, subtle or otherwise, to reach their quotas. On March 30, 1943, Army reserve officials in Stuttgart complained to OKW that the Waffen SS was using "illegal means" to recruit for a "so-called HJ Division to be presented to the Führer on his birthday." "It would be totally false, however," the report continued, "if the Führer were under the impression that he was dealing with purely voluntary recruits." The report cited several incidents in which Hitler youths had been forcefully "moved" (bewegt) to volunteer; they had even had their "ears boxed" for failure to respond to SS appeals. When Berger was forced to investigate, the SS Recruiting Station in Stuttgart denied the charges, claiming that it could not find the allegedly responsible persons because the Army had given "imprecise information." Berger, in an explanation to Himmler, simply dismissed the affair as another example of the Army "raising a stink against the SS."[17]

In November 1943, the commander of the Hitler Youth Division would order an investigation to determine just how many of the teenagers had been inducted against their will. Undoubtedly, most of the boys had volunteered their service with enthusiasm, animated as they were by youthful idealism and romantic notions of heroic combat. A significant minority, however, appear to have joined because of personal or institutional pressures; others were simply drafted. Thus, claims that the division was a purely voluntary formation must be viewed with some skepticism.

WEL courses for the first batch of 17-year-old recruits commenced at the beginning of May 1943, and, to expedite transfer to active military service, were shortened from six to four weeks.[18] Given their brevity, the courses could do little more than inculcate the basics of military service, harden the youths physically, and help to ease the transition from civilian to military life. At the WELs the boys were also to receive their uniforms and basic equipment--an intent, it turned out, that was only partially fulfilled.

At the end of May, the 39 SS Military Instruction Camps transferred the youngsters to the Waffen SS in a uniform ceremony. Speeches by HJ and SS leaders, and the singing of songs such as "Ein junges Volk steht auf," and "Es zittern die morschen Knochen," accompanied by HJ and SS musical units, characterized these solemn martial events. At the ceremony in WEL Wildflecken, Axmann and Himmler were the honored speakers–their speeches tailored to appeal to the boys' idealism and sense of eliteness. Axmann spoke first:[19]

---

[17]It seems the boys were imprisoned in a room guarded by SS soldiers and forced to sign "volunteer" papers. Ibid., pp 640-41. That coercion was practiced in some cases is openly admitted by former divison members. See for example, Meyer, K., *Grenadiere*, p 206; Hubert Meyer, P-164. "Der Einsatz der 12. SS-Panzerdivision 'Hitlerjugend' während der Invasionskämpfe in Frankreich von Juni bis September 1944." p 5 (Hereafter cited Meyer, H., P-164).

[18]In April 1943, Hitler had released these boys from the compulsory stint in the Labor Service.

[19]Excerpts from both the Axmann and Himmler speeches are found in Rempel, *The Misguided Generation*, pp 632-33.

Above all, you my comrades and young volunteers, who want to join the units of the Waffen SS, are a wonderful demonstration of the attitude and spirit of youth during this fourth year of war. We all feel the burning desire to create a military unit out of volunteer comrades from the Hitler Youth. The Führer was delighted with this wish of his youth. He counted on you and thousands of you responded to our call. You are the elite of German youth and I am happy and lucky that not one of you is here except by his own free will . . . In your unit, my comrades, the soldierly tradition of the Hitler Youth will find its ultimate expression. That is the reason why all German youths direct their attention to this unit, to you; that is why the honor of German youth depends on you; that is why you must embody the virtues inherent in the best of Germany's youth. So, we expect you to be idealistic, selfless, courageous and loyal!

The Reichsführer SS was equally to the point:

Since the years of struggle, throughout the years of growth before the war and during the war years themselves, a tie of particular intimacy and inner fellowship bound the Hitler Youth and the SS together. Not only the time of struggle, the combat of fists, but much more, the battle of spirits and hearts for our eternal Germany has brought us together and will forever unite us. Now, during the war, ten thousands of Hitler youths have volunteered for the Waffen SS; they have fought honorably and creditably; many of them became casualties. The class of 1925 participated in the great battle of Kharkov courageously and successfully. It can be said in all candor that half of the Waffen SS divisions that reconquered Kharkov, were volunteers from the classes of 1924 to 1925. For all of them this difficult battle was the first taste of combat . . . In these weeks, when the sacrifice of Stalingrad was on everyone's mind, when the Russians mounted massive attacks, your Youth Leader made the decision to offer to the Führer the best young boys of the new class for a new Waffen SS division. The Führer agreed happily. After eight years of training in the Hitler Youth, you have now assembled in your Waffen SS uniform with your old HJ armband. For four weeks you have lived together, worked together, trained together and prepared for military service. Today the Reich Youth Leader has released you from the Hitler Youth and presented you to the Waffen SS. Now, in your new Waffen SS uniforms, you will go home on a fourteen-day furlough (stormy applause!). After a few months in SS barracks you will enter a great formation, an SS Panzer grenadier division. You will then train some more, lose many drops of sweat in order to save drops of blood and finally will march alongside its sister division, the Leibstandarte SS Adolf Hitler. You will carry the name that the Führer gave you: SS Panzer Grenadier Division 'Hitler-Jugend.'

*   *   *

Waffen SS cadre and Hitler Youth recruits (note Waffen SS uniform and Hitler Youth armband) during the ceremonies at Wildflecken.

Clearly, Axmann, Himmler, and Berger envisioned the Hitler Youth Division as a second Leibstandarte, with equal élan and combat capability. The relationship was more than a symbolic one, for in the late spring of 1943, the Leibstandarte would provide its "sister division" with a nucleus of experienced officers, NCOs and technical specialists.[20] All regimental as well as numerous battalion and company commands in the HJ Division would be filled by LAH personnel. The LAH would also furnish elements of its armored regiment, artillery regiment, reconnaissance battalion, and tank repair and medical units, as well as its entire anti-tank battalion.[21] Thus, it was the Leibstandarte, a crack field division of the Waffen SS, that would impart spirit and substance to the nascent Hitler Youth Division, shaping its identity as a combat formation.

Formal organization of the HJ Division was delayed several weeks, the result of friction between Berger and Jüttner over the officer and NCO

---

[20]See Appendix 3 for a list of high ranking officers transferred from the LAH to the 12th SS Division. The LAH, like the Waffen SS in general, had always maintained close ties with the Hitler Youth; many boys had enlisted in the elite formation before and during the Second World War. In 1941-42, the RJF had even mounted special recruitment campaigns within the HJ for the Leibstandarte. Ibid., pp 603-5.

[21]According to Rudolf Lehmann, the transfer of LAH elements to the HJ Division would not be completed until February 1944. Kurt Meyer estimates that, in 1943, some 700 officers and NCOs from the Leibstandarte were detached to the HJ Division. They included several hundred Luftwaffe NCOs recently transferred to the LAH to help replenish the division following the costly defensive battles in the Kharkov area. Rudolf Lehmann, *Die Leibstandarte,* Band III (Osnabrück: Munin Verlag GmbH, 1982), pp 218-20; United States National Archives Record Group 238: Records of Proceedings (revised) of the Trial by Canadian Military Court of SS Brigadeführer Kurt Meyer, p 617 (Hereafter cited as Record Group 238: Records of Proceedings).

In late May 1943, the thirty-nine SS Military Instruction Camps (WELs) transferred the division recruits into the Waffen SS. The following photographs are from the ceremony at WEL Kaiserslautern.

RFSS Himmler arrives at Kaiserslautern.

Himmler marches past massed Hitler Youth banners.

Jost W. Schneider

Recruits in formation before the Kaiserslautern barracks.

Jost W. Schneider

Jost W. Schneider

An SS WEL instructor and recruits being reviewed.

RFSS Himmler, Gerhard Hein and Artur Axmann.

Jost W. Schneider

(Above) Himmler, unidentified, Axmann and Hein review the recruits.

Jost W. Schneider

problem. Possible delaying maneuvers by OKW and other manpower and supply agencies, as well as the unanticipated slowness of the recruitment process may have also contributed to the delay. On June 17th, Himmler met with Hitler at the Obersalzberg and informed him that the division was in the "build up" process. Finally, on June 24, 1943, Jüttner, whose headquarters was responsible for the assignment of officers and enlisted personnel, issued a directive officially establishing the 12th SS "Hitler Youth" Panzer Grenadier (armored infantry) Division. The troop training grounds at Beverloo, Belgium, situated northwest of Brussels, was to serve as the organizational and training center for the division. Reserves and replacements were to be supplied by the 12th SS Panzer Grenadier Training and Replacement Battalion (SS Panzer-Grenadier Ausbildungs und Ersatz Bataillon 12), located at Arnheim.[22] A month later, on July 27th, another Jüttner directive created the I SS Panzer Corps headquarters, with its training and replacement battalion situated at Berlin-Lichterfelde.[23] Both the 1st SS Leibstandarte and the 12th SS Divisions would serve under the Panzer Corps--commanded by SS-Obergruppenführer Josef Dietrich.

In June 1943, Fritz Witt, the commander of the LAH Division's 1st Panzer Grenadier Regiment, was appointed commander of the Hitler Youth Division. At the age of 35, Witt became one of the youngest divisional commanders in

Jost W. Schneider

Fritz Witt, here an SS-Obersturmbannführer.

---

[22]Hitler had originally ordered the formal establishment of the division for June 1, 1943. T-175/108/2631214-15. SS-Führungshauptamt. Betr.: Aufstellung der SS-Panz.Gren.Div. "Hitlerjugend." 24.6.1943; T-175/108/2631252. Führerbefehl, Führerhauptquartier. n.d.

[23]T-175/111/2635163-64. SS-Führungshauptamt. Betr.: Aufstellung des Gen. Kd. I.SS-Pz.Korps "Leibstandarte," Geheime Kommandosache. 27.7.1943.

the German armed forces. He had fought with distinction in the major campaigns of the war, earning many of Germany's most coveted military honors. A humane, yet hard-driving commander, Witt was held in high esteem by officers and enlisted men alike, and, despite a youthful, almost boyish physiognomy, he was typical of the dynamic breed of young SS officers who commanded from the front lines. A large, robust man who had a weakness for cigars, he would display a fatherly concern for the teenagers who made up his new command.

Witt's early life was similar to that of many young men who eventually found their way into the ranks of the Waffen SS. From a modest family background, he completed his elementary school education in 1922. A three year apprenticeship in the textile industry followed, after which he found employment as a shipping and correspondence clerk until the summer of 1931. In December 1931, after the bankruptcy of the firm for which he worked had left him unemployed, Witt joined the General SS (Allgemeine SS) in Hagen. On March 17, 1933, Witt became one of the original 120 hand-picked members of the Leibstandarte.[24] Service in the Waffen SS had a special attractiveness to this young man of modest social origin, who desired a career as an officer yet lacked the educational qualifications for such a career in the regular armed forces.

In January 1935, Witt's superiors transferred him from the LAH to the SS Regiment (Standarte) "Deutschland," quartered in Munich, where he took command of the regiment's 3rd Company. At the head of this company the young SS-Hauptsturmführer saw duty in the Polish campaign in 1939, earning the Iron Cross first and second class--the former for a boldly executed raid against the Polish fortress complex around Modlin. In October 1939, Witt was given command of the regiment's 1st Battalion, which he led with great distinction during the western offensive of 1940. On one occasion, at Merville on May 27, 1940, 20 enemy tanks supported by infantry suddenly attacked his battalion, which was deployed on the regiment's right flank. Because the battalion's anti-tank guns were still on the far side of the Lys Canal, and no bridges were available, they could not be brought forward to assist the defenders. Equipped only with light infantry weapons and grenades, Witt and his men repulsed the attack in savage close combat, disabling nine enemy tanks in the process.[25] For this and other actions, Witt received the prestigious Knight's Cross.

In October 1940, he returned to the Leibstandarte. As a battalion and later a regimental commander, Witt made a good account of himself in both the Balkan and Russian campaigns, participating in many of the LAH's notable

---

[24]See the following chapter for a detailed account of the origins and history of the Leibstandarte.

[25]According to Felix Steiner, the commander of the SS Regiment "Deutschland," Witt was the "heart of the resistance." Berlin Documentation Center. SS Personalakten, Fritz Witt. Vorschlagsliste Nr. 5 für die Verleihung des Ritterkreuzes des Eisernen Kreuzes. Div. St. Qu., den 18. Juli 1940. gez. Hausser; also, Klahn, Werner, "SS-Sturmbannführer Witt erhält das Ritterkreuz."

victories: the storming of the Klidi Pass (1940), the encirclement battle of Uman (1941), the capture of Rostov (1941), and the successful defensive battles around Kharkov (1943).[26] In recognition of his leadership qualities, Witt received the Oak Leaves to the Knight's Cross on March 1, 1943. Promoted to SS-Oberführer on July 1, 1943, Witt accepted the greatest challenge of his military career when he took command of the Hitler Youth Division. He would serve as its commander until his violent death early in the Normandy campaign.[27]

* * * * *

---

[26]Witt's brother, also a member of the LAH, was killed during the Greek campaign.

[27]The information on Fritz Witt's early life and subsequent military career from: SS Personalakten, Fritz Witt: Dienstlaufbahn, Lebenslauf, etc.; also author interview with Fritz Witt's son, Peter Witt, on June 8, 1981 in Bad Hersfeld, West Germany.

Chapter 3
THE LEIBSTANDARTE SS ADOLF HITLER

The Leibstandarte . . . shall not be a parade troop performing a purely ceremonial function. Rather, it shall be a community of soldiers welded firmly together through harsh training; a simple unspoiled world in which decisive virtues prevail; a world in which the heart questions and is answered by other hearts. Youth found it magnificent. Sepp Dietrich and his Leibstandarte, that was stirring.

(Ernst-Günther Krätschmer)

In case there were ever an attempt at a revolt in Berlin by foreign workers, the Führer would send his *Leibstandarte* to the capital; it would make an example of them that would make every lover of such excesses lose all itch for them.

(Joseph Goebbels)

The origins of the Leibstandarte reach back to the spring of 1933, when, for the third time in ten years, the need for personal security compelled Hitler to establish a small "household" guard, unquestionably loyal to him and suited for internal security duties. On March 17, 1933, Hitler formed a headquarters guard (SS-Stabwache) consisting of 120 specially selected SS men commanded by his long-time associate and supporter, **Josef (Sepp) Dietrich.**[1] At the same

---

[1]Dietrich had joined the SS in 1928 at the lowest rank (SS Mann), but advanced quickly in Himmler's rapidly expanding organization. After organizing the SS in southern Bavaria, Dietrich became head of the SS Oberabschnitt Nord in Hamburg. In April 1931, he played a major part in crushing the Stennes putsch--an incipient revolt of the refractory northern-radical SA. During 1932, Dietrich accompanied Hitler on his electoral tours across Germany, serving as his personal bodyguard. Throughout the pre-war period he remained a member of Hitler's personal entourage, often accompanying the Führer on maneuvers and formal inspections of military installations. A charismatic leader with a passion for hunting and auto racing, Dietrich possessed the rare ability to inspire and to motivate. His technical acumen as a soldier, however, was decidedly limited. As SS-Obergruppenführer Wilhelm Bittrich recalled: "I once spent an hour and a half trying to explain a situation to Sepp Dietrich with the aid of a map. It was quite useless. He understood nothing at all." In the last analysis, Dietrich's "Landsknecht personality, combined with a rough intelligence and sense of loyalty to Hitler explain his rise to a moderately lofty status within the Nazi hierarchy." Heinz Höhne, *The Order of the Death's Head. The Story of Hitler's SS* (New York: Ballantine Books, 1966), pp 496-97; James J. Weingartner, *Hitler's Guard. The Story of the Leibstandarte SS Adolf Hitler. 1933-1945* (London: Southern Illinois University Press, 1974), pp 16-17.

Josef (Sepp) Dietrich in 1933.

time, in key cities such as Hamburg, Dresden, and Munich, other small groups of armed SS men were formed into special detachments (SS-Sonderkommandos) to be used for police and other internal duties. Later known as political alarm squads (Politische Bereitschaften), these special detachments formed the foundation of the subsequent SS All-Purpose Force (SS-Verfügungstruppe), which, in turn, evolved into the Waffen SS.[2]

The SS-Stabwache moved into Lichterfelde Barracks on the outskirts of Berlin. A harsh, walled complex of brick buildings, the barracks in Imperial times had housed Germany's most prestigious military academy, the Hauptkadettenanstalt. At the Nürnberg party rally in September 1933, Hitler christened the new formation the Leibstandarte SS Adolf Hitler. As the title suggested, the Leibstandarte possessed a unique personal bond to the Führer, and, in a solemn midnight ceremony in Munich on November 9-10, 1933, Hitler and LAH strengthened this special relationship. Assembled by torchlight in front of the Feldherrnhalle (the site of the Nazi leader's abortive Putsch attempt in 1923), Dietrich's guardsmen swore an oath of allegiance to Adolf Hitler. In this manner, Reich Chancellor Hitler created an independent armed force at his sole disposal, elevating the Leibstandarte to the status of a true praetorian guard, above constitution, party, and state.[3]

The revolutionary implications of this new formation were not readily apparent to most Germans, for the functions and purpose of the LAH seemed to

---

[2]Hans Buchheim, et. al. *Anatomy of the SS State* (New York: Walker and Company, 1968), pp 142-43; for a still useful general history of the Waffen SS in English see George H. Stein's *The Waffen SS. Hitler's Elite Guard at War 1939-1945* (Ithaca, New York: Cornell University Press, 1966).

[3]Buchheim, *Anatomy of the SS State,* p 255.

assure a certain continuity with the past. Outwardly, the Leibstandarte was an armed unit organized to protect the Führer and to perform certain ceremonial tasks—its distinctive black dress uniforms, impeccable drill and incessant parading constituting a large part of its public image in the pre-war period.[4] But its actual significance was far greater and considerably more ominous, for the LAH would soon display its worth as Hitler's personal instrument of violence par excellence.

Jost. W. Schneider

Adolf Hitler leaving the Kroll Opera House in 1934. Note that he is flanked by LAH guards.

From the outset the armed SS, or Verfügungstruppe as it was soon christened with deliberate vagueness, was envisaged as an elite force with recruitment based upon rigid physical and racial standards. So selective were the SS examiners that, until 1936, a candidate could not have even one filled tooth. Dietrich and his Leibstandarte, however, though nominally a component of the Verfügungstruppe, remained "something special," an "elite within an elite," and were so regarded by Hitler.[5] Only the Leibstandarte enjoyed special recruiting privileges throughout Germany, while other armed SS units were confined in this respect to their particular Army corps areas. Dietrich's guardsmen also benefited from rail fare discounts for travel on official business or on furlough—a privilege also granted the Wehrmacht but denied to

[4]Weingartner, *Hitler's Guard*, p 144.

[5]James J. Weingartner, "Sepp Dietrich, Heinrich Himmler, and the Leibstandarte SS Adolf Hitler, 1933-1938." In: Journal of Central European History. Vol. 1. Number 3. September 1968. p 279.

The LAH marching past Hitler in Berlin. Note white leather accoutrements unique to this formation.

other armed SS formations. Only LAH soldiers wore smart white leather accoutrements with their black dress uniforms, and only they were permitted to wear the simple double Sig SS runes on their right collar tabs while "other (SS) units had to embellish and in a sense dilute them with an identifying mark."[6]

The Leibstandarte also enjoyed a degree of independence within the SS far greater than any other SS unit, for Dietrich, through his special personal relationship with Hitler, remained virtually immune to Himmler's control despite the LAH's formal subordination to the Reichsführer SS in April 1934. Furthermore, the LAH's links to the Wehrmacht in matters of training and equipment continued to grow, negating a good deal of the administrative control Himmler might have exercised over it. Relations between Dietrich's organization and local Army units of Military District III (Wehrkreis III) were almost uniformly cordial from the start of training operations in the summer of 1933. Conversely, the privileged status of the LAH often led to friction between its men and those of other SS units.

Much to Himmler's chagrin, the principal loyalty of Dietrich and his men would remain to Adolf Hitler. For Leibstandarte soldiers the link to Hitler was no mere abstraction. Many of them served in close proximity to the Führer as guards at the Reich Chancellery and at the Obersalzberg, or filled the open black limousines that accompanied the Nazi leader when he ventured out. A few even saw duty on Hitler's personal staff.

When in the early summer of 1934 Hitler decided to eliminate the revolutionary wing of Ernst Röhm's storm troops (Sturmabteilung, or SA), he turned to the Leibstandarte to perform the task. From June 30th to July 2nd, LAH soldiers manned the firing squads at Munich's Stadelheim Prison and at the Lichterfelde Barracks in Berlin. Although impossible to determine how many participated in these shootings, on July 5, 1934, 25 men including Dietrich (whom the Führer personally promoted to the rank of SS-

[6]Ibid., p 279.

Obergruppenführer) were advanced in rank for "distinguished service" in the purge, and although the "cleansing action" (Säuberungsaktion), as it was called, was not commemorated on the Leibstandarte's regimental standard, all participants later received commemorative daggers. The entire LAH swore an oath of secrecy concerning the affair, breaches of which were to be severely punished. The significance of the Leibstandarte's role in the purge is clear: for the first time the LAH had demonstrated its value as a pliant instrument of counter-revolutionary violence, conducting its operations in absolute loyalty to Hitler.[7]

* * *

The pre-war years brought a steady expansion of the Leibstandarte, which from early 1934 on was clearly being organized and trained along the lines of an infantry regiment. By March 1934, it had increased in size to about 1,000 men, distributed into four rifle companies, a machine gun company, a motorized company, a reconnaissance company, and support units. The LAH grew to roughly regimental strength by the fall of 1934, and three years later (fall of 1937) numbered 3,622 men; in terms of numbers and motorization it moved far ahead of the other armed SS formations--a fact that clearly demonstrated its favored status within the Verfügungstruppe.[8]

The Wehrmacht High Command contemplated the growth of the Leibstandarte, and of the Verfügungstruppe in general, with increasing alarm. The High Command, convinced that the existence of armed SS units posed a threat to its jealously guarded prerogative as the sole bearer of arms for the German nation, attempted to limit the expansion of such units--an effort that was largely successful during the period before the war.[9] The SS, for example, was forbidden to recruit through the press, forcing it to rely principally upon verbal propaganda within other National Socialist organizations, particularly the Hitler Youth.[10]

In its early conflict with the SS, the Army discovered an unlikely ally in Hitler, who could ill-afford a confrontation with the institution that would be fundamentally responsible for implementing his plan of territorial expansion via military conquest. Hitler, to defuse Army anxiety concerning the purpose of the armed SS, issued a top secret military directive on August 17, 1938. The directive clearly separated the functions of the armed SS from those of the Wehrmacht, stipulating that the true purpose of the SS units was for use at home. Hence, these units were to be organized, trained, and equipped to fulfill "internal political tasks," such as the suppression of revolutionary unrest, thereby releasing the Army from a responsibility it had always found repugnant. The Verfügungstruppe, moreover, was to be neither a component of the Wehrmacht nor of the police, but a standing force exclusively at Hitler's dis-

---

[7]Ibid., p 277.

[8]Weingartner, *Hitler's Guard*, p 23.

[9]In May 1940, General Alfred Jodl, Chief of the OKW Operations Staff (Wehrmachtführungsstab), would register in his diary his anxiety concerning Himmler's "limitless plan of expansion for the SS." Wegner, *Hitlers Politische Soldaten*, p 303.

[10]Buchheim, *Anatomy of the SS State*, p 259.

posal. In the event of mobilization for war, however, its troops were to come under the operational control of the Army.[11]

Hitler's directive served a distinct purpose--that of reassuring the Wehrmacht--and thus does not signify an accurate reflection of either Hitler's, or Himmler's, ultimate plans or intentions vis-à-vis the Verfügungstruppe. There was, in fact, "a more compelling reason for the existence of the armed SS," which went far beyond the goal of a militarized police force and aimed at nothing less than the creation of an independent and specifically National Socialist army. Himmler remained realistic enough to know that he lacked the resources to build a force large enough to supplant the Wehrmacht; yet through the instrument of the Verfügungstruppe (and later the Waffen SS), its prestige elevated by service at the front, he hoped to eliminate the political influence of the traditional armed forces. This intent is perhaps the most logical explanation for the expansion of the military wing of the SS well beyond the requirements of a militarized police--an expansion that would reveal an unbroken line of continuity right up to the collapse of the Third Reich in 1945.[12]

Despite the resistance of the conservative military establishment, the Leibstandarte continued to enjoy a steady flow of volunteers. Some came as fervently committed National Socialists, but many others enlisted for extraideological reasons, such as the desire to join the guard regiment of the Führer. On the surface, the functions of the LAH appeared definable in traditional ways, for guard regiments serving autocratic rulers were a glamorous component of Germany's martial past. The public perception of the Leibstandarte was certainly that of a super-elite formation--a perception sedulously promoted by Goebbels' propaganda machine. Others joined out of a spirit of adventure, or perhaps because of enthusiasm for the smart black dress uniforms worn by LAH members. Simple pragmatism was also a factor, since the educational requirements for officer training in the SS were lower than in the Wehrmacht, thereby attracting youths who found officer careers in the traditional services barred to them. Consequently, the LAH, and the Verfügungstruppe in general, provided individuals from lower middle class (Mittelstand) and from peasant backgrounds an opportunity to lead prestigious military careers, but without the traditions and social pretensions of the Wehrmacht.[13]

In view of the significance of non-ideological determinants for enlistment in the SS, it is not surprising that ideological indoctrination played a relatively

---

[11]Ibid., pp 262-64.

[12]For an insightful discussion of this problem see Wegner, *Hitlers Politische Soldaten,* pp 301-3; 316; also Stein, *The Waffen SS,* pp 16-17.

[13]According to Höhne, the Verfügungstruppe "remained an army of peasants and artisans. In Schleswig-Holstein, Lower Saxony, Franconia and the Saar, one out of every three farmers' sons joined the Verfügungstruppe or, later, the Waffen-SS." Höhne, *The Order of the Death's Head.* p 505.

[14]As Hans Buchheim pointed out in his "Gutachten" for the Eichmann trial, this held true for the entire SS: "the body of ideological doctrine and theoretical dogma available in the SS was astonishingly meagre . . . the SS had no strict ideological training or educational discipline, nothing which can even remotely be compared with that of the communists." Buchheim, *Anatomy of the SS State,* pp 319-20.

minor role in the Leibstandarte.[14] Schooling in National Socialist Weltanschauung there was, and it concentrated upon standard themes: the threat posed to the German people by the Jews, the corrosive effects of Christianity and of pacifism upon the German spirit, and the superiority of the "Aryan" race, to name a few of them. Despite such indoctrination, Himmler's attempt to forge the armed SS into the ideological cutting-edge of National Socialism remained a "largely futile enterprise when applied to the Leibstandarte, for the men who had joined it had done so for the purpose of leading lives as soldiers, albeit soldiers who were attracted by the unique status conferred by membership in that company." Many LAH members were not even party members, let alone fanatical Nazis.

It was Sepp Dietrich, however, who ultimately set the tone for the LAH, which, in a very real sense, was his own personal creation. Dietrich evinced little concern for either National Socialist party affairs or ideology; his lack of enthusiasm for Himmler's "blood and soil" vaporizings derived in part from the concerted effort to shape the Leibstandarte into a technically refined, professional combat unit--an effort that demanded adoption of the more utilitarian attitudes of the regular Army. The assimilation of such attitudes appears to have taken place within the Verfügungstruppe in general;[15] and just as the process of modern total war tends to blur boundaries that divide a nation's social classes and institutions, so too the identification of the field formations of the armed SS with those of the Wehrmacht would grow stronger as the Second World War progressed.

If the Leibstandarte did possess a distinctive ideology, it can perhaps best be understood as an ideology of activism. Indeed, a kind of primitive activism, ultimately lacking a rational purpose or concrete goal, was one of the driving forces behind the National Socialist movement as a whole. A former Leibstandarte soldier has characterized the pre-war LAH as a world in which "the rules of Germanness were not read out; one learned them by leaps from ten meter towers, by 20 mile marches, and by the most severe training on the exercise grounds."[16] It was this spirit of unadulterated soldiering that furnished the LAH with its particular élan and appeal.

Although difficult to pinpoint a specific ideological character, the Leibstandarte clearly did possess a distinctive mentality. The early 1920s had witnessed the bifurcation of German military development into separate and distinct lines. For one group of Germans the line went through the regular armed forces, from the Reichswehr of the Weimar period to Hitler's Wehrmacht. For a second, tributary group the path was much different, leading from the post World War One Free Corps (Freikorps) movement into the SA and the SS.[17] It

---

[15]Weingartner, "Sepp Dietrich, Heinrich Himmler, and the Leibstandarte SS Adolf Hitler, 1933-1938." pp 281-83.

[16]Ernst-Günther Krätschmer, *Ritterkreuzträger der Waffen-SS* (Göttingen: Plesse Verlag, 1957), pp 10-11.

[17]The Freikorps comprised irregulars, mostly former soldiers, who preferred the security and predictability of military life to the harsh and uncertain realities of a civilian career during the Weimar period. Often assisted by the Reichswehr, the Freikorps passed its time beating up on communists and other perceived enemies of the Reich, until eventually disbanded. Andreas Hillgruber, "Die 'Endlösung' und das

was the violent milieu of the Freikorps--its nihilism and elitism--that most closely captured the spirit of the Leibstandarte. Dietrich himself had served with the elite assault troops of the Bavarian Army in World War One; thereafter, he had joined the Bund Oberland Freikorps and battled the Polish volunteer army in upper Silesia. Through the charismatic leadership of Dietrich, and of other remnants from the earliest stratum of Leibstandarte membership, the freebooter (Landsknecht) mentality so typical to the Freikorps would remain pronounced within the LAH as well.[18]

An integral component of the LAH mentality (and of that of the entire armed SS) was the apotheosis of "toughness" (Härte). Paradoxically, SS "toughness" reflected both the pronounced idealism and the underlying inhumanity of the SS spirit. The phenomenon of Härte, however, is not easy to define, for it was, in fact, many things: the subjugation of oneself and of others to iron discipline, the attempt to push oneself to physical and psychic limits, the refusal to accept that any task, no matter how great or small, was impossible. Ideologically, Härte demanded an uncompromising posture, even ruthlessness, towards one's enemies, and, if necessary, towards one's own comrades. Training to be tough, of course, is intrinsic to a soldier's education everywhere, but in the armed SS such training often assumed exaggerated dimensions. The result would be a specific brand of soldiering that often led to great victories, but at a terrible price in casualties.

Through his battlefield exploits and uncompromising behavior, Kurt Meyer would earn a reputation for Härte perhaps unsurpassed in the Leibstandarte. For the SS as a whole, the prototype of toughness was undoubtedly SS-Obergruppenführer Reinhard Heydrich, the Chief of the Reich Main Security Office of the SS (Reichssicherheitshauptamt) until mortally wounded by Allied agents in May 1942. The memoir of a former SS cadet illustrates just how far Heydrich was able to carry the ideal:[19]

> My account would not be complete without a reference to the 'blond God' Reinhard Heydrich. At that time Heydrich was already almost a mystic figure. There was hardly a room in the Cadet School without his picture--many more than of the Reichsführer. I cannot repeat all the qualities attributed to him, but one was outstanding--his (toughness). There can be no better proof of the iron discipline to which he subjected both himself and his body than the moments immediately after he had been attacked when, mortally wounded and in agonizing pain, he still mustered the strength to reach for his holster, open it and send five shots after his attackers. It is significant that almost without exception his pictures showed him as the winner of the 'Reich Route March.'

---

deutsche Ostimperium als Kernstuck des rassenideologischen Programms des Nationalsozialismus." p 270. In: *Deutsche Grossmacht-und Weltpolitik im 19. und 20. Jahrundert* (Dusseldorf: Droste Verlag, 1977).

[18]Weingartner, *Hitler's Guard*, p 145; Stein, *The Waffen SS*, pp 290-92.

[19]Wounded on May 29th, Heydrich died on June 4, 1942. The quote is from Buchheim, *Anatomy of the SS State*, pp 339-40.

With its diminutive size and carefully selected personnel, the Verfügungstruppe was able to introduce a number of innovations in actual military training. In contrast to the Wehrmacht, the armed SS made organized sport and physical conditioning an integral part of its training routine. Long distance running, boxing, rowing, and track and field events were regular activities for officers and enlisted men alike. This training regimen not only fostered a high degree of physical fitness, but also served to promote a special camaraderie and mutual respect between officers and enlisted personnel. Thus, in its training as well the Verfügungstruppe displayed an egalitarianism uncommon to the regular armed forces. At no time, however, was the SS soldier permitted to forget that he belonged to a highly elite military organization. Until 1939, SS infantrymen trained principally as assault troops, similar perhaps to British Commandos and United States Army Rangers.[20] Such training demanded a very personal type of leadership, and, like the SS emphasis upon toughness, would contribute to alarming losses among both officers and NCOs.

*　　　*　　　*

From the summer of 1934 until the outbreak of war in 1939 the Leibstandarte settled into a relatively passive routine, punctuated only by its participation in the bloodless victories of Hitler's "flower war" (Blumenkrieg). Symbolic of its growing prestige, the LAH was the first German unit to enter Saarbrücken during the remilitarization of the Rhineland in March 1936. When German troops advanced into Austria two years later during the Anschluss, a motorized contingent of the Leibstandarte was also there, serving with General Heinz Guderian's XVI Army Corps. In October 1938, Dietrich's soldiers participated in the occupation of the Sudetenland.[21]

On the eve of the Second World War the Leibstandarte moved out of Lichterfelde Barracks, its quarters since 1933, and would never return again as a complete unit. A week later, on September 1, 1939, the Wehrmacht poured into Poland, slicing through the defenses of a poorly prepared and technically inferior opponent. As a motorized infantry regiment, the LAH fought briefly with General Johannes Blaskowitz's Eighth Army, and, later, with General Walther von Reichenau's Tenth Army. Dietrich's infantrymen played an important role in the battle of the Bzura pocket, which yielded some 105,000 prisoners. Throughout the Polish campaign Hitler maintained a keen interest in the formation that carried his name, tracing its movements on a large map in the Reich Chancellery marked with the simple notation, "Sepp."[22]

In May 1940, Hitler began his offensive in the West against France and the Low Countries. For the next six weeks the Leibstandarte would see almost continuous action, developing the style of aggressive mobile warfare that would become its trademark. Brought up in strength to a reinforced infantry regiment (motorized), the LAH began the campaign attached to Army Group B, and took part in the invasion of Holland. At dawn on May 10th, the motorcycle company commanded by Kurt Meyer burst through the Dutch border

[20]Stein, *The Waffen SS,* p 13.
[21]Ibid., pp 8, 19, 24.
[22]Weingartner, *Hitler's Guard,* p 36.

defenses and covered some 48 miles in six hours' time, reaching the line of the Yssel river at Zwolle--its first objective.[23] Meyer immediately seized a Dutch civilian vehicle, raced off to meet with the mayor of the town, and successfully negotiated its surrender. Farther south, at Zutphen, the lead elements of the Leibstandarte's 3rd Battalion had also reached the Yssel by mid-day, only to find the bridges over the river destroyed by their Dutch defenders. Undaunted, the SS troopers paddled across in small boats (Schlauchboote) despite exposure to intense enemy machine gun fire.[24]

Following a 36 mile advance beyond the Yssel by the evening of the 10th, Dietrich's regiment was withdrawn and directed southwest to support the drive of the 9th Panzer Division on Rotterdam. Elements of the Leibstandarte occupied Rotterdam on the afternoon of May 14th, just hours after waves of Heinkel 111 bombers had blanketed the city with bombs.[25]

Following the Dutch capitulation, the LAH took part in the drive towards the Channel coast and in the battle along the Dunkirk perimeter. On the evening of May 24, 1940, the German High Command issued its controversial order that temporarily halted the general advance on Dunkirk at the line of the Aa Canal, leaving to Göring's Luftwaffe the task of eliminating Allied forces bottled up within the perimeter. The Leibstandarte received the order just as it was poised to launch an attack across the canal, but Dietrich, his regiment in an exposed position under heavy artillery fire, elected to ignore it and attacked as planned. The next morning, a battalion of his SS troops crossed the canal and captured the high ground near Watten. In view of the precarious position of his men, Dietrich's breach of the halt order represented a "sound tactical decision displaying an intelligent sense of initiative."[26]

The victorious romp through Holland and Flanders had led to curious behavior on the part of some LAH soldiers, and following the successful forcing of the Aa Canal, Dietrich was forced to reassert soldierly discipline. He ordered his men to "cease wearing civilian business suits, which some had apparently 'liberated,' and to banish dogs, dolls and stuffed animals from their vehicles, which in Dietrich's words had taken on a 'gypsylike appearance.' "[27]

The Leibstandarte now temporarily withdrew from the front to refit for Case Red (Fall Rot)--the forthcoming offensive against the French forces south of the Somme-Aisne line. Back in action by early June, the LAH participated in the main German drive towards Paris as a component of Panzer Group Kleist. The Panzer Group, however, slowed by stiffening enemy resistance north of the French capital, would soon shift its attack further to the east. Consequently, by June 12th, the LAH had reached the Marne near Château-Thierry and secured a bridgehead across the river at St. Aulde. In the final days of the French campaign, the Leibstandarte spearheaded the Panzer

[23]Meyer, K., *Grenadiere*, p 20.
[24]Rudolf Lehmann, *Die Leibstandarte.* Band I (Osnabrück: Munin Verlag GmbH, 1977), pp 226-29.
[25]Meyer, K., *Grenadiere*, p 24.
[26]Weingartner, *Hitler's Guard,* p 42.
[27]Ibid., p 43.

Group's drive southward in pursuit of the beaten adversary, demonstrating once again the war of movement at which it had come to excel: spraying the enemy with automatic weapons fire from moving vehicles, smashing barricades with armored cars and mortar fire, and, for a three-day period, even racing so far ahead it lost contact with Panzer Group headquarters. In one of the deepest German penetrations of the campaign, the LAH seized St. Etienne and its garrison on June 24th.[28]

Following the victory over France the Leibstandarte retired to Metz for additional training and refitting. Here, it became temporarily involved in the preparations for Operation Sealion, the planned invasion of England. During this period the LAH also underwent significant expansion, for on August 6, 1940, Hitler authorized its enlargement to the size of a reinforced brigade.

The peaceful interlude was abruptly shattered on April 6, 1941, when large German forces smashed into Yugoslavia and Greece. Once more the Leibstandarte was at the forefront of the assault, and once more its performance was nothing short of spectacular. In a violent two-day engagement with veterans of the British Expeditionary Force, an LAH battlegroup commanded by SS-Sturmbannführer Fritz Witt forced open the strategic Klidi Pass, the gateway to Greece. But the price for the victory was high: 37 dead and 98 wounded.[29] Shortly thereafter, the LAH's reconnaissance battalion stormed the stoutly defended Klissura Pass, capturing more than 600 prisoners at a loss of nine men killed and 18 wounded.[30] Meyer, who commanded the battalion, describes the operation in his war memoirs, offering vivid insight into the aggressive, if unorthodox, combat leadership so distinctive of the Waffen SS.[31] While two of his companies struggled up the cliffs to outflank the defenders, Meyer and a small group advanced along the road through the pass; mortars, medium field pieces, and dual purpose 88mm guns supported the attack. Above him, Meyer could hear the crackle of machine gun fire and the dull thud of hand grenades as his troops stormed the enemy strongpoints. Suddenly, one violent explosion shook the earth, and then another: the Greek defenders had just set off the main demolition charges, ripping huge gaps in the road and sending portions of it crashing to the valley below. "We crouch behind the rocks," writes Meyer,[32]

> and dare not move. A sick feeling nearly chokes me. I scream to Emil Wawrzinek that he must continue the attack, but he stares at me as if he doubts my sanity. Machine gun fire spatters the rocks in front of us. Our lead group consists of about 10 men. Damn! We can't simply stay where we are while craters are being blown in the road and machine gun fire sweeps the rubble. But even I am crouching in complete cover and fear for my life. How

---

[28]Stein, *The Waffen SS,* pp 85-86.

[29]Lehmann, *Die Leibstandarte,* Band I, p 378.

[30]Ibid., pp 385-86.

[31]The term Waffen SS was first introduced in the fall of 1939; within a year it had superceded the older term Verfügungstruppe to describe the armed formations of the SS. Wegner, *Hitlers Politische Soldaten,* p 127.

[32]Meyer, K., *Grenadiere,* p 64.

SS-Hauptsturmführer Kurt Meyer after the French campaign in 1940.

(Below) Himmler congratulates LAH officers after the successful Greek campaign. (Left to right) Keilhaus, Himmler, Meyer, Sukkow and Mertsch.

can I get Wawrzinek to move? In desperation I feel the smooth roundness of a potato masher in my hand and yell to the group. Thunderstruck, they stare at me as I show them the grenade, pull the pin, and lob it directly behind the last man. Never again as in this moment have I seen such a uniform leap forward. As if possessed we rush around the rocky crag and into the freshly blown crater. The spell is broken. The hand grenade has brought an end to our paralysis. We grin at one another and continue the advance.

The next day, Meyer's motorcycle troops captured the important town of Kastoria, bagging an additional 1,200 prisoners. Meyer, for the achievements of his battalion during this 24 hour period, would receive the Knight's Cross.

By April 20, 1941, the Leibstandarte had captured the Metzovon Pass, cutting across the withdrawal route of the Greek Epirus Army and forcing the capitulation of its 18 divisions. That evening, high atop the pass, beneath shadowy pines and flickering candlelight, Dietrich and the Greek commander signed the surrender documents.[33]

Only weeks later, on Sunday morning June 22, 1941, Hitler unleashed the greatest gamble of his military career--Operation Barbarossa, the attack on Soviet Russia. More than 3,000,000 men organized into 153 divisions (of which 19 were armored and 14 motorized) advanced along a front that stretched 1,800 miles from the Arctic tundra to the Black Sea coast.[34] For the soldiers of the Waffen SS in particular, Hitler's war of extermination (Vernichtungskrieg) against the hated communist enemy would be one of unparalleled ferocity. And in the crucible of the eastern front they would establish once and for all their reputation as an elite fighting force.[35]

Subordinated to Colonel-General Ewald von Kleist's 1st Panzer Group, the armored striking force of Field Marshal Gerd von Rundstedt's Army Group South, the Leibstandarte (now a full-fledged motorized division) entered the fighting on July 1st in the vicinity of the Luck bridgehead across the Styr river. Already on June 22nd, the tanks of the Panzer Group had crossed the frontier north of Lemberg (Lvov), achieving tactical surprise along the entire front. Under a glowing, oppressive sun, Kleist's III and XLVIII Panzer Corps had punched a deep hole in the Soviet bunker positions along the Bug river. However, in marked contrast to Army Group North and Army Group Center, Rundstedt's forces quickly encountered vigorous opposition. The Russian defenders, deployed in great strength and depth across the axis of Kleist's advance, recovered rapidly from the initial shock of invasion and fought with a skill and a ruthlessness to which the Germans were not accustomed. Behind stacks of straw and in trees and farmsteads lurked enemy sharpshooters outfitted with telescopic sights; the ubiquitous cornfields teemed with Soviet infantry in well-concealed positions that were only cleared through bitter hand-to-hand combat. General Franz Halder, Chief of the German Army General Staff, noted in his diary the tenacity of individual enemy units in battle, and the fact that some Russian bunker crews preferred to blow themselves up with their bunkers rather than to face captivity.[36]

For the Leibstandarte, its first days in the field would bring a chilling awareness that the war in the east would be a struggle of apocalyptic dimensions. Again, Kurt Meyer:[37]

---

[33]Lehmann, *Die Leibstandarte,* Band I, pp 398-401.

[34]Horst Scheibert and Ulrich Elfrath, *Panzer in Russland. Die deutschen gepanzerten Verbände im Russland-Feldzug 1941-1944* (Dorheim: Podzun-Verlag, 1971), p 8.

[35]My reference here is only to the "classic" SS divisions, that is, to the Leibstandarte, Das Reich, Totenkopf, and Wiking. Members of these divisions garnered approximately 55 percent of all Knight's Crosses awarded to formations of the Waffen SS. Wegner, *Hitlers Politische Soldaten,* p 281.

[36]Generaloberst Franz Halder, *Kriegstagebuch. Tägliche Aufzeichnungen des Chefs des Generalstabes des Heeres 1939-42.* Band III (Stuttgart: W. Kohlhammer Verlag, 1964), p 10.

[37]Meyer, K., *Grenadiere,* pp 80-81.

The road leads in a straight line to the southeast . . . On the horizon clouds of smoke climb vertically into the sky. I am moving behind the lead platoon and scour the terrain with my field glasses. On a slope I recognize an abandoned artillery piece and among the fresh green corn I can make out several clear patches. The gun is a German light field howitzer that has been abandoned in its firing position and it has a depressing effect upon us. For the first time we've discovered a German weapon abandoned on the battlefield. Several feet from the gun stands a ransacked field ambulance. Its doors have been ripped open and are smeared with blood. In silence we observe this scene of devastation. No soldiers, either living or dead, are to be found. Slowly we motor up the hill.

The conspicuous clear patches become more evident. We can now clearly make out one large and one small patch. I drop my field glasses and rub my eyes, then I take another look. My God, that can't be possible what I've just seen. We cover the final two hundred yards quickly. The lead platoon dismounts and runs with me to the clear patches in the corn. Our steps grow slower, then we stop suddenly. No one dares to go farther. We remove our steel helmets as if in prayer. No words desecrate the scene. Even the birds are silent. Before us lies a company of naked and brutally slaughtered German soldiers. Their hands have been bound with wire and their eyes ripped open. Perhaps the officers of this company have met an even more terrible end. They lie several yards from their comrades. We find their bodies in the green clover--torn to pieces and trampled . . .

My soldiers stand before me. They expect an explanation from me, or at least instructions for their further conduct in Russia. We look at one another. I search the eyes of every soldier. Without saying a word I turn around and we continue on towards an unknown fate.

Kurt Meyer, obviously fatigued, during the early stages of the Russian campaign.

Advancing southeast along the Kiev highway, and through the dark, primeval forests of Galacia, the Leibstandarte was entangled in fierce fighting west of Zhitomir until mid-July. It then took part in the encirclement battle of Uman, a classic military operation that harvested more than 100,000 enemy prisoners. Following a brief stay in a quiet area south of Kirovograd to refit, the division returned to action in early September. Now subordinated to General Erich von Manstein's Eleventh Army, the motorized units of the LAH helped to breach the defenses of the Crimea. In October, Dietrich's SS troops were advancing along the northern coast of the Sea of Azov, once again assigned to Kleist's armored forces. Securing a bridgehead across the lower Mius on October 12th, the LAH then pushed on towards Rostov.

But by now there were disturbing auguries. Fuel shortages appeared, and heavy rains began to fall, transforming the dirt roads into quagmires of mud. Icy winds sweeping off the Sea of Azov portended the approach of winter, for which the LAH was neither clothed nor equipped. By the end of October, dysentery and combat attrition had reduced the division to roughly one half its normal combat strength.[38] The advance slowed.

Reduced in strength and low on fuel the Leibstandarte made a final, desperate lunge towards Rostov. On November 20, 1941, it burst into the city along with the 14th Panzer Division and swept forward to the Don, establishing a bridgehead on the far side of the river. Rostov fell after furious house-to-house combat. Yet the success was short-lived, for determined Soviet counterattacks with infantry and armor soon compelled Kleist to order a general withdrawal from the Rostov sector. On November 28th, Kleist's exhausted divisions began to jerk backwards in retreat to the line of the Mius and Ssambek rivers some 50 miles west of Rostov.

The abandonment of Rostov heralded the first major German setback on the eastern front--a sudden shift in fortune that sobered the Wehrmacht but enraged Hitler. The dictator's extraordinary decision to fly to Russia to learn directly from Dietrich the causes for the defeat was indicative of his growing trust and confidence in the LAH commander. Dietrich managed to persuade Hitler that the defeat had not resulted from deficiencies within the Army Group South leadership.

By December, the Leibstandarte was firmly ensconced along the Mius - Ssambek river line, subjected to fierce enemy counterattacks in the savage Russian winter. Here it would remain until the end of May 1942, when it was finally removed from the front for reorganization as a Panzer grenadier division. On Hitler's order, the LAH received an armored detachment composed of three companies equipped principally with 75mm Panzer IV tanks. In October 1942, this detachment was expanded to regimental size, and, in November, the Leibstandarte was given a company of the brand new super heavy and thickly armored Tiger tanks. The complement of Tigers was quickly increased to battalion strength.[39]

---

[38]Weingartner, *Hitler's Guard,* pp 59-64.
[39]Ibid., pp 66-73.

On June 28, 1942, the Germans launched their summer offensive in southern Russia. Hitler, however, convinced that a British descent on the Atlantic coast to help relieve the hardpressed Soviets was imminent, decided to send the Leibstandarte to France. By now, the LAH had become an "elite fire brigade," to be dispatched at a moment's notice to crisis points along the periphery of Hitler's empire. But the five month hiatus in the West would prove relatively uneventful as the division continued to refit and to reorganize. It conducted training exercises in Normandy, in the flat, open country south of Caen.[40]

In November 1942, the Leibstandarte was involved in the occupation of Vichy France, and, by January 1943, was back in Russia to help shore up the crumbling southern front following the Stalingrad disaster. Dietrich's veterans, fighting alongside the SS Divisions "Das Reich" and "Totenkopf," were hurled into the grinding defensive battles around Kharkov; despite appalling losses (including over 40 percent of combat strength) they played a major role in the recapture of the city in mid-March and in the stabilization of the German front.[41] Exultant over the Kharkov victory, Hitler awarded Dietrich the Oak Leaves with Swords to his Knight's Cross. Clearly, the Leibstandarte had reached the "apex of its prestige and its attainment, in Hitler's mind at least, of a reputation as a military force of almost superhuman qualities."[42]

Ironically, the elite qualities of the LAH were already undergoing a certain dilution, for to replenish its depleted ranks large numbers of Luftwaffe ground personnel were incorporated into the division in May 1943. The decision to extract the cadre personnel for the Hitler Youth Division from the Leibstandarte would result in a further diminution of its quality. By mid-June, LAH personnel destined for the HJ Division were entraining and chugging westward in anticipation of their new assignment.[43] Many of them now veterans of nearly four years of war, they would spend the better part of the next year imparting the special sense of elitism and the aggressive combat technique of the Waffen SS to the young recruits of the Hitler Youth Division.

*　　*　　*　　*　　*

[40]Meyer, K., *Grenadiere*, p 281.

[41]Lehmann, *Die Leibstandarte*, Band III, p 219.

[42]Weingartner, *Hitler's Guard*, p 57.

[43]Leibstandarte personnel destined for the HJ Division began to entrain between June 7-12, 1943. The LAH's anti-tank battalion, as well as elements of its medical and tank repair units, would be transferred to the HJ Division between September 1943 and February 1944. Lehmann, *Die Leibstandarte*, Band III, pp 220, 223.

Chapter 4
THE TRAINING OF THE HITLER YOUTH DIVISION

Modern trench warfare demands knowledge and experience; a man must have a feeling for the contours of the ground, an ear for the sound and character of the shells, must be able to decide beforehand where they will drop, how they will burst, and how to shelter from them. The young recruits of course know none of these things.

(Erich Maria Remarque)

The Hitler Youth Division will fight [fanatically] . . . The enemy will be struck with wonder.

(Adolf Hitler)

The problem of filling officer and NCO positions in the 12th SS Hitler Youth Division would persist throughout the entire training period. Although the Leibstandarte veterans incorporated into the division provided a small nucleus of experienced officers and NCOs, there remained an urgent requirement for additional company commanders and platoon and squad leaders. To become squad leaders (Gruppenführer), a number of youths who had performed well in the pre-military instruction camps received noncommissioned officer training at the SS NCO school at Lauenburg; other recruits, who had demonstrated leadership ability early in their basic training, participated in special NCO courses within division itself. The outcome of this approach was certainly unique, for the divisional noncommissioned officers were, in part, the same age or barely a year older than the boys they would lead into battle.

To fill vacant company commands, the division had no alternative but to turn to young platoon leaders (Zugführer), and, under the guidance of Knight's Cross holder SS-Hauptsturmführer Wilhelm Beck, the division organized a special officer training course. The shortage of technical specialists (for instruction in artillery use, etc.) caused particular concern, especially following the commencement of unit training early in 1944.[1] However, several "raids" at the Army Personnel Bureau (Heerespersonalamt) in Cottbus managed to

---

[1]The divisional escort company (Begleitkompanie), for example, experienced "special difficulties" training its light infantry gun platoon, for no officer with the requisite knowledge of the weapon was available. Bundesarchiv-Militärarchiv. RS 3-12/1. Tagebuch Divisions-Begleit-Kompanie der 12. SS-Pz. Div. "H.J." 1943-1945. 24.2.1944. (Hereafter all references to this Bundesarchiv cited BAMA.)

Klaus Bartels

SS-Hauptsturmführer
Wilhelm Beck.

secure the transfer of some 50 Wehrmacht officers, most apparently with a technical background, to the Hitler Youth Division.[2] Despite such efforts, the division would enter combat in June 1944 with a shortage of 144 officers and 2,192 NCOs–given an authorized strength of 664 and 4,575, respectively.[3] The 48 percent shortfall in noncommissioned officers was particularly crippling, and for a formation lacking the peculiar motivation and thorough training of the Hitler Youth Division might have had disastrous consequences. Conversely, the paucity of small unit commanders was bound to undermine efforts to hone the division into a professional fighting force, and to adversely affect its performance in battle.

Despite such obstacles, by the end of July 1943 most of the top officers--the regiment and battalion commanders--had been assigned. The great majority of them were quite young, in their late twenties or early thirties; the company commanders and platoon leaders were younger still, mostly in their early twenties.[4] The rank and file recruits, of course, and a portion of the NCOs were barely 17 years of age at the start of the training period. A small percentage of the recruits were younger still (16½).

The Hitler Youth Division was indeed a youth division–a fact that discomfited not only the RJF but Propaganda Minister Goebbels as well. Goebbels feared that Allied propaganda might interpret a division made up of teenagers as a sign of desperation. His fear did not lack substance, for Allied propaganda broadcasts and leaflets did refer sarcastically to the "Baby Division," with a milk bottle as its symbol![5] Hitler's attitude was quite different, and at his mid-

---

[2]Meyer, H., P-164, p 3; Hubert Meyer, *Kriegsgeschichte der 12.SS-Panzerdivision "Hitlerjugend."* Band I (Osnabrück: Munin Verlag GmbH, 1982), pp 18-19. (Hereafter cited *Kriegsgeschichte.*)

[3]Apparently, those concerned with the initial organization of the Hitler Youth Division had planned an establishment of 840 officers (see Chapter Two, p. 27); however, the division's situation report for June 1, 1944, shows an authorized strength of 664 officers. BAMA RH 10/321. Zustandsbericht 12.SS Pz. Div. "H.J.," Meldung vom 1.6.1944.

[4]T-175/18/2521572, 2521760. Führerstellungbesetzung der 12. SS Pz. Gren. Div. "H.J.," 31.7.1943.

[5]Rempel, *The Misguided Generation,* p 646.

day military conference on July 26, 1943, he lectured Himmler on the utility of military formations composed of young boys. Referring to the youthful recruits of the Hermann Göring Panzer Grenadier Division, Hitler exclaimed:[6]

> The youngsters from the Hitler Youth fight fanatically . . . young German lads, some only sixteen. Most of these Hitler youths fight more fanatically than their older comrades . . . The enemy reports that they only got hold of them after every man had fallen . . . The Hitler Youth Division will fight the same way, like the rest of youth. They are already uniformly aligned. The enemy will be struck with wonder.

*   *   *

In July and August 1943, the first 10,000 recruits arrived at the Beverloo training grounds in Belgium.[7] Basic training commenced at once, and with the gradual arrival of additional recruits the division was almost full strength by the end of September. The organization of divisional sub-units also began immediately--a process largely completed by mid-September. Most of the sub-units were quartered and trained at various locations east and southeast of Antwerp. The two Panzer grenadier (motorized infantry) regiments of the 12th SS, for example, underwent basic training at Beverloo. The artillery regiment also occupied quarters near the Beverloo training grounds, in the area of Mol. The reconnaissance battalion, signal, and medical units were situated in Turnhout; the division's headquarters (Stabsquartier) was located just outside the city (Zwanestrand). The engineer battalion was stationed at Herentals on the Albert Canal. The tank regiment, in contrast, was assigned the former French tank training grounds at Mailly-le-Camp, some 20 miles south of Chalons-sur-Marne and roughly 150 miles from divisional headquarters.[8]

The decision to organize the division as a Panzer grenadier formation had come as a surprise to the divisional command, which seized the occasion of a visit by General Heinz Guderian, now Inspector General of Panzer Troops, to request reorganization as a full-fledged tank unit. The request brought swift results: on October 21, 1943, Hitler ordered that the division, along with the formations of the I and II SS Panzer Corps in general, be reorganized into Panzer divisions. A corresponding directive from the Waffen SS operational headquarters (SS-Führungshauptamt) followed on the 30th.[9]

---

[6]Helmuth Heiber (ed.), *Hitlers Lagebesprechungen. Die Protokollfragmente seiner militärischen Konferenzen, 1942-1945* (Stuttgart: Deutsche Verlags-Anstalt, 1962), p 334.

[7]For the division's 25th SS Panzer Grenadier Regiment there are two surviving company lists. They show that the great majority of the recruits for the two companies came from the class of 1926, and had backgrounds in vocational training. T-354/154/3798022-28. Kompanieliste 3./Pz.-Gren. Rgt. 25; Kompanieliste 10./Pz.-Gren. Rgt. 25.

[8]Meyer, H., *Kriegsgeschichte,* p 20.

[9]Jüttner's directive referred to the Hitler Youth Division only. T-175/111/2635155. Führerhauptquartier, 21.10.1943; T-175/108/2631204-5. SS-Führungshauptamt. Betr.: Umgliederung der SS-Panz. Gren. Div. "Hitlerjugend." 30.10.1943.

One problem the 12th SS Panzer Division "Hitler Youth," as it was now designated, could do little about was its subordination to an unduly complex chain of command. As an SS division, it looked to Jüttner's Führungshauptamt in Berlin on matters concerning personnel and equipment. For training purposes the division was now subordinated to General Leo Freiherr Geyr von Schweppenburg's Panzer Group West, a training staff with no operational responsibilities. Operationally, the 12th SS came under the control of the I SS Panzer Corps (itself in the process of organization) and the Fifteenth Army.[10] Commanded by General Hans von Salmuth, the Fifteenth Army defended a critical stretch of the Atlantic coastline from Antwerp to the Orne river. Finally, German ground forces in the western theater, from the Zuider Zee in Holland to the French Mediterranean coast, came under the supreme command of Field Marshal Gerd von Rundstedt, the Commander-in-Chief West (Oberbefehlshaber West, or OB West) since March 15, 1942. With the arrival of Field Marshal Erwin Rommel and his Army Group B staff in the fall of 1943, the German command structure in the West would become even more complex, generating fundamental disagreements over strategic policy and undermining efforts to devise a uniform plan for the defense of the Atlantic coastline.

The beginning of basic training, however, confronted the Hitler Youth Division and its 35-year-old commander, SS-Oberführer Fritz Witt, with more immediate concerns. Because few of the distinctive SS camouflage uniforms were immediately available, most of the boys began training in civilian clothes, or in their Hitler Youth uniforms. Army and Luftwaffe personnel transferred to the division also served initially in their old uniforms. A more serious obstacle was the shortage of heavy weapons and armored fighting vehicles. The artillery regiment boasted but a few field howitzers, while the armored regiment possessed just four Panzer IV and two outmoded Panzer III tanks--all filched from the Leibstandarte. Damaged in Russia, the tanks had gone first to the Allkett tank factory in Berlin for repairs, then to the Hitler Youth Division. By the end of November, the regiment would have an additional ten Panzer IV's available for training purposes. Ammunition of all types and gasoline were also in short supply; trucks, armored personnel carriers, and motorcycles were practically non-existent. Eventually, the division would be outfitted with a colorful assortment of captured Italian vehicles, but these would not arrive until December 1943 - January 1944; once pressed into service, the Italian trucks and half-tracks broke down repeatedly.[11] After a corps-size communications exercise near Dieppe had demonstrated the complete unreliability of these vehicles, the divisional command requested their replacement with more efficient German models--a conversion only partially completed by early June 1944.[12]

[10]The I SS Panzer Corps would not become operational until the spring of 1944. Meyer, H., P-164, p 4.

[11]The engineer battalion for one appears to have devoted a good deal of time to repairing broken down vehicles. T-354/155/3798847, 3798863. Darstellung der Ereignisse, SS Pz. Pi. Btl. 12.

[12]BAMA Zustandsberichte, 12. SS Pz. Div., 1.11.1943, 1.1.1944; Meyer H., P-164, pp 4-5; Meyer H., *Kriegsgeschichte*, pp 17, 21.

Field Marshal Gerd v. Rundstedt, Commander-in-Chief West.

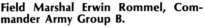

Field Marshal Erwin Rommel, Commander Army Group B.

A report by SS-Obersturmführer Karl Kugler, a platoon leader in one of the division's infantry battalions, offers insight into the frustrations occasioned by the shortages of equipment, fuel, and other critical resources:[13]

> Gasoline for our motor vehicles was the principal shortage during the training period. It didn't even suffice for the motorcycle messengers. Merely a messenger with an Italian single-seat motorcycle (Solo-Maschine) was available to the battalion. Thus, at first it was not possible to train the motorcycle messengers with the companies. Training with armored personnel carriers was a rare event, and, when it did take place, was almost considered a holiday. Most of the time just one of the carriers was refuelled, and then used for training exercises by all of the companies. An 'operational reserve' of barely 3,000 litres was available, which was sealed and carefully watched. Replacement parts for the maintenance echelons were not available; tools only in small measure. Grease and oil were 'represented through flags . . .'

---

[13]Meyer, H., P-164, p 7.

It so happened that in the 2nd Company, several youths stole some grease from a French merchant so they could lubricate their vehicle. The theft was discovered, and the lads placed under three days house arrest. As they admitted themselves it wasn't the arrest that was most painful, but the fact that they had to return the **grease.**

Of course an additional problem, as the division noted in its situation report for November 1943, was the shortage of training personnel, especially for instruction in the use of heavy weapons. Another concern was the physical immaturity of many of the young recruits, which rendered tasks such as lifting or moving heavy equipment particularly burdensome.

*　　*　　*

Clearly, the goal of transforming almost 20,000 teenagers into an efficient fighting force posed a formidable challenge--one that would require patience, understanding, and an innovative approach. Most of the boys had fathers or older brothers serving in the Wehrmacht or Waffen SS, many of whom had been killed or wounded; with fathers at the front, the task of raising the youngsters had been left largely to their mothers and to the Hitler Youth. The destruction wrought by the aerial bombing of German cities had caused additional hardship for many.

Sensitive to the special wartime conditions under which these boys had grown up, Witt required unit leaders to assume a fatherly responsibility for their young charges, and to help fill the gaps in their education. Many officers and NCOs, in fact, took a special interest in the boys, providing support in family matters, assisting with official business such as letters to authorities, and even comforting them when homesickness struck.[14] Divisional policy in general promoted an unusually close relationship between unit leaders and their troops. The result of such a bonding process would be poignantly evident during the Normandy campaign, when, on occasion, young soldiers risked their lives to retrieve the bodies of fallen leaders.

As much as possible, the youngsters' parents were included in the educational process, and the ties to the Reich Youth Leader were carefully maintained.[15] Discipline was strict, the youths forbidden to drink, smoke, or to patronize the local brothels. In fact, any relationship with girls was prohibited for those under 18.[16] The boys were given sweets instead. To promote physical development, they also received special rations, the outcome of an agreement between the German High Command and SS-Obergruppenführer Oswald Pohl, the Chief of the SS Economic and Administrative Main Office (Wirtschafts-und Verwaltungshauptamt). The weekly ration, which, according to Pohl, was considerably more substantial than that allotted to workers in heavy industry, consisted of the following:[17]

---

[14]Gurowski, Fragebogen.

[15]Axmann conducted formal inspections of the HJ Division on a number of occasions, including December 1943, and March and April of 1944. *Die 3. Kompanie. SS-Panzer-Regiment 12, 12.SS-Panzerdivision "Hitlerjugend"* (Kompanie-Kameradschaft, Eigenverlag, 1978), pp 13, 25, 31.

[16]Record Group 238: Records of Proceedings. pp 552-53.

SS-Obergruppenführer Oswald Pohl, Chief of the SS Economic and Administrative Main Office.

3.5 liters fresh milk
1,750 grams of bread
200 grams of meat
140 grams of lard
120 grams of sugar
245 grams of (other) nutrients

Although the discipline of the boys was generally good, youthful enthusiasm and immaturity did cause occasional problems. Some serious incidents occurred when recruits "used weapons to even scores in personal disputes. One such incident sent a young soldier to the hospital, but his adversary was excused on grounds of immaturity–of engaging in 'child's play.' " A more common breach of discipline was theft, which appears to have taken place with alarming frequency. The boys stole from civilians and fellow soldiers alike, finding valuables in letters and packages a particular enticement, and forcing Witt to order close surveillance of the mails.[18]

Despite repeated warnings by Witt, some lower echelon officers and NCOs evinced little sensitivity for the youthfulness of their recruits, and persisted in practicing bizarre punishments for minor disciplinary infractions-- punishments that included electrifying door handles, shaving heads, and forcing the boys to clean their weapons between one and three in the morning. Less than two months before the Allied invasion of Western Europe, on April 12, 1944, Witt complained in a special directive that "many unit leaders still do not seem to grasp . . . that their principal duty is to shape our young soldiers into straight and decent (gerade und anständig) SS men." He ordered platoon and squad leaders to live in the same rooms with their troops to demonstrate concern for the youths' welfare.[19]

*   *   *

[17]T-175/70/2586532-3. Pohl to RFSS, Verpflegung der Angehörigen der SS Pz. Gren. Div. "H.J.," 25.6.1943; Rempel, *The Misguided Generation,* p 644; Meyer, K., *Grenadiere,* p 208.

[18]Among the few surviving records of the 12th SS is an order from its tank regiment dated March 7, 1944; it notes that "reckless handling" of pistols by soldiers under the influence of alcohol had led to several recent accidents within the regiment. T-354/155/3798702. Regimentsbefehl Nr. 20/44. SS-Panzer-Regiment 12. 7.3.1944; Rempel, *The Misguided Generation,* pp 649-50.

[19]T-354/154/3797992-3. Witt, Kdr. Tgb. Nr. 237/44, "Sonderbefehl," 12.4.1944; Rempel, *The Misguided Generation,* pp 651-52.

Actual military training witnessed a number of innovations designed to exploit the natural enthusiasm of the seventeen year olds. Training personnel limited formal military drill to the essentials, and excluded entirely from the training program such traditional methods as weapons practice on the firing range and marches with heavy packs. Similar to the Waffen SS in general, the divisional leadership placed great emphasis upon sports to harden the youths physically. To familiarize them with actual battlefield conditions, most training took place in the field, often with live ammunition. Even instruction in weapons use was conducted in the field under realistic battle conditions.[20] In one exercise (Scharfschiessübung), heavy machine guns were fired over the heads of the advancing infantry while 81mm mortars lobbed their shells barely 50-100 yards in front of them.[21] Although such activities prepared the recruits for the rigors of combat, they also led to occasional mishaps; by the beginning of April 1944, the division had suffered 15 dead--most of them, no doubt, through training accidents.[22]

On the suggestion of General Geyr von Schweppenburg, the division also emphasized close combat training and the proper use of camouflage. Most of the training personnel had learned the art of camouflage from their Russian opponent; they now passed on their knowledge and experience to the young recruits. Gradually, the boys became masters of camouflage, capable of "reading" terrain, taking advantage of the natural cover it provided, and concealing helmets, vehicles, and weapons with branches, leaves, or straw.[23] The

Woscidlo

[20]Meyer, H., P-164, p 6.
[21]Interview with Günther Burdack, May 21, 1983, Bad Hersfeld.
[22]BAMA Zustandsbericht, 12.SS Pz. Div., 3.4.1944.
[23]Gurowski, Fragebogen.

General Geyr v. Schweppenburg talking to two boys from the Hitler Youth Division during their training.

recruits of the two Panzer grenadier regiments devoted particular attention to reconnaissance, night fighting, and to flexible shifting from attack to defense. Training personnel also stressed the critical importance of proper radio discipline, and for intercepting enemy communications the division was equipped with a special radio monitoring unit (Nachrichtennahaufklärungszug); it would perform valuable service during the Normandy battle.

To toughen recruits mentally, build confidence, and enhance knowledge of weapons and equipment, the division sometimes resorted to curious procedures. The commander of one infantry battalion concocted a special exercise (Mutübung) that required his soldiers, fully equipped with weapons and accoutrements, to leap into a sand pit 30 feet deep. Through such trials the boys learned never to hesitate to do what was necessary in a combat situation. One recruit would later recall that his instructor, to demonstrate the explosive effect of a hand grenade, had detonated the weapon atop his head, on his helmet. The instructor was not hurt, for as the demonstration showed the grenade splinters only travelled laterally and upwards. In another exercise, the youths disassembled and rebuilt their machine guns with their eyes bound or while in the dark.[24] The youngsters were clearly fascinated with their weapons and vehicles and handled them with genuine care and enthusiasm.

---

[24]Burdack interview; interview with Heinz Berner, June 1, 1983, Normandy.

TRAINING OF THE DIVISION IN BELGIUM

Woscidlo

Division Ia Hubert Meyer (left) and Fritz Witt.

Woscidlo

Woscidlo

Woscidlo

Woscidlo

Divisional members
in training.

Woscidlo

Woscidlo

Woscidlo

Motorcycle training near Turnhout, Belgium.

69

The organization and training of the division's tank regiment commenced at the end of July 1943. Upon arrival in Mailly-le-Camp, the prospective tankmen joined the special training companies established for tank commanders, gunners, loaders, drivers, and radio operators, respectively.[25] The majority of the tank commanders were from the class of 1925, and had successfully completed (or were candidates for) their college entrance examinations. Like the infantry recruits, the Panzer trainees received little formal military drill, concentrating instead upon weapons and combat training in the field. The shortages of tanks and gasoline disrupted and slowed the training program, and the few available tanks often had to be distributed to individual companies for a few hours at a time. Thanks to the personal initiative of SS-Obersturmbannführer Max Wünsche, the regiment commander, the tank crews did have the opportunity to work 8-14 days in tank production at an armament plant in Nürnberg; some crew members participated in gunnery or anti-aircraft training, or received instruction in driver training at the Waffen SS Motor Vehicle Technical Training Institute (Kraftfahrtechnische Lehranstalt) in Vienna.[26]

Panzer trainees from the division's tank regiment.

Despite the rigorous schedule, the young tankmen took advantage of their stay in France to visit local sites of historical interest. Not far from Mailly-le-Camp were the Verdun battlefields, where, 27 years before, their fathers' generation had fought its most desperate struggle. Duly impressed, the youths toured the battered forts and the still thoroughly cratered landscape on the outskirts of the city. A happier excursion took them to Reims, one of France's cultural treasures with its historical buildings and inspiring Gothic cathedral.

---

[25]The regiment, however, would not approach full strength in personnel until late December 1943, when it received some 600 recruits from the SS Tank Instructional Battalion of the SS Tank Training and Replacement Regiment (SS-Panzer-Lehrabteilung des SS-Panzer-Ausbildungs-und Ersatzregiments) in Latvia. *Die 3. Kompanie,* pp 13-14.

[26]Meyer, H., *Kriegsgeschichte,* pp 21-22.

Although the boys had undergone eight years of incessant ideological schooling in the Hitler Youth, and most of them four additional weeks of intensive indoctrination in the pre-military instruction camps, Witt still considered weekly sessions in ideological training a necessity within the division as well. He found two principal reasons for this: the German collapse in 1918 and the struggle against Bolshevism. Every soldier, he felt, had to realize what Germany was fighting for, and it was the responsibility of officers and NCOs alike to make sure that the weekly ideological theme was hammered home. These themes included "Germany's demand for living space," and "the enemies of Germany are the enemies of Europe,"--National Socialist platitudes no doubt familiar to the boys from the age of ten, when they had first entered the Hitler Youth. The indoctrination sessions also included lectures in which the youngsters were reminded of the destruction wrought by the Anglo-American bomber offensive against Germany. From their quarters in Belgium, in fact, the boys could often hear the drone of the Allied bomber fleets high overhead as they approached the cities and factories of the Reich. The purpose behind such indoctrination was "to make every man of the division a convinced carrier of our ideology, so that every last man of the division understands what he is fighting for, and to transform the Hitler youth into an SS man who lives according to the fundamentals of the SS as a fanatic warrior."[27]

Although shortages in training personnel, equipment and supplies persisted, by January 1, 1944, the 12th SS Panzer Division had made substantial progress in its training efforts. It now had 40 Panzer IV tanks at its disposal and many more were on the way, for on November 3, 1943, Hitler had ordained that all armored divisions in the West be equipped at once with 93 Panzer IVs.[28] By the beginning of 1944, the 12th SS had also received most of its artillery, anti-tank guns and machine guns; trucks, motorcycles and armored personnel carriers had arrived in significant numbers. The division had conducted training exercises on the squad, platoon, company, and battery level, and while far from fully operational, portions of it were now ready for such tasks as providing security or cover (Sicherungsaufgaben).[29]

*   *   *

Assisting Fritz Witt in his efforts to prepare the division for combat were the commanders of his two Panzer grenadier and single tank regiments. Commanding the 25th and 26th SS Panzer Grenadier Regiments were SS-Standartenführer Kurt Meyer and SS-Obersturmbannführer Wilhelm Mohnke, respectively.[30] Standing approximately 5'10", broad shouldered and athletic in

---

[27]T-354/156/3800397-8. 12. SS Pz. Div., Abt. IIa, Die weltanschauliche Schulung in der SS-Panzer-Division "Hitlerjugend," 22.11.1943; Rempel, *The Misguided Generation*, pp 656-57; B.J.S. MacDonald, *The Trial of Kurt Meyer* (Clarke, Irwin and Company, Ltd., 1954), p 16.

[28]Walther Hubatsch (editor), *Hitlers Weisungen für die Kriegführung 1939-1945. Dokumente des Oberkommandos der Wehrmacht* (Frankfurt am Main: Bernard und Graefe Verlag für Wehrwesen, 1962), p 234.

[29]BAMA Zustandsbericht, 12. SS Pz. Div., 1.1.1944.

[30]Both Meyer and Mohnke had received promotions to these ranks on June 21, 1943. SS Personalakten, Kurt Meyer and Wilhelm Mohnke.

SS-Obersturmbannführer Wilhelm Mohnke.

Kurt Meyer, here an SS-Obersturmbannführer.

build with penetrating grey-blue eyes, Kurt Meyer combined the cool recklessness (Draufgängertum) of the Landsknecht with the ideological fanaticism of the political soldier. Like Hitler, whom he ardently admired, Meyer was steeped in the racialism and Social Darwinism so prevalent in Europe in the late 19th and early 20th centuries; in fact, his whole political outlook was dominated by the threat he saw in Bolshevism and in the Asiatic peoples to western culture and civilization.

His father, a factory worker, had died of wounds suffered in World War One. Following an elementary school education, Meyer studied to be a merchant, thereafter finding employment for brief periods in the late 1920s as a miner and in a sugar factory. In 1929, he joined the Mecklenburg armed provincial police, with which he served until May 1934. Meyer had already joined the SS in October 1931, and, in the spring of 1934 he entered the Leibstandarte. He never belonged to the Hitler Youth. In the pre-war LAH he served in its anti-tank company (Panzerjägerkompanie), first as a platoon leader and later as company commander.

In September 1939, the 28-year-old SS-Hauptsturmführer entered the Polish campaign at the head of his Panzerjäger, launching a spectacular combat career that would make him a legend and earn him the sobriquet "Schnelle Meyer." (He was also called "Panzermeyer.") In a periodic review, Dietrich characterized Meyer as a "passionate soldier," and he certainly was that.[31] A classic example of the aggressive and ruthless Waffen SS officer, he pushed his

---

[31]Interrogated by the Canadians shortly after the war, Meyer appeared to view the struggle in Normandy as "magnificent in the best Wagnerian tradition. As he described his actions and those of his men, it seemed as though he liked to consider himself as Siegfried leading his warriors to their death." Public Archives of Canada (Ottawa). Special Interrogation Report, Brigadeführer Kurt Meyer. HQ Cdn. Forces in the Netherlands, 24 August 1945. (Hereafter documents from the Public Archives of Canada cited PAC.)

men (and himself) to their limits. He was also a dare-devilish motorcycle man, and would suffer some 18 broken bones and four concussions in the course of his military career.

Meyer, as the commander of a motorcycle company in France, and of the reconnaissance battalion of the Leibstandarte in the Balkans and in Russia, demonstrated an instinctive grasp of the techniques of modern mobile warfare. A first rate leader of men, he possessed a keen tactical sense and a flexibility of mind; he also provided his superiors with accurate reports--"a good index, when in action, of a straight character." His unorthodox methods in Russia, where he and his troops sometimes ventured far behind enemy lines and then blasted their way out, were legendary. By early 1943, this reckless, albeit highly effective, style of combat à 'outrance had already earned him the Iron Cross first and second class, the Knight's Cross, and the Oak Leaves to the Knight's Cross.

Following the completion of a training course for regimental commanders at Wünsdorf (Pz.Tr.Schule Wünsdorf) in August 1943, Meyer was transferred to the Hitler Youth Division. Despite his methods, which were often harsh, Meyer was no "drill sergeant," and was genuinely loved and honored by his young troops.[32] An incident witnessed by a former 12th SS Division recruit reveals a more gentle side to the man:[33]

> In Beverloo a young soldier has run away. For desertion in the LAH one would certainly be punished with penal company duty, and, in some circumstances, even with death. On his way home to Germany the youth was nabbed by the military police and his capture reported to the regiment. At once, SS-Standartenführer Kurt Meyer ordered that the boy be picked up and brought to his company . . . Trembling, the youngster reported to his unit. The regimental commander somewhat curtly asked him why he had deserted. 'I was homesick,' the youth replied. Panzermeyer blustered and swore as follows: 'I have here 10,000 young men, just like yourself, but they did not run away from me. Are you aware what it means to be absent without leave?' Well, we thought, at least that was not desertion. The boy replied, 'jawohl, Standartenführer;' whereupon Panzermeyer said, 'in that case I will punish you. Take off your steel helmet.' The youth complied. Panzermeyer then boxed the boy's ears and said, 'that's in

[32]Something of Meyer's popularity can be gauged from the fact that thousands of former Waffen SS soldiers attended his funeral in Hagen in December 1961, following his sudden death on his 51st birthday. Jost W. Schneider, *Verleihung Genehmigt! Eine Bild-und Dokumentargeschichte der Ritterkreuzträger der Waffen-SS und Polizei, 1940-1945* (San Jose: Bender Publishing, 1977), p 241.

[33]Material on Kurt Meyer's early life and subsequent military career has been gleaned from the following sources: SS Personalakten, Kurt Meyer: Dienstlaufbahn, etc.; United States National Archives Record Group 218: Supplementary Report of the SHAEF Court of Inquiry re: Shooting of Allied Prisoners of War by 12. SS Panzer Division (Hitler-Jugend) in Normandy, France, 7-21 June, 1944. Exhibit 8. Testimony of Brigadeführer Kurt Meyer (Hereafter cited Record Group 218: Supplementary Report SHAEF Court of Inquiry.); Record Group 238: Records of Proceedings, p 557; MacDonald, *The Trial of Kurt Meyer*, p 190; Grabher-Meyer, Fragebogen.

place of your father. Now off with you, and do your duty like the others. The matter is forgotten.'

We all breathed a sigh of relief, and our esteem for our brave commander rose immensely.

Like Fritz Witt, SS-Obersturmbannführer Wilhelm Mohnke, the commander of the division's 26th SS Panzer Grenadier Regiment, was also one of the original 120 members of the Leibstandarte. In April 1945, he would end his military career among the flames and rubble of Berlin, where, as the commander of an SS battlegroup, he conducted the defense of the governmental quarter of the city.[34]

Mohnke, after a modest education and employment as a clerk in the procelain trade, enlisted in the General SS in September 1931. Early in 1933 he saw brief duty with the auxiliary police before his transfer to the Leibstandarte on March 17, 1933. His surviving SS personnel records are sketchy, but do indicate that in the mid 1930s he took part in a training course for company commanders, and in a course at the Panzerschule Wünsdorf.

During the war he had fought in Poland, France, and in the Balkans, was wounded repeatedly and decorated with the Iron Cross first and second class. In France in 1940, he had commanded a battalion, and in September of that year was promoted to the rank of SS-Sturmbannführer. Early in 1942 he served temporarily as the commander of the LAH's armored detachment, which was then in the process of initial organization; shortly thereafter (March 1942), he assumed command of the Leibstandarte's replacement battalion.

Harsh and austere in appearance, Mohnke was a man of violent emotions, distant, and even brutal. He was not popular with fellow officers and enlisted men. Severely wounded during the Greek campaign he had lost a foot, and, most likely, acquired an addiction to morphine. However, he was a man of some personal courage–an assertion supported by his many wounds, as well as his willingness to assume the responsibility of a regimental command despite a severe physical handicap.[35]

Cutting a sharply contrasting figure was SS-Obersturmbannführer Max Wünsche, the dashing 29-year-old commander of the division's 12th SS Panzer Regiment. Tall, slim, blue-eyed and blond, with regular handsome features, Wünsche was a charismatic leader; like Kurt Meyer, he also had a reputation as a Draufgänger. However, unlike either Witt, Meyer, or Mohnke, the younger Wünsche had served in the Hitler Youth, joining the organization in November 1932 after serving as a department head at a bookkeeping and ac-

---

[34]In Berlin, Mohnke's SS battlegroup would include the LAH's 1st Guard Battalion (SS Wach-Bataillon 1). Thus, in their determined defense of the approaches to the Reich Chancellery, with Hitler's bunker located beneath the building, Mohnke and a part of the Leibstandarte "would experience a reversion to first principles"--the protection of the Führer. Mohnke, after setting fire to the deserted bunker on May 1, 1945, attempted to escape but the Russians captured him. Weingartner, *Hitler's Guard*, p 138.

[35]Discussions with former members of the 12th SS have confirmed the impression that Mohnke was not popular with his men. SS Personalakten, Wilhelm Mohnke: Lebenslauf, Dienstlaufbahn, etc.; MacDonald, *The Trial of Kurt Meyer*, p 30.

SS-Sturmbannführer
Max Wünsche.

counting agency. He joined the SS in July 1933, and came to the Leibstandarte in October 1934. Thereafter, Wünsche attended a series of officer training courses at Jüterbog, Bad Tölz (SS Junkerschule), and at Dachau. On his birthday, April 20, 1936 (also Hitler's birthday), he was promoted to SS-Untersturmführer, and given command of an infantry platoon in the LAH. Following a promotion to SS-Obersturmführer in September 1938, Wünsche was detailed to Hitler's personal escort detachment (Begleitkommando des Führers), with which he served as an orderly—a post he continued to fill during the attack on Poland a year later.

Wünsche, as a platoon leader and company commander in the LAH during the western offensive, won the Iron Cross first and second class. He also nearly lost his life: continuing its advance towards the Dunkirk perimeter, the LAH, supported by tanks and additional infantry, attacked Wormhoudt on May 28, 1940. British infantry and artillery vigorously defended the town. Dietrich and Wünsche, to gain a clearer appreciation of the situation, drove forward that morning to locate the LAH's forward elements. Unwittingly drawing to within 50 yards of the enemy, their staff car was stitched by machine gun fire and burst into flames. The two men sought shelter in a culvert, pursued by the flaming gasoline that poured from the disabled vehicle. The culvert provided protection from the enemy fire, but not from the intense heat of the gasoline, forcing Dietrich and his subordinate to blanket themselves with mud. After repeated German efforts to extricate the two men had failed due to the intense enemy machine gun and artillery fire, an assault group from the LAH finally succeeded in rescuing them from their uncomfortable hiding place by late afternoon.[36]

---

[36]Meyer, K., *Grenadiere*, pp 29-30; Weingartner, *Hitler's Guard*, p 43.

During the Balkan campaign, Wünsche served as divisional adjutant and, in 1941, continued to perform duties as a staff officer with the Leibstandarte on the eastern front. In Russia, Wünsche ably demonstrated his intelligence and versatility as a soldier, taking temporary command of units whose commanders had been killed or wounded, flying battlefield reconnaissance in a Fieseler Storch, and even serving briefly on two occasions as the LAH's chief of operations (Ia). In February 1942, Wünsche took over the assault gun battalion (Sturmgeschützabteilung) of the LAH, and played a significant part in the successful defensive battles on the southern front. After the withdrawal of the LAH from Russia, he attended the Kriegsakademie in Berlin, and, in October 1942, assumed command of a tank battalion in the Leibstandarte's Panzer regiment. By late January 1943, Wünsche was back in action, skillfully leading his tank unit in the battles around Kharkov. On one occasion, his tanks ploughed their way through a violent snow storm to open a supply route to Meyer's reconnaissance battalion, which had become cut off. In recognition of his soldierly abilities, Wünsche was awarded the Knight's Cross on February 28, 1943.[37]

* * *

Such were the fighting qualities of the top commanders who would lead the 12th SS Panzer Division into battle in June 1944. Young, charismatic officers such as Witt, Meyer, and Wünsche, steeled by years of combat in the most elite unit of the Waffen SS, were the best Germany had to offer. By January 1944, moreover, they had made great strides in shaping the youngsters of the HJ Division into soldiers with extraordinary élan and fighting capability. As basic training neared completion, unit training (Verbandsausbildung) commenced, and was well underway by early February 1944.[38] Because coordinated unit exercises would require the presence of the tank regiment, it moved in mid-January from Mailly-le-Camp to Beverloo. However, the potential vulnerability of a large troop training grounds to attack from the air soon compelled Witt to shift the regiment into the area around Hasselt, a short distance from Beverloo.[39] By early February, the Panzer regiment had received most all of its Panzer IVs, but only eight of the newer and heavier Panther tanks that were to equip one of its two tank battalions.[40] The Panther battalion's 3rd Panzer Company, quartered in Winterslag, was one of the companies waiting impatiently for its armored fighting vehicles; while it waited, training continued on foot--the endless marches through the Belgian countryside becoming even more distasteful after the company commander,[41]

> invented his famous flag-signal system. This signal
> system would be used in an emergency, when no contact
> by Morse code or radio was possible. To master such a
> system in combat, however, demanded intensive training--
> a procedure roughly as follows: The company marched

---

[37]SS Personalakten, Max Wünsche: SS Stammkarte, Dienstlaufbahn, Lebenslauf, etc.

[38]BAMA Zustandsbericht, 12. SS Pz. Div., 5.2.1944.

[39]*Die 3. Kompanie*, pp 15-16.

[40]On February 5, 1944, the division reported 79 Panzer IVs operational and 18 under short-term repair. BAMA Zustandsbericht, 12. SS Pz. Div., 5.2.1944.

Max Wünsche atop one of the first Panther tanks received by the division's tank regiment.

from its billets into the countryside. Once there, the recruits were divided into tank crews, and the crews widely separated. They then began to advance on foot. While the company or individual platoons moved forward in accordance with the given flag signal, our commander followed the spectacle with a critical eye from his command car atop the next small hill. First platoon forward, third platoon forward . . . and so it went mile after mile through the knee-high brush, and we wondered repeatedly what it was all for . . .

Now although the signal system included signs for halt and reverse, these commands had not yet been practiced, and, after hours of marching, one crew suddenly became mischievous. Arriving at a (small) stream it signalled, 'company halt, swamp!' That went like a sigh of relief through the widely scattered tank crews, and we immediately took cover, which, considering the high brush, was hardly difficult. Our commander had already motored on to the next little hill and was unaware of our action. After a short wait he came roaring up in his command car to look for the company. It took some time, however, until he tracked down the first crew.

His ensuing rage still rings in our ears . . . (but) all our commander's efforts to determine who had given the, in his opinion, 'idiotic halt order' were in vain. With some satisfaction the company renewed its advance, but not, of course, until we had received a thorough dressing-down, which was directed mainly at the platoon leaders. But what did that matter . . . in comparison to the splendid rest we had just gotten.

On February 6, 1944, elements of the Panzer regiment conducted a training exercise attended by Guderian, Geyr, and Sepp Dietrich, the commander of

---

[41]*Die 3. Kompanie,* pp 20-21.

the I SS Panzer Corps. The tankmen won high praise, which led to the accelerated outfitting of the division with Panther tanks.[42]

For the 3rd Panzer Company the arrival of its first Panthers later that month was something of an event. One young loader, perhaps overwhelmed by the prospect of his first exercise with live ammunition, absent-mindedly slammed an armor piercing round into the breech of his cannon, despite an order to load with high explosive. To his horror, the lad soon discovered that the armor piercing shell had a greater muzzle velocity than high explosive ammunition; it sailed over the target, located on a small forward slope, and crashed into the field beyond, where other companies were busy with their own training exercises. Happily, the only injury was to the young man's pride, and, after a thorough dressing-down, his punishment consisted of dragging a heavy hatch cover from the training ground all the way back to his quarters.[43]

In March, the division conducted another major training exercise, this time with infantry from the 26th Regiment and several companies of tanks. The Commander-in-Chief West, Rundstedt, observed this exercise, and once more the participants won recognition for their high state of preparedness. Pleased with the progress of his command, Fritz Witt declared on March 16, 1944, that the "training situation happily is a good one. Our Hitler Youth boys during these eight months have been transformed into young men who know the military craft." To celebrate this "miraculous transformation," he ordered the replacement of candy rations with cigarettes and tobacco.[44]

The March 1944 training exercise is observed by GFM v. Rundstedt, Kurt Meyer, Sepp Dietrich and Fritz Witt.

[42]*Die 3. Kompanie,* pp 22-23; Meyer, H., *Kriegsgeschichte,* p 22.
[43]*Die 3. Kompanie,* pp 24-25.
[44]Rempel, *The Misguided Generation,* p 655.

H.P. Taylor

V. Rundstedt and Witt review members of the division in March 1944.

By early April, the I SS Panzer Corps considered the 12th SS Panzer Division ready for action (einsatzbereit). Problems persisted, however, as the division duly noted in its monthly situation report. Fuel for training purposes remained in short supply. The tank regiment suffered from a shortage of armored command vehicles, and had yet to acquire the majority of its Panthers. The artillery regiment's 1st Battalion still lacked its armored observation vehicles. In addition, some sub-units were not yet fully motorized, and the division was still in the process of exchanging its Italian vehicles for German ones.[45] Despite such concerns, the division remained confident that it would be fully operational in time to meet the expected Anglo-American invasion of western Europe.

* * * * *

---

[45]BAMA Zustandsbericht, 12. SS Pz. Div., 3.4.1944.

Chapter 5

TRANSFER TO NORMANDY AND FINAL PREPARATIONS

Everyone waited for the cross-channel attack. We clearly understood that decisive battles lay ahead. Our baptism of fire was imminent. We awaited it anxiously. Would we meet the challenge? It became bitterly serious. I had already written my father how I wanted my obituary to read in the newspaper. Without apparent cause I often felt agitated. During duty-free hours I tried to be alone, repaired to the forest and passed time in quiet introspection. My confidence remained.

(SS-Sturmmann Jochen Leykauff, 12th SS Panzer Division)

The beginning of spring 1944 brought the transfer of the 12th SS Panzer Division from Belgium to France. The encirclement of General Hans Hube's First Panzer Army by Russian forces in the Ukraine in late March had led to the OKW decision to dispatch the II SS Panzer Corps (9th and 10th SS Panzer Divisions) to the rescue.[1] As a result, the 12th SS Panzer received instructions to occupy the area vacated by the 10th SS Panzer between the lower reaches of the Seine and the Orne in Normandy.

At the end of March, SS-Sturmbannführer Hubert Meyer[2] (the chief operations officer of the 12th SS), accompanied by a small staff, drove into Normandy to reconnoiter the newly assigned sector. Meyer, arriving at the former headquarters of the 10th SS near Lisieux, was surprised to learn that the division had been stationed directly behind the coastline, where, in the event of an Allied invasion, it would immediately have faced the full weight of enemy air and naval power. Deeply concerned, Meyer drove at once to Panzer Group West headquarters in Paris, where he conferred with the Panzer Group's Chief of Staff, Brigadier-General Edler von Dawans. Both men agreed that the decision to place the 12th SS so close to the coastline was "indefensible " and in violation of the strategic thinking of the Panzer Group (see pp 86-87), to which the division was still subordinated for training purposes. Consequently,

---

[1]Among the formations swept into the pocket was the Leibstandarte, by now a shadow of its former strength. Following its rescue, the LAH was sent to Belgium to refit.

[2]The 30-year-old Meyer (no relation to Kurt Meyer) had served as a company and a battalion commander in the LAH. His decorations included the Iron Cross first and second class. In September 1943, he completed a General Staff training course at the Kriegsakademie, qualifying him to serve as chief operations officer in an armored division. SS Personalakten, Hubert Meyer.

von Dawans promised to discuss the matter with his superiors at OB West. The next day, the division was assigned a cantonment area farther back from the beaches, south and southwest of Rouen.[3]

On April 1, 1944, the trains transporting men and equipment began to roll southwest towards Normandy--a process that would take some two weeks to complete and require about 90 trains in all. The division's new quarters encompassed a large area, stretching from Elbeuf, near the Seine, all the way to Sées, southeast of Argentan, and from there to Dreux, located west of Paris. The Panzer regiment settled near the Seine crossings, in the area Elbeuf - le Neubourg - Louviers, from where it could intervene rapidly against an enemy landing either north or south of the river. For the same purpose, the engineer battalion was also situated near the Seine--astride the Eure from Pacy to Autheuil.[4] The special task of the engineer battalion was to keep the crossings open for the Panzer regiment. The artillery regiment's sector was south of Evreux (Damville); the sector of the reconnaissance battalion around Rugles. The 26th SS Panzer Grenadier Regiment occupied positions south of the tank regiment, around Houdan, while the 25th SS Panzer Grenadier Regiment took up quarters in the western portion of the cantonment area: Bernay - Orbec - Vimoutiers - Sées. From the latter positions the 25th Regiment could move swiftly in a westwardly direction, towards Caen and Falaise. Finally, the Flak battalion was ensconced near Dreux to provide anti-aircraft cover for the local airfields. Fritz Witt established his headquarters (Divisionsstabsquartier) at Acon, roughly in the center of the divisional sector.[5]

*   *   *

The transfer to Normandy proceeded smoothly, with the exception of an incident involving the French underground and the division's 12th SS Reconnaissance Battalion. Elements of the battalion had entrained and begun to move southward from Turnhout on the evening of April 1st. Following some ten minutes behind the Anvers - Paris express, they crossed the Franco - Belgian frontier at Baisieux, arriving in Ascq (near Lille) at precisely 10:45 p.m. A few hundred yards from the Ascq train station, and in the path of the convoy, an explosion shook the tracks, causing the derailment of two flat cars and the disruption of some cargo and equipment. Yet damage was negligible, and despite hostile small arms fire the Germans incurred no casualties.

The commander of the troop convoy, SS-Obersturmführer Walter Hauck, immediately ordered the town searched for weapons and the seizure of its entire male population between the ages of 17 and 50. A thorough search of the

[3]Meyer, H., *Kriegsgeschichte,* p 40.
[4]T-354/155/3798863. Darstellung der Ereignisse, SS-Pz. Pi. Btn. 12. Stabs-Kp.: Menilles; 1. (gp.): Autheuil; 2.Kp.: Pacy-sur-Eure; 3.Kp.: Chambray; 4.(s.): Hardencourt; Br.-Kol(B): Jouy-sur-Eure.
[5]Meyer, H., *Kriegsgeschichte,* p 40; PAC. Special Interrogation Report, Kurt Meyer. Interviews with and questionnaires completed by former division members also provided valuable information concerning the location of the various sub-units.

On April 1, 1944, the division supplied an honor company (one officer, three NCOs and thirty-five men) to escort the Sturmbrigade Wallonien from Cherleroi to Brussels, Belgium, after breaking out of its encirclement at Cherkassy/Ukraine. The brigade's commander, Leon Degrelle, was awarded the Oakleaves to his Knight's Cross at this time and a number of his troops were presented with decorations by SS-Oberführer Witt.

SS-Sturmbannführer Leon Degrelle at a march-past in the Belgian town of Cherleroi. His small children are with him.

Woscidlo

Witt, Wünsche and Kurt Meyer were among those at the return ceremony.

The Sturmbrigade on its march from Cherleroi to Brussels.

Woscidlo

Degrelle (left) talks to Dietrich (right) in Brussels.

streets and houses netted several groups of 20 to 30 suspects, who were led in swift succession to the train station and lined up along the railway track near the damaged train. Up to this point, Hauck had apparently acted in accordance with a strict new set of guidelines issued by OB West on February 3, 1944, to combat French underground attacks against German military personnel and installations. Such attacks had increased alarmingly in recent months; in Ascq alone the Resistance had recently conducted two similar attempts to sabotage German rail traffic, forcing local German military authorities (Oberfeldkommandantur in Lille) to dispatch a guard unit there to provide additional protection.

The tragic conclusion to "l'Affaire d'Ascq" is difficult to reconstruct. According to French trial records, Hauck, in extreme agitation, ordered the groups of suspects to be shot in the roadbed beside the railway cars--a task allegedly carried out at once. A fourth group was only spared a similar fate through the intervention of the German military police (Feldgendarmerie), who, alerted by the frantic telephone calls of a French railway employee, arrived from Lille in time to put an end to the massacre. German sources insist that the search of the town had uncovered large quantities of weapons, explosives and radio equipment, and that the roundup of suspects was conducted in a proper soldierly fashion; only after several of them had attempted to escape had the Germans opened fire, killing at least 77 Frenchmen with no losses of their own. A subsequent investigation by the Germans led to the capture of a number of participants in the sabotage actions in Ascq; following a military trial, seven of them were condemned to death on June 16, 1944.[6] Once in Normandy, and even during the fighting there, the 12th SS would experience no further problems with the French Resistance; on the contrary, relations with the local population would often be cordial in nature.

*   *   *

While the division settled into its new quarters, Fritz Witt and his chief operations officer, Hubert Meyer, contacted local Wehrmacht units and their commanders in an effort to acquire a picture of the German defenses in Normandy. They motored first to St. Lô, where they conversed with General Erich Marcks, the commander of the LXXXIV Army Corps. Marcks, who had lost a leg while fighting in Russia, made a strong impression upon his visitors. His Army Corps, he pointed out, was weak in strength, yet responsible for the defense of the Normandy coast from Merville, just east of the Orne, to the base of the Cotentin Peninsula at Avrances. The Anglo-American invasion, he insisted, would come in June, perhaps between the Orne and the Vire and on

---

[6]SS-Obersturmführer Hauck and seven other former members of the 12th SS Reconnaissance Battalion were sentenced to death by a French military tribunal in Metz on August 6, 1949; eight additional men were sentenced to death in abstentia. One man received 15 years hard labor. However, thanks in part to the efforts of the French defense lawyers, at least two of the men eventually received pardons. The others were released from captivity in 1954. Walter Hauck, *L'Affaire D'Ascq*. Acte d'Accusation, Tribunal Militaire Permanent Metz. Expose des Faits (Paris: 1949), pp 13-20 (document located at Hoover Institute Library, Palo Alto, California); Meyer, H., P-164, p 11; Meyer, H., *Kriegsgeschichte*, Band II, pp 556-57.

Fritz Witt and division Ia, Hubert Meyer, at the divisional head-quarters, Spring 1944.

the east coast of the Cotentin Peninsula, but he questioned the ability of his own meager forces to turn back such an attack.

Duly concerned, Witt and Hubert Meyer decided to inspect for themselves the vital stretch of the Normandy beaches from Bayeux to the Seine--an undertaking that confirmed Marcks' pessimistic assessment. Defending the Calvados coastline from Merville to Asnelles-sur-Mer (some 6 miles northeast of Bayeux) was Major-General Wilhelm Richter's 716th Infantry Division. This formation was a static (bodenständig) coastal defense unit, poorly equipped with artillery and anti-tank weaponry. Its forward defenses consisted principally of a line of 40 to 50 strongpoints (Stützpunkte), but were lacking in depth; most of the division's artillery and other heavy weapons were still without protective concrete bunkers.[7] Behind the 716th Infantry Division, in reserve around Caen, stood the 77th Infantry Division. Together, these two

---

[7]Wilhelm Richter, B-621. ''Kampf der 716. Infanterie Division in der Normandie vom 6.6.-23.6.1944.'' pp 2-4.

formations formed the right flank of the LXXXIV Army Corps, which was subordinated to General Friedrich Dollmann's Seventh Army. Dollmann's responsibility was a large one indeed–the defense of the Atlantic coastline from the Orne to the Loire. Positioned on the right flank of the 716th Infantry was another static formation, the 711th Infantry Division; this unit, with a defensive front extending to the mouth of the Seine, belonged to the LXXXI Army Corps, and formed the westernmost flank of von Salmuth's Fifteenth Army.

The inadequate strength and depth of the coastal defenses convinced both Witt and his operations officer that an Anglo-American landing in Normandy could not be prevented,[8] and that a successful outcome to the battle would hinge in large part upon a timely commitment of the German armored reserves. By the spring of 1944, however, the concerned German staffs had not been able to forge a uniform policy governing the deployment of the Panzer divisions in the western theater–the result of a spirited controversy that had followed the arrival of Field Marshal Rommel in the West by early December 1943.

Adolf Hitler, to accelerate preparations to meet the anticipated invasion of western Europe, had issued Military Directive No. 51 on November 3, 1943; two days later, he had commissioned Rommel and his Army Group B staff to inspect the "Atlantic Wall" from Denmark to Brittany to determine its state of readiness. In his new post, Rommel exercised at first a purely advisory function, but in mid-January 1944, he requested and received command of the Seventh and Fifteenth Armies.

Rommel tackled his assignment with great energy and resolve, in the process devising a concept for the defense of the Atlantic coastline that reflected his experiences in North Africa, where the Allied air forces had disrupted with paralyzing effect the operations of his Africa Corps in the final phase of the campaign. In Rommel's view, "the first 24 hours (of the invasion) would be decisive," for once the Allies had established a beachhead it would be impossible to drive them out because of their great superiority in materiel. Thus, he was convinced that the only chance of thwarting an amphibious assault lay in offering "the strongest possible resistance to the actual landing." To accomplish this, Rommel planned to declare the beaches the main battle line (Hauptkampflinie), and to place the Panzer divisions directly behind them so they could intervene at once. The crushing Allied superiority in the air, he insisted, would render impossible a rapid shifting to the invasion front of any mobile reserves located deep inside France.[9]

Rommel's ideas were unorthodox and did not meet with approval from either Rundstedt or Geyr. Field Marshal Rundstedt, who had studied every major Allied amphibious assault of the war, considered the success of the initial landing a "foregone conclusion," given the enemy's enormous material

---

[8]Meyer, H., *Kriegsgeschichte, p 41.*
[9]Friedrich Ruge, A-982. "Rommel and the Atlantic Wall." p 9; Hans Speidel, B-720. "Gedanken Rommels über Abwehr und Operationen im Westen." pp 16-17.

superiority and his ability to drop large airborne units well behind the German forward defenses. He hoped to strike the Allies at their weakest moment, when the separate landing forces were still isolated on their beachheads and not yet reinforced or resupplied. Rejecting Rommel's concept of a linear tactical deployment of the armored divisions, the elderly Field Marshal wanted to hold back the tanks beyond the range of the enemy battleships' heavy guns and the aerial bombardment of the coastal defenses. The mobile reserves, in fact, were to be located just close enough to the shoreline to enable them to intervene in the first day's combat; options for shifting or withdrawing the Panzer units were to be kept open at all times.[10]

The arrogant and intellectual Geyr was largely in sympathy with OB West. Geyr, who had commanded a tank corps in Russia, advocated a traditional, mobile deployment of the tank forces. He wanted to assemble the Panzer divisions in the great forests north of Paris. The Allied forces would then be drawn into the interior of France and destroyed in a classic battle of maneuver. Like Rundstedt, Geyr feared an enemy airborne assault of operational scope well behind the coast–a possibility, he believed, that further justified his strategic concept. In addition, Geyr recognized that a fundamental weakness of the Wehrmacht in the West was the lack of a powerful, centralized strategic reserve, and for such a reserve he would argue vigorously, albeit with disappointing results.[11]

The outcome of this "cock fight," as Geyr characterized it, was an illogical compromise. Hitler, on April 29, 1944, placed the 2nd, 21st, and 116th Panzer Divisions under the operational control of Rommel's Army Group B; the 1st SS, 12th SS, 17th SS (a Panzer grenadier division with no tanks) and the Panzer Lehr, he declared an OKW reserve. In the event of invasion, the latter formations could not be moved or committed without the prior approval of OKW (i.e., Hitler himself). In this manner, Hitler "divided the control of the armored forces, with the result that there was neither a strong tactical reserve, nor a strong strategic reserve" in the western theater. The compromise satisfied no one, certainly neither Rommel nor Geyr, each of whom continued to plead his own cause until the very eve of the invasion.[12]

This dualism in the control of the German tank forces reflected a more fundamental concern: the absence of a unified German command structure in the West. Rundstedt, despite his position as commander-in-chief, had no authority beyond the two army groups (four armies) under his immediate command.[13]

---

[10]Bodo Zimmermann, B-308. "OB West: Atlantic Wall to Siegfried Line, A Study in Command." pp 49-51.

[11]"With the dispatch of Rommel to the West," writes Geyr, "there developed a sharp intellectual controversy between the views of the Field Marshal and myself." General Leo Freiherr Geyr von Schweppenburg, B-466. "Geschichte der Panzergruppe West." pp 8-9; Zimmermann, B-308, pp 41-42.

[12]Chester Wilmont, *The Struggle for Europe* (New York: Harper and Row, 1952), p 193.

[13]At Rundstedt's urging, OKW created an additional army group staff, Army Group G, on April 26, 1944. Commanded by General Johannes Blaskowitz, the new staff took command of the First and the Nineteenth Armies, which defended the less threatened stretch of the French coastline along the Bay of Biscay and the Mediterranean Sea.

Rommel and General Erich Marcks (far left), commander of LXXXIV Army Corps, reviewing Normandy defenses in the spring of 1944.

And even this authority was seriously limited, for Rommel, by virtue of his favored standing with Hitler, actually enjoyed substantial independence from OB West. Rundstedt had no control over Navy and Luftwaffe forces in the West, or over the Organization Todt, which was responsible for the major construction projects along the Atlantic Wall; the staff of Geyr's Panzer Group took its orders directly from the Wehrmacht High Command. Hitler, moreover, through the machinery of OKW, kept a firm grip on the activities of his field commanders, his constant interference and unrealistic directives representing an additional source of anxiety. All attempts to establish more rational policies floundered on the Führer's opposition.

If the Germans could not agree on how to best deploy their armor, they were also at odds concerning potential enemy invasion sites. By late February 1944, Hitler had developed a keen interest in Normandy, and, in the coming months, he would order the reinforcement of its defenses. He reasoned that the Allies would require a large port to sustain a major amphibious operation; the port of Cherbourg, located at the tip of the Cotentin Peninsula, appeared particularly vulnerable to him.[14] Consequently, Hitler feared that the enemy would at least attempt an initial landing in Normandy to isolate the peninsula and to capture the port. In March, therefore, he ordered the 352nd Infantry Division (with its nucleus of eastern front veterans) inserted into the coastal defenses on the left flank of the 716th Infantry Division. By the beginning of

---

[14]Hitler's concern for the defense of the Cotentin Peninsula and for its vulnerability to an enemy amphibious assault is first evident in his Directive No. 51a, issued on December 12, 1943. Hubatsch, *Hitlers Weisungen für die Kriegführung,* pp 238-40.

May, the 21st Panzer Division was also in Normandy, replacing the 77th Infantry Division in the Caen - Falaise sector. The latter formation was relocated to the westernmost foot of the Cotentin Peninsula. In addition, Hitler dispatched the 91st Air Landing Division (Luftlande-Division) and the 6th Parachute Regiment to the peninsula.[15]

While Hitler perceived the danger to Normandy, OKW, OB West and Army Group B did not--rather, these staffs focused their concern upon the sector defended by General von Salmuth's Fifteenth Army. In 1940, Rundstedt's plans for the invasion of England had envisioned a crossing at the Channel's narrowest point, the Pas-de-Calais. Applying his logic in reverse, he now assumed that the Allies would attempt a similar maneuver. Rommel's view was that the mouth of the Somme and the stretch of coastline from the Somme to Le Havre represented the most probable invasion sites, and although he at least contemplated shifting the 12th SS Panzer to an area directly south of the Cotentin Peninsula, his overriding attention remained riveted on the Fifteenth Army.[16] The weekly situation reports of OB West and Army Group B, moreover, reveal no particular concern for the possibility of an enemy landing in Normandy.[17]

Long after D-Day, the major German commands in the West would cling to the delusion that the Normandy operation was merely a diversion intended to siphon forces from the Fifteenth Army, in whose sector the main enemy landing would still be expected. Contributing to the German disorientation--with disastrous results for their conduct of the entire Normandy battle--was a brilliant Allied deception, called Fortitude, as well as duplicity within the Germans' own intelligence community (see Chapter 10, p 197).

Because the Germans lacked secure knowledge of enemy intent, the 12th SS received instructions from Panzer Group West to prepare three separate approach routes (Aufmärsche) for the division's deployment at sectors along the French coastline. Aufmarsch "A" foresaw the commitment of the division between the Somme and the Seine; "B," its deployment between the Seine and the Orne; and, "C," an advance to the coast west and northwest of Caen. Later, Geyr ordered the division to work out an approach march for operations farther west, at the mouth of the Loire. The staff of the 12th SS prepared the various contingencies in meticulous detail, dividing divisional elements into march columns that were fully operational battlegroups (Kampfgruppen). To enable each battlegroup to move at a uniform pace, the wheeled vehicles were separated from the tracked vehicles, and the latter assigned to a separate marching column (the first):

[15]Heinz G. Guderian (Jr.), "Noch einmal: Zu: Friedrich Ruge, *Rommel und die Invasion.*" In: Europäische Wehrkunde 2/80. p 89.

[16]Rommel, on May 12, 1944, proposed moving the 12th SS into position behind the Cotentin Peninsula in a conversation with General Alfred Jodl, the OKW Chief of Operations. The proposal was quickly dropped.

[17]Heinz G. Guderian (Jr.), "Noch einmal: Zu: Friedrich Ruge, *Rommel und die Invasion.*" In: Europäische Wehrkunde 2/80. pp 89-90.

1. 12th SS Panzer Regiment, with
   one infantry battalion (with half-track carriers)
      from the 26th Regiment
   one engineer company (with half-track carriers)
   one self-propelled artillery battalion
   one self-propelled Flak battery
2. 25th SS Panzer Grenadier Regiment, with
   one artillery battalion
   one Flak battery
3. 26th SS Panzer Grenadier Regiment (less one battalion), with
   one artillery battalion
   one Flak battery

The remaining divisional sub-units, such as the reconnaissance and engineer battalions (less the latter's 1st Company) were grouped with the two Panzer grenadier regiments. As a precaution against attack from the air, all vehicles were to maintain 100 yard intervals during the approach march; to prevent the division from becoming too strung out, each approach route comprised four major thoroughfares, three for the wheeled and one for the tracked vehicles. Once completed, the plans were distributed in sealed envelopes to all regiments and independent battalions, and copies provided for Panzer Group West.[18]

* * *

As the warm spring days of April and May followed in swift succession, the division completed its final preparations for battle. Although shortages of gasoline persisted, posing a particular problem for the tank crews, unit training progressed at a vigorous pace. To avoid attack from the Allied fighters and fighter-bombers that now roamed the skies over Normandy, most training was conducted at night, the boys sleeping during the day.[19] As an added precaution, all vehicles, including the tanks, were dug in and carefully camouflaged. With the threat of invasion growing more imminent, the division performed frequent alarm exercises, as well as maneuvers calculated to meet the challenge of an enemy airborne (paratrooper) assault. To combat an airborne attack, all sub-units provided for the all-around defense of their respective quarters. In mid-May, Witt shifted the 12th SS Flak Battalion from Dreux into the area around Louviers, where it took over the air defense of the local Seine bridges. The battalion's 1st and 3rd Batteries (88mm guns) were positioned about Elbeuf; its 2nd and 4th Batteries (88mm and 37mm guns, respectively) were stationed initially near Pont-de-l'Arche, and later near Gaillon. Although the destruction of the bridges could not be prevented, the battalion's Flak would send four or five heavy bombers tumbling out of the sky in the remaining weeks before the invasion.[20]

---

[18]Meyer, H., P-164, pp 12-13; Meyer, H., *Kriegsgeschichte,* p 42.

[19]Returning from a divisional communications exercise on the eve of the invasion, SS-Obersturmführer Rudolf von Ribbentrop, the commander of the division's 3rd Panzer Company and the son of the German foreign minister, was badly wounded in a Spitfire attack. *Die 3. Kompanie,* pp 32-33.

SS-Hauptsturmführer Wilhelm Beck, leader of the officer candidate course at Evreux, awards prizes to winners of a military sports competition, 20 April 1944.

D. Rose

Tillières-sur-Avre castle, 55 miles south of Rouen, was Fritz Witt's quarters from April to 6 June 1944. The photo below was taken there.

Jost W. Schneider

36th birthday celebration for divisional commander, Fritz Witt, on 27 May 1944 in Tillières. 1st row, 3rd from left: Schürer (Ordnance Officer), Springer (Adjutant), K. Meyer (CO Rgt. 25), Witt, Mohnke (CO Rgt. 26), Schröder (CO Art. Rgt.), Rothemund (Adjutant). 2nd row: von Reitzenstein, Manthey (Div. Engineer), Pandel (CO Sig. Btl.), Wünsche (CO Pz. Rgt.), H. Meyer (Div. Ia), Buchsein (Div. IIa), Schuch (CO Div. HQ). 3rd and 4th row: Weiser (Corps Adjutant), Krause (CO 1st Btl, Rgt. 26), Urabl (CO Field Replacement Btl.), Bremer (CO Recce Btl.), Dr. Kos (Commissariat Officer), Müller (CO Eng. Btl.), Waldmüller (Co 1st Btl., Rgt. 25), Siebken (CO 2nd Btl., Rgt. 26), Kolitz (CO Div. Supply Troops), Hanreich (CO Antitank Btl.), and Ritzert (CO 15th Co., Rgt. 25).

By May 1944, the great majority of the division's weapons and vehicles had arrived. In field maneuvers attended by the Inspector General of Panzer Troops, Heinz Guderian, the 12th SS Panzer Division "Hitler Youth" demonstrated that, after nine months of determined preparation, it had reached a state of near complete operational readiness. In the first days of June, the final Panther tanks arrived, and their crews labored feverishly to ready them for combat. Thus, the division had attained a strength that included some 20,500 soldiers, 177 tanks, 52 pieces of artillery, more than 1,600 machine guns, and over 300 armored personnel carriers and scout vehicles.[21] Clearly, it represented one of the better equipped and more thoroughly trained German formations of the Second World War.

River crossing exercise by SS-Panzerpionierbataillon 12 and SS-Panzerregiment 12. This bridge was constructed over the Seine at Elbeuf in May 1944.

---

[20]Meyer, H., P-164, p 14; Meyer, H., *Kriegsgeschichte,* p 43.

[21]The division, however, would enter the Normandy battle without its tank destroyer and rocket projector (Nebelwerfer) battalions, which were not yet fully operational (See Appendix 4 for a complete order of battle for the 12th SS). The figure for tank strength signifies operational tanks as of June 6, 1944. The 177 tanks included 94 Panzer IVHs, 63 Panther Gs, 12 Panzer 38(t)s, and eight command tanks. The Panzer 38(t) was a Czech armored fighting vehicle that the Germans had continued to manufacture as late as 1942; although obsolete by 1941, it had continued to see service as an artillery observation vehicle. The shortage of 144 officers and 2,192 NCOs was made good numerically through the addition of some 2,360 personnel not originally included in the division's organizational tables. According to Kurt Meyer, the 12th SS also had roughly 500 Italians, Russians, and ethnic Germans (Volksdeutsche) who served with the support units. In any case, as all sources differ to some degree, it is impossible to determine the personnel and weapons strength of the division with total accuracy. BAMA Zustandsbericht, 12.SS Pz. Div., 1.6.1944; BAMA RH 19IX/3. Generalkommando I.SS-Panzer Korps. Ia Tgb. Nr. 44/g. Kdos.; Record Group 218: Supplementary Report SHAEF Court of Inquiry. Exhibit 8. p 16.

The months of training against the backdrop of a military situation that had grown progressively worse for Germany had transformed the 17 and 18-year-olds of the 12th SS into a professional fighting force of superior quality. The youngsters were convinced that Germany's fate would be determined by the outcome of the invasion battle; confident, even arrogant, they waited impatiently for the opportunity to prove themselves at the front. Already the front had drawn perceptively closer to them, for daily the enemy bombers passed overhead on their way to smash the bridges across the Seine or the rail installations around Paris upon which the resupply and reinforcement of Rundstedt's divisions in Normandy depended. Letters from home often brought news of family members and friends killed or wounded at the front, or by the saturation bombing of Germany's cities. One young soldier had lost his mother to a bombing attack on Berlin; two months later his parents' home was struck again and his father reported missing.

On the night of June 4-5, 1944, the division moved elements of its 1st and 2nd Panzer Battalions into the cantonment areas of the 26th and 25th SS Panzer Grenadier Regiments, respectively. A new issue of gasoline had just arrived, prompting Witt to order joint exercises of armor and infantry--an activity that the insufficient stocks of gasoline had hitherto sorely limited.[22] The exercises were necessary, and with poor weather predicted for the English Channel, the likelihood of an imminent enemy descent appeared remote. Rommel himself, reassured by the reports of his chief meteorologist in Paris, had left his headquarters at La Roche-Guyon on June 4th to meet with Hitler at the Obersalzberg. He planned to make one final attempt to bring both the Panzer Lehr and 12th SS Panzer Divisions under his direct control.

Such optimism, however, was without foundation, for by the evening of June 5th, an immense armada of 6,483 ships--including six battleships, 23 cruisers, and 104 destroyers--was approaching the Normandy coastline. All day long the wind-swept, surging sea had carried the invasion fleet towards German-occupied France. Along the coast and in the interior from Holland to the French Riviera, 58 German divisions stood guard--a force, to be sure, of uneven quality,[23] yet potentially formidable if its armored fist could move swiftly into battle at the decisive point. And it was upon their chances to do just this that the Germans pinned their hopes.

*   *   *   *   *

---

[22]Meyer, H., *Kriegsgeschichte*, p 50.

[23]Of the 58 German divisions available in the West, 33 of them were weak coastal defense units; only ten were armored or armored infantry divisions. According to Müller-Hillebrand, the Germans possessed 1552 tanks and 310 assault guns and tank destroyers in the western theater on June 10, 1944. The tank strength broke down as follows: Pz. III: 39; Pz. IV: 748; Pz. V (Panther): 663; Pz. VI (Tiger); 102. Burkhart Müller-Hillebrand, *Das Heer 1933-1945. Entwicklung des organisatorischen Aufbaues.* Band III: Der Zweifrontenkrieg (Frankfurt am Main: Verlag E.S. Mittler und Sohn, 1969), p 151.

Division headquarters in Normandy, May 1944. Sepp Dietrich and Fritz Witt watch American bombers heading inland. The Knight's Cross holder at far left is H. Weiser.

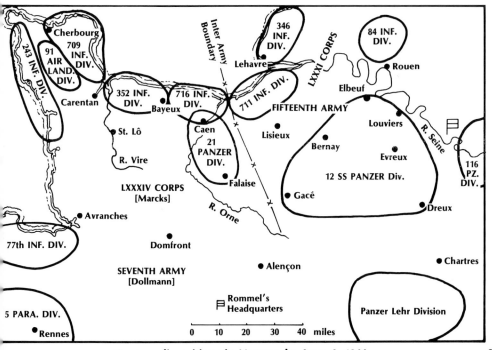

German dispositions in Normandy--June 6, 1944.

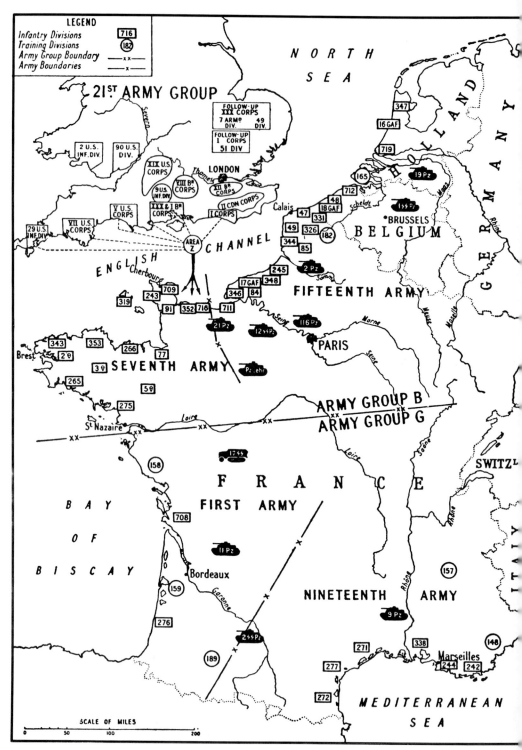

German dispositions in the West--June 6, 1944.

Chapter 6
THE INVASION: JUNE 6, 1944

To 12th SS Panzer Division: Division to move forward immediately . . .
Assignment: Operating on the left flank of the 21st Panzer Division, to throw the enemy . . . into the sea and destroy him.

(Order from Seventh Army)

In familiar fashion my trusted driver plunges forward. Dark
clouds rise up out of the west . . . On the road from Caen to
Falaise we encounter fleeing civilians. An omnibus burns violently. Heart-rending cries come from the bus but we can do
nothing to help. The door is jammed and blocks the way to
freedom . . . But we cannot stop. We must move on and gain
ground towards the front. Patches of forest attract us like
magnets. More and more fighters fill the sky. They attack remor-
selessly but we must continue. The march column must roll!

(Kurt Meyer)

At precisely 12:15 a.m., the gliders transporting the vanguard of the 6th
British Airborne Division slipped the towropes of their Halifax bomber tugs
and began their descent into German-occupied France. Commanded by
Major-General Richard Gale, the 6th Airborne Division was to perform a task
vital to the success of the entire invasion plan–that of seizing and holding the
open left flank of the Normandy bridgehead, against which the main weight of
the German counterattack was expected to fall as the Panzer divisions moved
up from their garrisons east and southeast of Caen. While the red and
yellow tracers of the German Flak discomfited the bombers, which flew on to
raid Caen, the small glider force of less than 200 men plunged undetected
towards its objectives: the bridges on the only through-road over the Orne
river and the canal between the city and the sea. In a coup-de-main the
paratroopers overwhelmed the defenders of the canal bridge and occupied it.
The capture of the Orne bridge one half mile to the east posed less of a
challenge, for its defenders had fled. Both bridges were taken intact.

By 12:50 a.m., the parachutists of Gale's main force were floating towards
their drop zones directly east of the Orne. They rapidly secured their objectives, which included the demolition of five bridges in the flooded Dives valley
to frustrate an approach of German reinforcements from that direction, and
the destruction of a coastal gun battery at Merville. Soon after dawn the at-

tackers were moving their anti-tank guns into place to cover the open ground south of Ranville, and waiting for the tanks of the 21st Panzer Division.[1]

Shortly after midnight the first report of enemy airborne drops east of the Orne reached the headquarters of the 12th SS Panzer Division in Acon. At once, the officer on duty relayed the information to Fritz Witt at his quarters in Tillières-sur-Avre, about a mile outside Acon. According to the report, which originated from a Luftwaffe command post in Evreux, uniformed straw dummies had been dropped by parachute in the vicinity of several airfields near the Normandy coast between the Seine and the Orne; although unconfirmed, actual airborne landings appeared to have taken place in the sector of the 711th Infantry Division, which defended the stretch of coastline from the mouth of the Seine to an area just east of the Orne. Hoping to clarify the startling information, 12th SS Panzer immediately telephoned the headquarters of both the 711th Infantry and 21st Panzer Divisions. The infantry division confirmed the drop of the dummy parachutists, but not the landing of hostile airborne troops. 21st Panzer Division had received no reports of enemy activity. Off the coast the weather was stormy, and no Allied naval units had been observed. Intermittent rains battered the shoreline.[2]

Woscidlo

A shot-down glider of the 6th British Airborne Division near Caen, June 6.

[1]Wilmont, *The Struggle for Europe*, pp 238-42.
[2]Meyer, H., *Kriegsgeschichte*, p 52; Meyer H., P-164, p 15.

Woscidlo

Antiaircraft fire from the invasion fleet searches out menacing German aircraft.

Part of the Allied armada off the coast of Normandy.

99

Woscidlo

The British landing fleet as seen through a German telescope.

Witt, Hubert Meyer, and several other members of the divisional staff carefully weighed the available intelligence and concluded that the invasion had not yet begun; rather, they thought the unusual enemy activity signified an attempt to probe German countermeasures against a possible airborne assault. Confident in their analysis all retired to bed, with the exception of their reflective commander. Subsequent reports, however, soon conveyed the seriousness of the Allied operation in Normandy, and, about 1:30 a.m., an agitated Witt awakened Meyer and informed him that the invasion had indeed begun. Meyer dressed quickly and then hurried to the telephone. The 711th Infantry Division, he learned, was engaging enemy paratroopers on its left flank; the 21st Panzer reported that Allied parachutists had touched down in the area of Troarn, east of Caen. Although Witt had yet to receive instructions from a higher headquarters, he placed the 12th SS Panzer on alarm—a move accomplished at exactly 3:00 a.m. according to surviving divisional records.[3]

With the speed and precision born of constant rehearsal, the youngsters of the Hitler Youth Division hurried into their uniforms, gathered weapons and

[3]Kriegstagebuch I./25. SS-Pz.Gren.Rgt. 6.6.44 (Hereafter cited KTB I./25. SS-Pz.Gren.Rgt. Document is a typed transcription of the hand-written diary located in United States National Archives Microcopy T-354: Miscellaneous Records of the 12th SS Panzer Division); BAMA. Tagebuch Divisions-Begleit-Kompanie. 6.6.44.

equipment, and loaded their vehicles. The hum of the troop carriers and the deep growl of the tanks as they fired up their powerful Maybach engines shattered the stillness of the early morning hour. The weeks of waiting and anticipation were finally over and many could scarcely contain their excitement. Some knocked one another playfully on the shoulders; others embraced. Tankmen tossed their distinctive black caps high into the air. The prevailing mood could not be mistaken: "The Tommies will get it now!" Unexpected encouragement came later that morning, when 30 to 40 sleek Messerschmitt fighters, hugging the treetops, swept through the divisional sector on their way to the battlefront, rocking their wings in response to the cheers and hurrahs from below. What the young soldiers could not know was that the Luftwaffe, a spent force by June 1944, would rarely be seen in the skies over Normandy in the coming weeks of battle.

Within an hour the regiments and independent battalions of the division stood ready at their alarm stations. On his own initiative, Kurt Meyer dispatched elements of his 25th SS Panzer Grenadier Regiment to reconnoiter in the direction of Caen. The division reported its readiness to I SS Panzer Corps headquarters in Rouen, but received no marching orders, for Dietrich's tank corps had yet to receive its own operational instructions. Repeated inquiries at corps headquarters, moreover, were unable to cast added light on the events unfolding along the coast. The lack of a telephone link to Army Group B proved a further frustration.[4]

*   *   *

Between one and two in the morning, reports of the landings began to filter back to OB West and Army Group B,[5] where they were greeted with considerable skepticism. At 1:30 a.m., Naval Group West telephoned Rundstedt's headquarters and notified it of reported airborne landings in the sectors of the 711th and 716th Infantry Divisions; the LXXXIV Army Corps, defending western Normandy, had ordered the highest state of alarm. Five minutes later, Major-General Max Pemsel, the Seventh Army Chief of Staff, conveyed a similar message to his counterpart at Army Group B, Major-General Dr. Hans Speidel. Pemsel also mentioned enemy airborne activity along the east coast of the Cotentin Peninsula, near Montebourg and Marcouf.[6] At 2:15 a.m., Pemsel once again rang up Speidel, informing him that the 91st Air Landing Division was already locked in combat with American paratroopers on the Cotentin Peninsula; fifty of the enemy, in fact, had been taken prisoner at a bridge. The Seventh Army chief of staff assured Speidel that a major Allied operation was underway, and that Army and Luftwaffe reports alike confirmed this impression.

---

[4]Meyer, H., P-164, pp 15-16; Meyer, K. *Grenadiere*, p 208.

[5]There are no reports of enemy landings in records of the Seventh Army, or in the war diaries of Army Group B and OB West, prior to 1:30 a.m., June 6th.

[6]The American 82nd and 101st Airborne Divisions had landed in the southeast corner of the Cotentin Peninsula, where they were to perform the same mission on the western flank as Gale's 6th Airborne Division east of the Orne.

Major-General Dr. Hans Speidel.

Speidel was not convinced. At 1:40 a.m., he got a report of landings farther up the coast, in the Fifteenth Army's sector, but they appeared to be limited in scope. Shortly thereafter, he learned that straw dummies had been discovered in Normandy. These revelations reinforced Speidel's own conviction that the actual invasion could only come at Pas-de-Calais. Throughout the early morning hours he repeatedly told Seventh Army, which stood in the path of an enormous assault, that the enemy must be staging a purely local action in Normandy. At 3:00 a.m., he even went so far as to reassure Rundstedt's staff that he was taking it all very calmly. "It's possible," he asserted, "that bailed-out airplane crews are being mistaken for paratroopers."[7]

In defense of Speidel, his lack of concern was hardly unique; it only reflected the reigning opinion at OB West and among the Navy and Luftwaffe high commands in the West--an opinion due in large measure to a lack of secure knowledge of enemy intent. With the German coastal radar stations bombed out of action or jammed, and Luftwaffe aerial reconnaissance unable to penetrate the thick screen of fighter protection above the Allied convoys, the passage of the invasion fleet through the Channel had gone undetected.[8] Thus

---

[7]T-312/1568/000939. 7 AOK. Messages Received Re Operations along Invasion Front (Hereafter cited Telephone Log. Seventh Army.); T-84/281/000737. Kriegstagebuch Heeresgruppe B (Hereafter cited KTB Heeresgruppe B.); BAMA. RH 19IV/43. Kriegstagebuch OB West. 6.6.44. (Hereafter cited KTB OB West); BAMA. RH 19IV/134. Telefonkladde. Meyer-Detring (Ic OB West). 6.6.44.

[8]The Germans, to provide early warning of the approach of hostile air and naval forces, had established an elaborate network of radar blanketing the Atlantic coastline from Kirkenes in northern Norway to the Spanish frontier. Along the shores of Holland, Belgium, and northwestern France the coverage was particularly thorough, with a major radar station every ten miles, supported by an inland system not so dense, albeit still comprehensive. Consequently, the Germans were confident that they could not be surprised--that their electronic sentries would furnish ample warning of invasion. They had not reckoned with the Allied countermeasures, which, on the eve of the invasion, were swift and surgical. In the week before D-Day the RAF heavily and accurately bombed six major radar stations between Boulogne and Cherbourg; during the night before the invasion, most of the remaining installations in that sector were effectively jammed. Wilmont, *The Struggle for Europe*, pp 246-47.

blinded, Seventh Army did not report the presence of warships off the coast of France until 2:15 a.m., and then the detection was made by sound, not by radar![9] Denied proper intelligence, the staffs at OB West and Army Group B were unable to gauge the significance of the early messages from along the invasion front; not until late morning would the scope and direction of the assault begin to become apparent. The disruption of vital communication centers by Allied air and naval forces further aggravated the situation, which prevented a swift and telling response to the landings. Perhaps the gravest consequence of the prevailing disorientation was that it would adversely affect the deployment of both the 12th SS and the 21st Panzer Divisions (the two armored formations nearest the Normandy beaches) during the critical morning hours of June 6th.

Further crippling the defenders' reactions was the disarray in the German command structure in France on the eve of the invasion. Among the senior commanders most deeply concerned, only Rundstedt, Geyr and Marcks, the commander of the LXXXIV Army Corps, were at their respective posts.[10] The commander of the 21st Panzer Division, Brigadier-General Edgar Feuchtinger, had absented himself to Paris for unexplained reasons, and had taken his capable operations officer with him. Sepp Dietrich, the commander of the I SS Panzer Corps, was in Brussels. General Dollmann had already left Seventh Army headquarters for Rennes, in Brittany, where he planned to direct a training exercise. But by far the most significant absence was that of Rommel. The energetic Field Marshal had always stressed the need to crush an enemy invasion within its first few hours, yet he was 500 miles away at Herrlingen, and would not return until late that evening. Had Rommel been at his post the response to the landings would very likely have been a more determined one.[11]

As the morning progressed the reports of invasion multiplied. Gradually, OB West began to stir. At 3:25 a.m., Naval Group West informed Rundstedt's headquarters that landing craft had appeared off the Calvados coast–at Port-en-Bessin and Grandcamp. Swarms of Allied aircraft towing gliders had also been sighted, drifting slowly southward above the Channel islands. At last aware that a large enemy operation was underway, OB West, at 4:10 a.m., placed both the Seventh and Fifteenth Armies on highest alert;[12] at the same time, it ordered the 12th SS Panzer, the Panzer Lehr and the 17th SS Panzer Grenadier Division–OKW reserves--to prepare to march. In partial defiance of his standing orders, Rundstedt had already dispatched elements of the 12th SS

---

[9]T-312/1568/000938. Telephone Log. Seventh Army.

[10]Alarmed by a sudden surge in enemy air activity, General Marcks had entered his command bunker in St. Lô late that evening (June 5th). Following reports from Richter's 716th Infantry Division, Marcks alarmed his LXXXIV Army Corps at eleven minutes past one. June 6th was the General's birthday. Friedrich Hayn, *Die Invasion, Von Cotentin bis Falaise.* Wehrmacht im Kampf series. Bd. II (Heidelberg: Kurt Vowinckel Verlag, 1954).

[11]Wilmont, *The Struggle for Europe,* p 282; David Irving, *The Trail of the Fox* (New York: E.P. Dutton, 1977), pp 361-62.

[12]Seventh Army, however, had already issued the alarm more than two hours earlier, at 1:40 a.m. T-312/1568/000938. Telephone Log. Seventh Army.

towards the Normandy coastline to carry out a reconnaissance. At 4:45 a.m., the aging Field Marshal followed these moves with the first formal request to OKW for release of its reserves. He argued that if these forces were set quickly in motion, they would be able to reach the battle area that day.[13]

While Rundstedt impatiently awaited the release of the strategic reserves, the 146 tanks of the 21st Panzer Division stood idly by in the fields and orchards east and northeast of Falaise.[14] Feuchtinger's armor could have moved up to Caen unmolested under the cover of darkness--the tragedy for the Germans was that it did not do so. At 4:20 a.m., the determined Pemsel again spoke with Speidel at Army Group B, this time requesting that the 21st Panzer be deployed at once against the enemy airborne bridgehead east of the Orne. With Rommel absent, however, Speidel was reluctant to commit the formation until the Schwerpunkt (point of main effort) of the Allied operation had become more clear. Not until 6:45 a.m., perhaps after conversing with his commander by telephone,[15] did Speidel release the 21st Panzer to Seventh Army; fifteen minutes later, Seventh Army subordinated the division to Marcks' LXXXIV Army Corps, with orders that the division attack the enemy paratroopers. Due to a breakdown in communications, another two hours elapsed before Marcks was able to pass on his instructions to Feuchtinger, who was now back at his post. In the interim, Feuchtinger had sent a portion of his armor rumbling towards the airborne bridgehead without waiting for orders. Thus, it was not until well after dawn that the German striking force closest to the Calvados coastline was set in motion. The great irony was that, by that time, the principal threat had shifted to the sector west of the Orne, where the Allied seaborne landings were now well underway.[16]

*　　　*　　　*

At 2:30 a.m., OB West had issued its reconnaissance order to 12th SS Panzer via Panzer Group West; the division then relayed the directive to its reconnaissance battalion, commanded by SS-Sturmbannführer Gerhard Bremer.

[13]BAMA. KTB OB West, 6.6.44.

[14]Following its destruction in North Africa, the 21st Panzer had been reformed beginning in the spring of 1943. In addition to its large complement of tanks (Panzer IVs) the division possessed 51 assault guns, as well as some specialized weapons designed and built by the division itself. Still, the division suffered from numerous shortcomings. Except for its weapons, it was heavily dependent upon French and English vehicles captured in 1940. Replacement personnel were often poor, including numerous ethnic Germans (Volksdeutsche), many of whom did not understand the German language. Despite such concerns, Feuchtinger considered his tank division sufficiently trained and of "average mobility" by the time of the invasion. The 21st Panzer would fight alongside the 12th SS Panzer Division during June and July 1944. Edgar Feuchtinger, B-441. "History of the 21st Panzer Division from the Time of its Formation until the Beginning of the Invasion." pp 4-5, 15-17.

[15]Although in his post-war memoirs Speidel places the time of his initial phone call to Rommel at 6:00 a.m., this call is not posted in the Army Group B war diary. In the diary there is no indication that Speidel telephoned the Field Marshal until more than four hours later, at 10:15 a.m. T-84/281/000745. KTB Heeresgruppe B.

[16]T-84/281/000741. KTB Heeresgruppe B; T-312/1568/000943. Telephone Log. Seventh Army; Feuchtinger, B-441, p 20.

[17]A veteran of the Leibstandarte, Bremer had participated in all of the division's

campaigns until his transfer to the 12th SS Panzer. Like Kurt Meyer, he had a reputa-

SS-Sturmbannführer Gerhard Bremer.

The 26-year-old, much decorated Bremer[17] conferred at once with the commander of the battalion's 1st Company, SS-Obersturmführer Peter Hansmann. Bremer informed him that enemy airborne landings had been reported along the Normandy coast and behind the coastal fortifications; the landings appeared to have taken place in the sectors west of the Seine and around Carentan. But the reports, Bremer continued, were imprecise and contradictory. Hansmann's company was to furnish needed intelligence by scouring the coastal region from the mouth of the Seine to the beaches north and northwest of Caen; if possible, the unit was to avoid battle, but to return with information on enemy strength and intentions, and, of course, with prisoners for interrogation.

Hansmann distributed his force into four separate patrols to provide thorough coverage of the assigned area. By 4:00 a.m., the armored scout cars and motorcyclists of the reconnaissance company were underway. Hansmann took direct command of the westernmost patrol, whose task it was to comb the beaches northeast of Bayeux as far as Courseulles-sur-Mer. The night was pleasantly cool, and a pale moon peeked occasionally through the clouds and the fog. Within an hour, the two eight-wheeled armored cars that composed Hansmann's patrol had reached Lisieux, a picturesque Norman town tucked in a valley some 25 miles east of Caen. Lisieux was already coming to life, as the

tion as a "Draufgänger." While in command of a reconnaissance company in Russia in the autumn of 1941, Bremer had become one of the first in the elite Leibstandarte to win the Knight's Cross. He also possessed the Iron Cross, first and second class. Personalakten, Gerhard Bremer. Lebenslauf, etc.

first farmers emerged from their half-timbered homes to begin another work-day. From there, the journey continued on the main highway towards Caen (Route Nationale 13), through the thickly wooded and sharply contoured landscape of the Dives valley.

It was now becoming lighter, and the patrol soon reached the outskirts of Caen. The scene that greeted them was one of frenzied activity. Wehrmacht vehicles choked the roadways, while a platoon of infantry, Panzer grenadiers of the 21st Panzer Division, moved into position. To the north the sound of battle was clearly audible. A captain explained to Hansmann that British paratroopers had landed astride the Orne and most likely seized the crossings there, for all communications with Ranville had ceased. While they conversed, enemy fighter-bombers swooped in and pumped their shells indiscriminately into the city. Civilians abandoned their dwellings and fled in panic.

In code the SS-Obersturmführer transmitted his first report to battalion headquarters. The patrol then wound its way through the center of Caen, navigating the narrow roadways lined with densely arranged stone buildings, and reached its western exit. Here the confusion was equally great, the roads jammed with men and vehicles, especially Luftwaffe ground personnel com-ing from the direction of the nearby Carpiquet airport. Leaving the city, the two armored cars motored on at high speed down the Route Nationale 13 towards Bayeux, 15 miles to the northwest. A gentle morning mist, as well as the many trees that lined the nearly perfectly straight highway, offered some concealment from the hostile fighter-bombers orbiting the battlefield.

Arriving in Bayeux the patrol encountered the now familiar scenes of panic and disorder. Townspeople ran from their homes, seeking safety in the coun-tryside; still others remained behind and discussed the unexpected turn of events with neighbors or local German garrison troops. Knots of civilians, soldiers and military vehicles were everywhere, thickening into an un-disciplined mass towards the center of the town. A platoon of German military police worked feverishly to impose order. Swept up in the confusion, Hansmann was unable to reach the city Kommandant. From a sergeant, however, he learned of heavy fighting along the coast, in the Bay of Arromanches, and that enemy seaborne landings were underway there. The distant crash of artillery supported the sergeant's claims.

All that remained was to observe the spectacle first-hand. To avoid detec-tion from the air, the patrol stayed off the main road leading northeast from Bayeux and advanced cross-country. The armored cars crept slowly forward, clinging to the stonewalls and hedgerows that furnished welcomed conceal-ment. When the patrol reached the high ground at Magny-en-Bessin, midway between Bayeux and the sea, they climbed the modest height, which overlooked the bay. The view below them was an extraordinary one. To the west, Hansmann could make out the steep bank of the bay. It shuddered under heavy artillery fire. Overhead, enemy aircraft, uncontested by the Luftwaffe, poured their rockets into the concrete fortifications along the shoreline. Through his field glasses he could discern the dark, menacing contours of the Allied invasion fleet--literally hundreds of warships stretching beyond the horizon and protected by a curtain of barrage balloons. In the background the big guns of the fleet punctured the steel grey sky with bright flickers of light. Closer in, swarms of landing craft ploughed through the dark green water towards the beaches, where they disgorged their human contents: British soldiers--easily recognizable because of their distinctive, flat helmets. Counterfire from German coastal batteries not yet subdued dropped among the invaders, sending great walls of water high into the air. The distinctive report of the German machine guns added to the deafening cacophony. Yet the enemy infantry, supported by amphibious tanks invented especially for the invasion, moved slowly inland through the dunes, encountering little organized resistance.

It was now nearly 8:00 a.m. What the bewildered patrol observed from their spectacular perch above the Bay of Arromanches were the first waves of the 50th Northumbrian Division. The division belonged to the Second British Army, commanded by Lieutenant-General Miles Dempsey. Following a powerful air and naval bombardment of the German coastal defenses, the lead battalions of Dempsey's three assault divisions--the 50th Northumbrian, the 3rd Canadian and the 3rd British Infantry Divisions--began to come ashore between 7:30 and 8:00 a.m. along a 25 mile front extending from the mouth of the Orne to Port-en-Bessin. The assault divisions of the First U.S. Army had started their landings east and north of the Vire estuary an hour earlier, at 6:30 a.m. The war diary of the German Seventh Army dolefully recorded, the landings came at low tide, rendering useless the bulk of the beach obstacles so assiduously planted closer to the shoreline.[18]

Convinced that the long-awaited invasion of Fortress Europe had begun, Hansmann radioed a clipped report to his superiors: "Hundreds of enemy ships sighted, protected by barrage balloons. British infantry and heavy equipment coming ashore virtually unopposed. A dozen heavy tanks counted. Coastal defenses either out of action or overrun. Enemy infantry in battalion strength moving south towards Bayeux. The city itself, and the roads leading into it, under naval bombardment."

Perhaps betrayed by the radio transmission, the patrol itself soon came under heavy shell fire. The violent explosions made the source of their discomfort abundantly clear: enemy naval artillery! The SS troopers sought safety inside their lightly armored scout cars, which rocked under the weight of the bombardment. Fortunately, the shelling ceased as abruptly as it had begun. There were no casualties. Following this narrow escape they continued to probe in the direction of Courseulles. Throughout the morning, Hansmann had received no additional instructions from the battalion; his three patrols farther east had also been silent with the exception of one, which had reported the capture of enemy paratroopers. By 11:00 a.m., Hansmann had completed his eventful mission and begun the return journey to battalion headquarters.[19]

---

[18]T-312/1569/000005. KTB Seventh Army.
[19]Hansmann's report, from which this account is gleaned, is found in Meyer, H., *Kriegsgeschichte*, pp 57-61.

While its patrols were racing towards the coastline the 12th SS Panzer Division had received its first marching orders. At 5:00 a.m., von Salmuth's Fifteenth Army, reporting that its 711th Infantry Division was still battling enemy paratroopers, petitioned Army Group B for the deployment of the 12th SS Panzer in that sector.[20] Simultaneously, OB West learned that more enemy naval vessels had been sighted off Port-en-Bessin, and that warships had also been observed near St. Vaast, well up the Cotentin Peninsula. It was now apparent that large enemy forces were approaching the Normandy coastline on a broad front. On his own initiative, Rundstedt decided to place the 12th SS Panzer under the control of Rommel's Army Group and to shift the formation into the Bernay - Lisieux - Vimoutiers area, from where it could intervene on the westernmost flank of the Fifteenth Army. A few minutes later, 5:20 a.m., following an inquiry from Panzer Group West, Rundstedt approved the return of the Flak battalions of the 12th SS and the Panzer Lehr--which were in position near crucial Seine crossings and around Paris, respectively--to their divisions.[21]

The march order reached Witt and his staff at approximately 7:00 a.m., and it had a shocking effect. The entire Panzer regiment, as well as the engineer battalion, were garrisoned well north of the Bernay - Lisieux axis. To reach the assigned assembly area, these units would have to move southwest, then to the north or northwest if deployed in the sector of the 711th Infantry Division: a gratuitous detour that would only cause delay. The OB West directive also failed to make use of the march plan (Aufmarsch B) already prepared by the division for a commitment between the Seine and the Orne; if executed, the directive would merely compress the division into a much smaller area, roughly 15 miles in depth and in length, from which fewer good roadways led to the coast. The roads leading in and out of Lisieux, moreover, were particularly vulnerable to air attack, for the town rested in a deep depression. At once Hubert Meyer got on the phone to I SS Panzer Corps headquarters and voiced the division's concerns, yet all attempts to overturn the order were useless.[22]

It is not clear what compelled OB West to issue such an order to the division. Throughout the morning Fifteenth Army had reported enemy airborne activity on its western flank, but landings from the sea had not taken place. Reports of Allied naval operations showed that they were concentrated farther west, from the Orne to the east coast of the Cotentin Peninsula. The most plausible explanation is that Rundstedt and his staff feared an extension of the Allied sea landings, which appeared imminent west of the Orne, at least as far east as the mouth of the Seine. The locations of the Allied airborne drops, however, as well as the destruction of the Dives bridges, should have made it apparent that the sea landings would be limited to the front of the Seventh Army.

---

[20]T-84/281/000741. KTB Heeresgruppe B.
[21]BAMA. KTB OB West. 6.6.44.
[22]Meyer, H., *Kriegsgeschichte*, p 62; Meyer, H., P-164, p 16; Meyer, K., *Grenadiere*, p 208.

Reluctantly, the division prepared its plans for the advance into the Lisieux area. At 10:00 a.m., the vast array of men and vehicles began to surge forward.[23] The divisional headquarters remained temporarily in Acon, where critical telephone links were available. In Lisieux a message center was established, while the 88mm and 37mm guns of the Flak battalion were ordered into position at important crossings near the town to furnish protection from air attack.[24] The low cloud cover, strong winds and intermittent rain favored the march, thus the advancing columns were not disrupted by Allied fighter-bombers–a happy state of affairs that would turn dramatically for the worse within hours.[25]

* * *

Without formal sanction from the Wehrmacht High Command, Rundstedt had set the 12th SS in motion to counter the threat as he perceived it. But at 9:30 a.m., his operations officer, Colonel Bodo Zimmermann, duly notified Rommel's headquarters that OKW had countermanded the subordination of the division to the Army Group. At 10:00 a.m., General Alfred Jodl, Chief of the High Command operations staff, firmly vetoed the OB West request--made more than five hours earlier--for release of the OKW armored reserves, although he did approve the move of the 12th SS Panzer to Lisieux. The powerful Panzer Lehr, however, which had begun to stir restlessly at its stations southwest of Paris, was to remain where it was, in march readiness.[26]

Based on available intelligence Jodl's 10:00 a.m. decision was a logical one. The first reports from Normandy had begun to reach his operations staff at Berchtesgaden between 3:00 and 5:00 a.m.[27] As the hours passed, it became evident that airborne drops had taken place across a wide front and that sea landings were underway along the Calvados coastline. Yet the situation remained obscure, and no one could gauge with certainty the magnitude of the enemy operation. Jodl's hunch was that it was a diversion, or holding attack, in prelude to the decisive main effort–an assessment he based principally on the choice of location as well as the prevailing weather conditions. Therefore, he elected to withhold commitment of the few available OKW reserves, no doubt hoping that the Seventh Army would master the situation with its own resources.[28] In any case, Jodl could not have released the formations without

---

[23]According to Kurt Meyer, his 25th SS Panzer Grenadiere Regiment got underway at 10:00 a.m.; the entire division was moving towards Lisieux by 11:00 a.m. KTB I./25. SS-Pz.Gren.Rgt. 6.6.44; Meyer, K., *Grenadiere*, p 209.

[24]Meyer, H., P-164, p 16; Meyer, K., *Grenadiere*, p 209.

[25]According to Rundstedt's operations officer, the misty, foggy weather prevailed until about 11:00 a.m., eliminating any significant fighter-bomber activity until that time. Other reports indicate that the poor weather most likely continued well into the afternoon. Zimmermann, B-308, p 76.

[26]BAMA. KTB OB West. 6.6.44.

[27]In June 1944 Hitler's headquarters (Führerhauptquartier) was located at the Berghof, high in the Bavarian Alps above Berchtesgaden. Both the chief of OKW, Field Marshal Wilhelm Keitel, and his deputy, Jodl, had their headquarters at Berchtesgaden.

[28]Brigadier-General Horst Buttlar-Brandenfels (Chief of Army Operations, Armed Forces Operations Staff), B-672. "OB West: Command Relationships. Annex Five: OKW Interpretation of the Normandy Landing at Noon on 6 June 1944." pp 37-40.

the explicit approval of Hitler. The dictator had awakened that morning about 8:00 or 9:00 a.m. and conferred with his chief military advisors. Certainly he forbade a commitment of the OKW reserves at that time; not until his military conference early that afternoon had the situation sufficiently clarified to justify their release.[29]

But the concerned commanders in Normandy were no more prepared than their superiors at Berchtesgaden to draw definitive conclusions. Entries in the OB West war diary at 9:30 a.m., and again at 11:00 a.m., show that despite the considerable enemy forces committed to the battle area, the staff was still uncertain whether it was facing a diversion or the main Allied assault. Army Group B and Seventh Army shared similar perceptions. At 10:20 a.m., Seventh Army even notified the Army Group that an extension of the landings into Brittany appeared possible.[30] Despite such confusion, one unpleasant fact was now all too apparent: the Allied attack was far too big to be cleared up by the forces of Seventh Army alone. At 9:10 a.m., Pemsel telephoned Speidel at La Roche-Guyon and informed him that enemy troops and tanks were pouring ashore in Normandy. Gradually, the scope of the Allied operation was becoming clear. Luftwaffe aerial reconnaissance as well as the continued flow of information from subordinate commands convinced OB West by late morning that the sea landings would be limited to an area west of the Orne. At 11:25 a.m., the LXXXI Army Corps reported to Rundstedt's staff that the situation in the sector of the 711th Infantry Division had stabilized: a battalion of enemy paratroopers had been destroyed and no further airborne activity had occurred. As a result of the diminishing threat east of the Orne, OB West by midday began to contemplate an eventual commitment of the 12th SS Panzer Division northwest of Caen.[31]

A deployment of the division in that sector could come none too soon, for along the coastline from Caen to Bayeux the German defenses were rapidly crumbling. At 9:25 a.m., General Marcks had lodged a frantic report with his superiors at Seventh Army: "The situation on the left bank of the Orne is dangerous. Enemy tanks have reached the artillery positions. The LXXXIV Army Corps has no mobile reserves equipped with anti-tank weapons." He pleaded for the immediate dispatch of the 12th SS to the area west of Caen, since the 21st Panzer was already committed east of the Orne. The 12th SS, of course, was still officially immobilized as a High Command reserve and could

---

[29]Even had Jodl released the 12th SS at 10:00 a.m., when, at least for the concerned staffs in France, the extent of the Allied operation in Normandy was beginning to clarify, the mass of the division could not have reached the battle zone in time to intervene on June 6th. At best, those elements stationed closest to the Caen - Falaise area--most notably Kurt Meyer's regiment--might have launched an attack during the late afternoon or early evening hours of D-Day. Still, had Meyer been able to attack in conjunction with the 21st Panzer, the results might have been significant. The Panzer Lehr Division, with even greater distances to cover from its garrisons in the Chartres - Le Mans - Orleans sector, could never have been a factor that day. The advance of both divisions was slowed appreciably by air attack, and by the inevitable requirements for maintenance and fuel.

[30]BAMA. KTB OB West. 6.6.44; T-84/281/000746. KTB Heeresgruppe B.

[31]T-84/281/000744. KTB Heeresgruppe B; BAMA. KTB OB West. 6.6.44.

offer no immediate support. An hour later, Marcks had no alternative but to instruct the 21st Panzer Division to suspend its advance towards the airborne bridgehead, cross the Orne, and move against the invaders from the sea.[32]

Despite the OKW refusal to commit its mobile reserves, Rundstedt continued to press for their release. At 2:15 p.m., he again petitioned the High Command for release of the 12th SS Panzer, arguing that the division was needed to help restore the situation in the seaborne bridgehead. Fifteen minutes later, and nearly ten hours after Rundstedt's initial request, Jodl freed both the 12th SS and the Panzer Lehr for deployment along the invasion front. At once OB West subordinated the divisions, along with Dietrich's I SS Panzer Corps headquarters, to Army Group B. At precisely 3:00 p.m., the Army Group placed all three formations under the tactical control of the Seventh Army.[33] At 3:05 p.m., some fifteen hours after Gale's paratroopers began their landings east of the Orne, the two tank divisions were finally ordered to commence the march into the killing zone. Seventh Army issued the order through Panzer Group West:[34]

> 1. To 12th SS Panzer Division: Division to move forward immediately north of the axis Alençon - Carrouges - Flers into the area around Evrécy. The division subordinated initially to the LXXXIV Army Corps.
> Assignment: Operating on the left flank of the 21st Panzer Division, to throw the enemy west of the Orne into the sea and destroy him.
> 2. To Panzer Lehr Division: As ordered by Army Group B, the division to advance immediately south of the said axis and reach initially the area Flers - Vire.

Upon reaching the battlefront they were to be assembled along with the 21st Panzer and the remnants of the 716th Infantry Division under the I SS Panzer Corps. With the concentrated striking power of three Panzer divisions at his disposal, Dietrich was to counterattack posthaste and to destroy the enemy between Caen and Bayeux. From his headquarters high atop the Obersalzberg, Hitler made only too clear what he expected from his generals; his hopeless injunction is preserved in the records of the Seventh Army:[35]

> The OB West operations officer stresses the desire of the High Command to have the enemy bridgehead annihilated by the evening of June 6th, since there exists the danger of additional air and sea landings . . . The beachhead must be cleaned up by tonight.

The march order from Seventh Army reached the headquarters of the 12th SS at roughly 5:00 p.m. Already elements of the division had arrived in their assembly areas near Lisieux. One of these was the 1st Battalion of Kurt Meyer's 25th SS Panzer Grenadier Regiment, which had motored into St.

[32]T-312/1568/000945. Telephone Log. Seventh Army.
[33]BAMA. KTB OB West. 6.6.44; T-312/1569/000006. KTB Seventh Army.
[34]Although the 12th SS Panzer was only subordinated to Panzer Group West for training purposes, orders to the division often came down through Geyr's staff. T-312/1568/000948. Telephone Log. Seventh Army.
[35]T-312/1568/000950. Telephone Log. Seventh Army.

Woscidlo

Panthers from the division rush towards the invasion front.

ECPA

This gun crew rushes through a French town to engage the invaders.

A 2cm four-barrelled Flak gun (Vierlings-Flak) protects advancing elements of the division against Allied fighter-bombers.

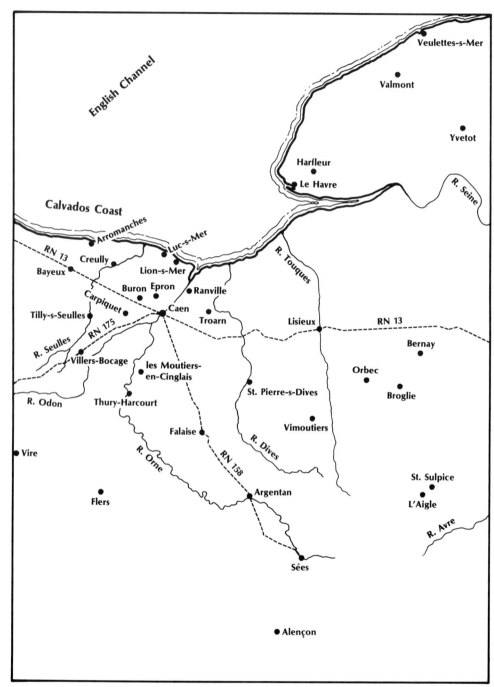

The March to the Front: June 6-8, 1944.

Pierre-des-Ifs, some four miles southwest of Lisieux, about 1:00 p.m.; there, the battalion's vehicles had taken cover astride the roadway.[36] Fortunately, for the advance to the Caen region the division could make use of the march routes previously laid out under Aufmarsch C. In a flurry of purposeful activity the division's radiomen, staff officers and motorcycle messengers relayed corresponding instructions to the divisional columns.[37]

Within an hour the regiments and independent battalions were underway; supported by tanks and artillery, both Panzer grenadier regiments marched as battlegroups capable of independent action.[38] The operations staff left Acon

Elements of the division are guided towards the invasion area.

---

[36]KTB I./25. SS-Pz.Gren.Rgt. 6.6.44.

[37]Unfortunately for the historian, the near total loss of the records of the 12th SS Panzer Division makes it impossible to reconstruct the actual routes taken by the division to the invasion front.

[38]Kurt Meyer's battlegroup consisted of his own regiment, portions of two tank companies of the 2nd Panzer Battalion (Panzer IVs), and the medium artillery (schwere Artillerie) of the artillery regiment's 3rd Battalion. The tanks were those that had been transferred into the regimental sector on the night of June 4-5 for the planned training exercise.

for les Moutiers-en-Cinglais—a village ten miles south of Caen abutting the southern rim of the Forêt de Grimbosq—where the division was to temporarily reestablish its headquarters. To be put in the picture, Fritz Witt had gone on ahead of his staff and made for the headquarters of the 21st Panzer Division in St. Pierre-sur-Dives. Indeed, as the shift towards Caen commenced, the division commander had little knowledge of the events that had transpired there. All he knew was that strong enemy forces had landed by air east of the Orne, and that sea landings had occurred along a wide front west of the river; he did not know how far inland the enemy had pushed, or even if they had already reached the division's intended concentration area around Evrécy, eight miles southwest of Caen. Adding to the uncertainty was the fact that all units of the 12th SS were observing radio silence—a procedure that not only frustrated enemy attempts to locate them, but Witt's own attempts as well.[39]

To minimize losses from air attack, the vehicles were well camouflaged and maintained 100 yard intervals. Whenever possible, the columns proceeded on secondary roads, the lines of troop transports, trucks and tanks stretching for miles along the arteries leading westward towards the front. Attacks from the

The Panzer regiment marches to the front with 100 yard intervals between vehicles as protection against air attacks. Note the divisional emblem on the front fender.

air had become more frequent early that afternoon; by now, however, the protective layers of cloud and mist had lifted, and the Spitfires and Hawker Typhoons of the Allied tactical air forces pounced on the division with a vengeance. Attacking out of the sun the planes dropped their bombs and loosed their rockets—white, feathery clouds trailing behind them as they left their racks. Soldiers sprang from their vehicles and sought available cover,

[39]Meyer, H., *Kriegsgeschichte*, p 65; Meyer, H., P-164, p 17.

while drivers struggled to remove their machines from the road. Some fought back with carbines or machine guns, only to find their tormentors invulnerable to such fire. The air attacks rolled on well into the evening hours, for the sun did not set over Normandy until 9:48 p.m. Where, the Germans wondered, was the Luftwaffe?[40]

The enemy air forces disrupted the cohesion of many of the marching columns and slowed their advance to a crawl. Although significant, the losses in men and materiel were not prohibitive; those elements without adequate anti-aircraft protection, such as supply columns, suffered most heavily.[41] Kurt Meyer lost most of the men and materiel of the medical company destined for his regiment; his 1st Battalion reported four dead, 12 wounded, and one missing, as well as the loss of insignificant quantities of vehicles, weapons and equipment. In marked contrast, the engineer battalion saw its entire bridging company destroyed--the pontoons and vehicles wiped out near Evreux. All told, the division suffered 83 casualties on June 6th--22 dead, 60 wounded, and one missing.[42]

But the 12th SS did not endure the Allied aerial assault alone. At 7:00 p.m., the Panzer Lehr Division began to move forward from its bases in the forests 75 miles southwest of Paris. Commanded by Major-General Fritz Bayerlein, the Panzer Lehr was the mightiest formation in the Wehrmacht. On June 6th it boasted a complement of 183 tanks (97 Panzer IVs and 86 Panthers), 40 tank destroyers and 658 armored personnel carriers.[43] A veteran of the North African campaign, Bayerlein was no stranger to the devastating effects of Allied airpower; he had pleaded with his superiors at Seventh Army to await the cover of darkness to begin the advance. But Dollmann was not to be swayed. The division, he insisted, had sat idle too long, and was to get moving at once.

---

[40]Many of the details in this section concerning the effects of Allied air activity have been drawn from interviews with former 12th SS Division members conducted in West Germany and Normandy in 1983. For example, Interview, Heinz Berner, June 1-2, 1983; Interview, Günther Burdack, May 21, 1983.

[41]Protected by a special mobile Flak unit, the Panzer regiment's 9th Panzer Company suffered no losses during the advance to Caen. The Flak unit, which was part of the Panzer regiment's 2nd Battalion, consisted of four 20mm "Vierlingflak," each mounted on the chassis of a Panzer IV. Each of the four Vierlingflak comprised four 20mm anti-aircraft cannon ensconced in an open armored turret. The weapon was a special invention of the division; with its rapid rate of fire it would do good service in Normandy. The Panzer regiment was also equipped with several 37mm Flak guns mounted on Panzer 38(t) chassis. Fragebogen, Ernst Haase; Fragebogen, Heinz Müller.

[42]KTB I./25. SS-Pz.Gren.Rgt. 6.6.44; Record Group 238: Records of Proceedings. p 598; Meyer, H., Kriegsgeschichte, p 68.

[43]The Panther battalion (I./Pz.Rgt. 6) was not available to the division on June 6, 1944. At the beginning of June, OKW had ordered the battalion to the eastern front. On June 5th, the lead train transporting the tanks was already rolling through Germany. At the request of OB West, OKW approved at 7:45 a.m. on June 6th the return of the battalion to the Panzer Lehr. The tanks would not reach the division until June 10th. BAMA. KTB OB West. 6.6.44; Helmut Ritgen, Die Geschichte der Panzer-Lehr-Division im Westen, 1944-1945 (Stuttgart: Motorbuch Verlag, 1979), pp 102, 134, 319.

Thus, the columns of the Panzer Lehr got underway, approaching the front along three parallel routes. Almost at once the clear blue sky above them filled with hostile aircraft. Wave after wave of Jabos (Jadgbomber, as the Germans called the Allied fighter-bombers) made their bombing runs, banked, circled, and came roaring in again. The same deadly game of hide and seek ensued: the Germans taking cover, the enemy overhead searching fresh quarry. A feeling of defenselessness pervaded the division, and even Bayerlein was shocked by the intensity of the aerial onslaught. The onset of darkness brought a brief respite, but then came the enemy night intruders, their targets illuminated by parachute flares. Because of such misfortune, the division's Panzer IV battalion had covered barely half of its 100 mile approach by the morning of June 7th. By the evening of the 7th, the division had lost 5 Panzer IVs, 84 half-tracks and prime movers, 90 trucks, and 40 petrol vehicles–roughly ten percent of its vehicles without having fired a shot![44] Not until June 8th would the Panzer Lehr limp into the area about Tilly-sur-Seulles, a village seven miles south of Bayeux.

*   *   *

Armored vehicles of the Panzer Lehr Division marching to the front.

[44]The figures are Bayerlein's; although perhaps exaggerated, they indicate the devastation wrought by the Allied tactical air forces in Normandy. Returning to his headquarters in Proussy on the evening of June 7th, Bayerlein would have his command car shot out from under him during a fighter-bomber attack, killing his driver and another companion. Incredibly, Bayerlein was only slightly injured. Franz Kurowski, *Die Panzer Lehr Division. Die grösste deutsche Panzer Division und ihre Aufgabe: die Invasion zerschlagen - die Ardennenschlacht entscheiden* (Bad Nauheim: Podzun Verlag, 1964), pp 40-41; Ritgen, *Geschichte der Panzer-Lehr-Division im Westen,* pp 105-6; Wilmont, *The Struggle for Europe,* p 300.

Grenadiers from the Panzer Lehr Division have reached the invasion front and look for Allied strongpoints.

As the night of June 6 wore on, the infantry, tanks and artillery of the 12th SS Hitlerjugend began to trickle into the rolling countryside southwest of Caen. For the young soldiers moving wearily towards the front, an ominous glow on the horizon gave vivid expression to the struggle that had preceded them. Throughout the day the heavy guns of the Allied battlefleet had pounded the city of Caen in an effort to deny its thoroughfares to German troops and vehicles. At 3:00 p.m., after leaflets had been dropped to warn the inhabitants that the railyards and electrical generating station were about to be hit, 600 bombers of the Eighth U.S. Army Air Force had dumped their loads on the city's historic center. The medieval quarters of St. Pierre and St. Jean were reduced to ash and rubble, and many civilians entombed in the cellars of their collapsed houses. Among the ruins fires took hold and raged for eleven days. The Normandy battle would bring untold agony to the city and transform it into a virtual wasteland.[45]

The battalions of the 25th SS Panzer Grenadier Regiment were the first to arrive, having averaged barely four miles per hour during the flame-licked approach from Lisieux. The regiment reached Bretteville-sur-Laize at about 10:00 p.m., and pushed on to Evrécy. From there, Meyer's 1st Battalion crossed the thickly wooded Odon valley and motored northwest to Missy, a small village astride the highway from Caen to Villers-Bocage (Route Nationale 175). The battalion then dismounted. Parking their transports in the woods beyond the village, the infantry advanced on foot to the rail line

[45]John Keegan, *Six Armies in Normandy* (New York: The Viking Press, 1982), pp 183, 185.

northwest of Noyers and established a covering position.[46] The tanks of the Panzer Regiment's 2nd Battalion as well as a portion of the artillery were also reaching their assembly areas. Still far back were the 26th SS Panzer Grenadier Regiment, the Panther tank and engineer battalions and the bulk of the division's artillery. Early the next morning a dead tired Fritz Witt arrived at his newly prepared command post south of Caen, having personally received from Dietrich in St. Pierre-sur-Dives the order to attack the enemy beachhead.[47]

At the head of his reconnaissance company, Kurt Meyer had crossed the Orne at St. André-sur-Orne; by dusk (June 6th), he stood south of Grainville-sur-Odon, near the Caen - Villers-Bocage road. As he describes in his post-war memoirs, the journey had not been a pleasant one:[48]

> In familiar fashion my trusted driver plunges forward. Dark clouds rise up out of the west. The city of William the Conquerer, from where he commenced his victorious march across the Channel in 1066, is destroyed.
> On the road from Caen to Falaise we encounter fleeing civilians. An omnibus burns violently. Heart-rending cries come from the bus but we can do nothing to help. The door is jammed and blocks the way to freedom. Mangled bodies dangle from shattered windows, further blocking the escape . . . But we cannot stop. We must move on and gain ground towards the front. Patches of forest attract us like magnets. More and more fighters fill the sky. They attack remorselessly but we must continue. The march column must roll!
> A swarm of Spitfires attacks the rear platoon of my company. Their rockets and machine guns reap a devilish harvest. The platoon is advancing through a defile and can take no evasive action. An elderly French woman comes towards us screaming, "murder, murder." An infantryman lies on the road and blood streams from his throat. A bullet has severed his artery. He dies in our hands. The ammunition in a transport explodes, sending tongues of flame high into the sky as the vehicle breaks apart. In minutes the debris is cleared. There is no stopping. We must advance!

Dispatching patrols to probe north towards Cheux and northwest towards Bayeux, Meyer continued on to Caen. In the city's southwest suburb of Venoix, he established an interim headquarters in a small château astride the

[46]Veterans of the regiment confirm its arrival at the invasion bridgehead on the night of June 6-7. KTB I./25. SS-Pz.Gren.Rgt. 6.6.44; PAC. Special Interrogation Report, Kurt Meyer, p 3; Fragebogen, Kurt Beyer; Fragebogen, Hans Dettmann.

[47]Sepp Dietrich and his Chief of Staff, SS-Brigadeführer Fritz Kraemer, had reached the headquarters of the 21st Panzer Division in St. Pierre-sur-Dives by a circuitous route at about 8:00 p.m. Their journey to the town was considerably delayed through air attack. Fritz Kraemer, C-024. "I. SS Panzer Korps im Westen." p 13; Meyer, H., *Kriegsgeschichte*, p 68.

[48]Record Group 238: Records of Proceedings, p 562; Meyer, K., *Grenadiere*, p 210.

Grenadiers watch fleets of Allied bombers fly overhead to hit advancing German reinforcements.

highway to Villers-Bocage.[49] Nestled among some tall, leafy shade trees, the
château offered protection from air attack. At midnight he reached the command post of the 716th Infantry Division, hidden deep in an underground
bunker on the outskirts of La Folie. Both the division commander, General
Richter, and the commander of the 21st Panzer Division, General
Feuchtinger, were present. Wounded men from both divisions lined the underground corridors, while doctors and their orderlies labored over them. In
few words, Meyer informed Richter that he had been underway to the General
for eight hours, four of which he had spent in roadside ditches hiding from
enemy aircraft. Still, the charismatic Meyer was bursting with confidence. The
English, he said, were "little fishes;" his Hitlerjugend would toss them back
into the sea.[50]

His audience was more than skeptical. Richter's poorly equipped formation
had borne the brunt of the British assault and had practically ceased to exist.
Some strong points, Richter stated, were still holding out along the coast;
beyond that he knew little, for all telephone lines to his regiments and battalions were severed. Nothing, it seemed, stood between the enemy and
Caen.[51] Feuchtinger's report was equally discouraging. The tank commander
was poorly informed of the whereabouts of his battlegroups, for he had neglected to bring a radio truck along! Although he lacked precise intelligence, he

---

[49]During trial testimony shortly after the war Meyer confirmed the establishment of a provisional headquarters in Venoix on June 6th. Record Group 238: Records
of Proceedings. pp 564-65.

[50]Record Group 238: Records of Proceedings, p 563; Meyer, K., *Grenadiere*,
p 211; PAC. Special Interrogation Report, Kurt Meyer, p 3; Richter, B-621, p 25.

[51]Richter estimates that he lost 80 percent of his infantry and artillery on June
6th. Richter, B-621, p 44; Meyer, K., *Grenadiere*, p 211.

General Edgar Feuchtinger, commander of the 21st Panzer Division.

was afraid that the enemy had already reached the Carpiquet airport, three miles west of Caen.

In fulsome detail Feuchtinger described the course of his ill-fated counterattack against the British beachhead. On orders from General Marcks, he had suspended his advance towards the airborne bridgehead late that morning and turned against the seaborne threat west of the Orne. Harassed by fighter-bombers and pounded by naval artillery, his tanks suffered severely as they approached their new assembly area north of Caen. On the western outskirts of the city, eight Typhoons dive-bombed a group of them, leaving two in flames and four others smoking. Not until shortly after 4:00 p.m. did the attack get rolling, the tanks advancing in two columns towards the beaches. Encountering a well-prepared adversary, a dozen more Panzer IVs were lost; the armor stopped in its tracks. By 7:00 p.m., a separate battlegroup of infantry managed to reach the coast at Lion-sur-Mer, where, for a short stretch, the German defenses were still intact. But two hours later, a large enemy glider-borne force landed beside the Orne, apparently across the path of the 21st Panzer's advance. In response to this sudden menace, the division broke off the attack--the infantry pulling back from the shoreline and the remaining tanks (70 in all) digging in north of Caen along a front extending from the west bank of the Orne to Epron.[52]

Finally put in the picture, Meyer sent his patrols to sweep the local villages west and northwest of Caen. At 1:00 a.m., they reported back: Carpiquet, Rots and Buron were free of the enemy; in Buron there were stragglers of the 716th Infantry Division. Carpiquet airport, on the other hand, was undefended, Luftwaffe Flak troops having fled its strong defenses earlier in the day. Les Buissons was in enemy hands. It was now clear to Meyer that there were no

---

[52]Shortly before 9:00 p.m., the British 6th Air-Landing Brigade, the final formation of Gale's 6th Airborne Division, swept in low over the coastline to reinforce the airborne bridgehead. A portion of the brigade landed beside the Orne canal, between St. Aubin d'Arquenay and Bénouville. Unnerved by the unexpected enemy activity, the Panzer division called off its attack. Wilmont, *The Struggle for Europe,* pp 286-87; Feuchtinger, B-441, pp 21-23; Kraemer, C-024, p 14.

organized German defenses covering the northwestern outskirts of Caen; to fill the gap he decided to position his regiment near St. Germain-la-Blanche-Herbe in readiness for battle.[53]

Preparing to return to his command post, Meyer was called to the telephone. It was Witt, calling from the headquarters of the 21st Panzer Division. Meyer quickly briefed his commander on the developments north of Caen. "The situation," Witt responded, "demands immediate action. Most of all, we've got to hold on to Caen and the Carpiquet airport." On orders from Dietrich's Panzer Corps, he continued, the 12th SS was to attack side-by-side with the 21st Panzer and to smash the enemy beachhead. Time of attack: 4:00 p.m., June 7th. Boundary between the two divisions: the rail line from Caen to Luc-sur-Mer.[54]

An eight-wheeled reconnaissance vehicle (Sd. Kfz. 231) rolling through the debris-strewn streets of Caen.

---

[53]The report of Meyer's reconnaissance company was largely accurate; les Buissons, however, would not be secured by the Canadians until later that morning. Record Group 238: Records of Proceedings. p 564; Meyer, K., *Grenadiere*, p 213.

[54]In his memoirs, Kurt Meyer asserts that the attack was to begin at 12:00 noon. However, the war diaries of Army Group B and Seventh Army confirm 4:00 p.m. as the time. Apparently, both Seventh Army and the I SS Panzer Corps had planned initially to attack with all three Panzer Divisions--12th SS, 21st Panzer and Panzer Lehr--on June 7th. The absence of the Panzer Lehr thwarted this intent. T-84/281/000779-80. KTB Heeresgruppe B; T-312/1569/000009, 000011-12. KTB Seventh Army; T-312/1568/000952. Telephone Log, Seventh Army.

Shortly thereafter, Meyer departed the gloom of Richter's bunker. The streets of Caen were empty now with the exception of soldiers still clearing away the debris. An unsavory odor gripped his nostrils: the smell of smoke and fire. His small party made their way back through the city, the burning buildings lighting the way. No one spoke. The destruction that engulfed them turned their thoughts to home and to the fires also raging there, in the cities of Germany. Overhead, solitary enemy planes circled the city, illuminating the sky as they photographed the damage below. Where, Meyer wondered, was the Luftwaffe?[55]

*　　*　　*

At 6:00 a.m., June 6th, SS-Obersturmführer Bernhard-Georg Meitzel had left Berlin by car carrying top secret documents intended for Panzer Group West, the I SS Panzer Corps and the 12th SS. Unaware that the invasion of France had begun, Meitzel, a staff officer with the 12th SS, paused briefly at the headquarters of the 1st SS Panzer Division east of Turnhout, in Belgium. Informed of the enemy landings in Normandy, he raced on into France. Delayed by at least a half-dozen punctures, he did not arrive at division headquarters until 7:00 a.m., June 7th. Witt's staff had stayed up all night and Meitzel could see the exhaustion in their faces. The enemy fighter-bombers, he learned, had taken their toll: two command cars had been shot up and a driver killed. Meitzel's own driver, who had not accompanied the officer on his mission to Berlin, was seriously wounded and would die three days later.

Though Meitzel himself had had no sleep, he was at once instructed to organize the transfer of Witt's headquarters from the Forêt de Grimbosq to the château in Venoix already occupied by Kurt Meyer.[56] SS Generals led from the front--from Venoix, Witt could keep his finger firmly on the pulse of the battle. Despite the myriads of hostile aircraft circling above them, the divisional staff reached their new quarters without incident. No sooner had they arrived--it was now mid-afternoon--than they were flooded with reports from the front: Kurt Meyer's infantry, supported by tanks and artillery, had swept into battle.[57]

*　　*　　*　　*　　*

[55]Meyer, K., *Grenadiere*, p 214.

[56]By midday, June 7th, Meyer had shifted his main regimental headquarters from Venoix to a small cafe in St. Germain-la-Blanche-Herbe.

[57]The divisional escort company went into position covering the new headquarters. Bernhard-Georg Meitzel, "Caen-Falaise." In: The Canadian Army Journal. Vol. 4. April-June, 1950; letter to author from Hubert Meyer, March 2, 1981; BAMA. Tagebuch. Divisions-Begleit-Kompanie. 7.6.44.

Chapter 7
BAPTISM OF FIRE: JUNE 7, 1944

Attack, counter-attack, charge, repulse--these are words, but
what things they signify!

(Erich Maria Remarque)

The gloom in Richter's bunker was more than justified. By the conclusion of
June 6, 1944, more than 150,000 enemy troops were ashore in Normandy. Supported by specialized armor as well as the unprecedented firepower of Allied
air and naval units, the assault divisions of the invasion force had cleaved deep
chunks from Hitler's vaunted Atlantic Wall. On the critical left flank, the infantry and armor of Dempsey's Second British Army held a nearly continuous
beachhead between Caen and Bayeux with a depth of four to seven miles.[1]
Anchoring the extreme left of this beachhead, the 3rd British Infantry Division
was within striking distance of Caen by late afternoon; at that time a battalion
of its lead brigade had made a spirited dash from Biéville down the road
leading into the city, only to be turned back by intense German fire from the
Lebisey Wood--a thickly timbered ridge athwart the road. To the right of the
3rd British, the 3rd Canadian Infantry Division had made the most progress of
any Allied division on D-Day, pushing inland for nearly seven miles; by
nightfall, the lead battalions of its 9th Brigade were barely three miles from
Caen's northwestern outskirts. Some Canadian tanks had even reached the
Caen - Bayeux road north of the Carpiquet airport, but had withdrawn
because of a lack of infantry support. Dempsey's final assault division, the
50th Northumbrian, was able to push southwest to within a mile of Bayeux,
thwarting German attempts to reform a line on the rising ground between the
coast and the town. The division would occupy Bayeux the next day.[2]

---

[1]By evening, the inner flanks of the 3rd Canadian and the 50th Northumbrian
Infantry Divisions had made contact, creating a continuous front some 12 miles in
length and six to seven miles in depth. But on the left, there still existed a strip of German held territory between the 3rd Canadian and the 3rd British Infantry Divisions.
Wilmont, *The Struggle for Europe*, p 276.

[2]PAC. War Diary. 3rd Canadian Infantry Division, 6 June 1944; L.F. Ellis, *Victory in the West*. United Kingdom Military Series. Sir James Butler, Ed. (London: Her Majesty's Stationery Office, 1962), pp 203, 223; Wilmont, *The Struggle for Europe*, pp 276, 283-84.

Woscidlo

These division members scan the skies over Normandy for Allied fighter bombers, June 1944.

In the skies above Normandy Allied dominance was absolute. On D-Day their strategic and tactical air forces flew 10,585 sorties. In response, the German 3rd Air Fleet managed 319 sorties, and most of these were either shot down or driven back. Throughout the day there was no sign of the Luftwaffe above the Normandy beaches, and it was nearly dark before the British saw their first hostile aircraft. Then four Heinkel 111 bombers sneaked in and scattered their bomb loads near the Canadian beaches before a squadron of Spitfires jumped them. None got away.[3]

Such was the unhappy situation that confronted the defenders of France, when, at 10:00 p.m., Field Marshal Erwin Rommel's car finally screeched to a halt before his château at La Roche-Guyon. Rommel spent most of that night, June 6-7, trying to find out what was happening in Normandy. Although the enemy was jamming German radios and many telephone lines were down, the commander of the Seventh Army, General Dollmann, managed to get through to the Field Marshal on the phone shortly before 11:00 p.m. Dollmann informed his superior that the counterattack of the 21st Panzer had failed, and that the enemy had reached the Caen - Bayeux road south of Ryes. The 12th SS Hitlerjugend, he assured Rommel, was scheduled to attack the next day, but Seventh Army was unsure of its whereabouts. Dollmann complained bitterly about the lack of air support, only to be told that Luftwaffe reinforcements would soon be moving up.[4]

---

[3]As of June 5, 1944, the units of the 3rd Air Fleet reported a battle strength (Kampfstärke) of 481 aircraft. Of these, 100 were fighter and 64 reconnaissance aircraft. Two weeks before the invasion, the Air Fleet had dispatched six of its best fighter squadrons to Germany. Reinforcements would bring the strength of the Luftwaffe in the West to about 1,000 planes of all types within a week after D-Day. Major O. Jaggi, "Die Auswirkungen der alliierten Luftüberlegenheit auf die deutsche Abwehr." In: Allgemeine Schweizerische Militärzeitschrift. Jg. 124. H. 5. 1958. p 335; Ellis, *Victory in the West*, p 567.

[4]T-312/1568/000951-52. Telephone Log. Seventh Army; Irving, *The Trail of the Fox*, p 372.

Because neither Rundstedt nor Rommel had faith in Dietrich's ability to orchestrate the counterattack of the Panzer divisions on his own, they decided to place Geyr and his Panzer Group West headquarters in overall command of the operation. At 9:30 a.m., June 7th, Speidel duly notified the High Command of this decision; an hour later, Rommel and his chief of staff briefed their counterparts at Panzer Group West concerning the new assignment. Subordinated to Seventh Army, Geyr's staff was to take control of all German formations between the Orne and Tilly-sur-Seulles.[5]

* * *

In the early morning hours of June 7th, Kurt Meyer devised his plan of attack; at 3:00 a.m., he issued verbal instructions to the commanders of his infantry battalions. Two of the battalions were to attack side-by-side; the third, echeloned to the rear. The whole line was to move forward towards the beaches, in conjunction, Meyer hoped, with Feuchtinger's 21st Panzer Division. To carry out this intent, the 1st Battalion was to assemble between Epron and la Folie and to make contact with the left flank of the 21st Panzer.[6] The 2nd Battalion was to go into position near Bitot, abreast of the 1st Battalion on its right. Forming the left wing, the 3rd Battalion was to occupy the ground southeast of Franqueville, on a reverse slope directly below the Caen - Bayeux road.   To furnish added firepower, a section of 150mm guns (two cannon) and a section of 20mm Flak from Meyer's heavy infantry gun (schwere Infanteriegeschütz) and Flak companies, respectively, were subordinated to each battalion. The batteries of the 12th SS Artillery Regiment's 3rd Battalion were to take up firing positions from where they could cover the advance of all three infantry battalions. The armor of the 2nd Panzer Battalion was to support the attack along a broad front; Meyer's reconnaissance company to secure the open left flank of his regiment. To be close to the action, Meyer ordered the establishment of an advance command post at the Abbey Ardenne, a formidable Gothic ruin in the fields north of St. Germain. The commander of the 3rd Artillery Battalion, SS-Sturmbannführer Karl Bartling, also set up a command post at the abbey.[7]

Under cover of darkness the battalions of the 25th SS Panzer Grenadier Regiment began moving up to their jump off positions.[8] Their transports carried them as far as the Caen - Bayeux road; there, the SS grenadiers sprang from the vehicles and continued on foot into the verdurous, open and

---

[5]T-84/281/000762, 000771, 000773. KTB Heeresgruppe B; Helmuth Greiner and Percy Ernst Schramm, *Kriegstagebuch des Oberkommandos der Wehrmacht* (Wehrmachtführungsstab) 1940-1945. Bd. IV: 1. Januar 1944 - 22. Mai 1945 (Frankfurt am Main: Bernard & Graefe Verlag für Wehrwesen, 1961), p 312.

[6]The war diary of the 1st Battalion states that there existed a rather large gap between the battalion and the left flank of the 21st Panzer Division. The gap was not closed until the afternoon. KTB I./25.SS-Pz.Gren.Rgt. 7.6.44.

[7]Meyer, H., *Kriegsgeschichte*, p 77; Record Group 238: Records of Proceedings, p 565; KTB I./25.SS-Pz.Gren.Rgt. 7.6.44.

[8]The 1st Battalion got underway at 3:45 a.m. It motored via Mondrainville and Bretteville-sur-Odon to the western edge of Caen, where the infantry dismounted. The vehicles were drawn up and camouflaged south of Caen. KTB I./25.SS-Pz.Gren.Rgt. 7.6.44.

gently undulating countryside that would soon become the killing ground. Meyer, from his provisional headquarters in Venoix, observed the migration of his young, untested soldiers towards the main battle line. They went forward calmly, and without emotion; some waved confidently to their revered commander, whose presence buoyed their confidence in these final hours before the baptism of fire. Although harassed by fighter-bombers and shellfire from Allied naval artillery, the grenadiers incurred few casualties.

Later that morning, Meyer and his driver struck out for the Abbey Ardenne. Hoping to make a less conspicuous target for the voracious Jabos, they had first exchanged their larger vehicle for a diminutive Volkswagen jeep. Despite the precaution, they had no sooner commenced the journey than enemy aircraft were upon them. Machine gun fire stitched the roadway about them; to avoid its deadly impact Meyer and his companion were compelled on more than one occasion to dive for cover. Only wild maneuvering by the driver managed to bring them to their destination intact.[9]

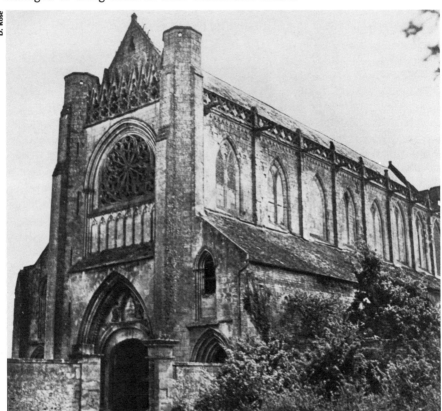

The Abbey Ardenne, Kurt Meyer's advance command post. The towers made excellent observation posts.

It was nearly 9:00 a.m. when Meyer reached the abbey. SS officers wearing camouflage uniforms and stiff black visor caps milled about the place; some

 [9]Meyer, K., *Grenadiere*, p 215.

wore long greatcoats with the SS runes on the collar. The abbey grounds consisted of many sturdy buildings and a lofty chapel--all enclosed within a massive stone wall. At each corner of the chapel stood a tall turret. Ascending a narrow, spiral stairway, Meyer climbed atop one of them and found that it made an admirable observation post. From the vantage point of the turret, he could make out the entire attack frontage of his regiment. The area was dotted with typical Norman farming villages, each consisting of little more than a cluster of stone houses, with neighboring orchards and tiny patches of forest. Fields of tall wheat and sugar beets stretched beyond the horizon. To the east, Meyer could see into the sector of the 21st Panzer; to the west, his view extended beyond the Mue, a little wooded stream that cut an irregular path northward until it emptied into the lower Seulles. Looking towards the coastline the silver barrage balloons were clearly visible floating serenely above the invasion fleet as protection against attack from the Luftwaffe--an unnecessary precaution Meyer thought to himself.[10]

Bartling, meanwhile, had reported his artillery ready for action. Three batteries of medium field howitzers were in position on the western fringe of Caen, while his fourth battery (105mm cannon) was situated south of Venoix, in the Odon valley. The Panzer grenadiers were also in place, and from the turret Meyer could see the companies of the 2nd Battalion stretched out before him. He watched as heavily armed patrols advanced towards the enemy and 20mm Flak shot it out with the pesty fighter-bombers, spattering the sky with small black puffs. The armor, however, had yet to reach the front, and without it, Meyer realized, his attack was doomed to failure. An anxious wait ended about 10:00 a.m., when the Panzer IVs of the tank regiment's 2nd Battalion finally began to arrive. The battalion commander, SS-Sturmbannführer Heinz Prinz,[11] reported 50 of his tanks (elements of all five companies) ready for action. The rest of his armor, he said, had been held up by air attack, mechanical breakdowns, or empty fuel tanks, and was not expected to arrive until the evening. Without delay the available tanks were shepherded into their staging areas: the 8th Company on the right, the 6th and 7th Companies straddling the abbey, and the 5th Company on the reverse slope southeast of Franqueville. The 9th Company was placed in reserve behind the left flank.[12]

[10]The author thoroughly examined this terrain, including the Abbey Ardenne, in June of 1983. The view from the abbey turrets is indeed extraordinary. Ibid. p 216.

[11]The 30-year-old Prinz had joined the Waffen SS in March 1935, serving initially with the SS Regiment "Germania." During the campaign in France he received the Iron Cross second class; in Russia in 1941 the Iron Cross first class. He was promoted to SS-Sturmbannführer on June 21, 1943. Prinz had a reputation as a cautious but capable tactician; for his role in the counterattack on June 7, 1944, he would receive the Knight's Cross. SS Personalakten, Heinz Prinz.

[12]According to Hans Siegel, the former commander of the battalion's 8th Panzer Company, at most 30 Panzer IVs participated in the attack on June 7th. Siegel had only five tanks ready for action that morning, and estimates that the other four companies of the battalion averaged no more than six available tanks. Fragebogen, Hans Siegel; Meyer, K., *Grenadiere*, pp 215-16; Meyer, H., *Kriegsgeschichte*, p 78; Hans Siegel, "Bericht des Kp.-Chefs 8./Pz.Rgt.12 - Ostuf. Hans Siegel aus der Erinnerung niedergeschrieben am 28.2.69;" Fragebogen, Willy Kretzschmar.

By midday, Meyer's battlegroup was ready for combat. Under a warm sun the SS grenadiers hunkered down in the fertile Norman fields. Their camouflage jackets a patchwork of green, brown and deep yellow, the youths blended imperceptibly into the terrain.[13] Anxiously, they clutched their weapons and awaited the Angriffsbefehl (order to attack). Behind them the low-slung Panzer IVs, hidden beneath straw and branches, trained their powerful 75mm guns towards the enemy. Exhausted from more than a day's constant marching, the tank commanders surveyed the battlefield through their field glasses.

W. Kretzchmar

A Panzer IV of the 5th Co., Pz. Rgt. 12, covered with grass as camouflage against air attack.

His force in position, Meyer left the abbey about 12:00 noon and visited his new main headquarters in St. Germain.[14] Fritz Witt and Max Wünsche were also at the headquarters, and together the three officers discussed the impending battle. Witt expressed concern about Mohnke's 26th Regiment, which was to go into the line on Meyer's left. Mohnke's battalions, however, were still far from the battle zone–strung out somewhere east of the Orne was all that Witt knew.[15] The Panthers of Wünsche's 1st Battalion were also stuck east of the Orne, awaiting a new issue of gasoline. With more than half of the division thus unavailable, Meyer would have to attack with his left flank completely exposed to the enemy–a dangerous undertaking at best. Undaunted, he quickly returned to the Abbey Ardenne. The front was beginning to throb, and he climbed atop the turret to take a closer look.[16]

*   *   *

---

[13]Most of the rank-and-file of the 12th SS Panzer Division wore camouflage jackets over their field grey uniforms; certain elements, however, such as the 3rd Battalion of the 26th SS Panzer Grenadier Regiment, were outfitted with complete camouflage uniforms.

[14]The times given for Kurt Meyer's movements on June 7th are approximate. During his trial testimony Meyer frankly admitted that he could not remember with precision the chronology of his activities that day. Record Group 238: Records of Proceedings, pp 568-69.

[15]The lead battalion of the 26th Regiment would not reach Grainville-sur-Odon until late afternoon, June 7th. Meyer, H., *Kriegsgeschichte*, p 88.

[16]Record Group 238: Records of Proceedings, p 568-69; Meyer, H., P-164, p 21; Meyer, K., *Grenadiere*, p 217.

ECPA

This grenadier, probably from the 3rd Battalion of the 26th SS Panzer Grenadier Regiment, wears the full camouflage uniform. See footnote 13 on previous page.

The night of June 6-7 was relatively quiet for the 3rd Canadian Infantry Division, nor did dawn bring the anticipated counterstroke, for the Germans were not ready. Forming the division's right flank, the 7th Brigade resumed its advance southward shortly after 6:00 a.m. Meeting only scattered and ineffective resistance, the lead battalions of the brigade--the Royal Winnipeg Rifles and the Regina Rifles--were soon going flat out for their objectives beyond the Caen - Bayeux road. By noon, both battalions were upon them, the Winnipegs in Putot-en-Bessin, and the Regina Rifles in Bretteville-l'Orgueilleuse and Norrey-en-Bessin.[17]

On the Canadian left, the 9th Brigade had skirmished briefly with infantry of the 21st Panzer early that morning. At 7:40 a.m., the brigade's advance guard, consisting of the North Nova Scotia Highlanders, commanded by Lieutenant-Colonel C. Petch, and the 27th Canadian Armored Regiment (The Sherbrooke Fusiliers) began to surge southwest along the main road from Villons-les-Buissons to Carpiquet. The light reconnaissance tanks of the armored regiment, American made Stuarts, led the way. Behind them followed "C" Company of the Highlanders, mounted in the battalion's troop carriers. Next came

---

[17]Colonel C.P. Stacey, *The Victory Campaign. The Operations in North-West Europe. 1944-1945.* Official History of the Canadian Army in the Second World War. Volume III (Ottawa: The Queen's Printer and Controller of Stationery, 1960), pp 125-26.

a platoon of medium machine guns (Vickers .303 inch), a troop of tank destroyers, two assault sections of pioneers and four 6-pounder guns. Behind this vanguard moved the main body of the advance guard—three companies of infantry riding on Sherman tanks.[18]

Sweeping aside slight opposition from snipers and machine gunners, the Canadians were clear of les Buissons by 9:30 a.m. Despite heavy mortar fire that soon set in from the left, they pushed on and were in Buron before noon. While "D" Company of the Highlanders cleared stragglers of the 716th Infantry Division from the village, "A" and "B" Companies moved up with their Shermans and began to advance upon Authie one-half mile beyond. "C" Company then passed two platoons in carriers through "B;" following a sharp skirmish with German machine gun posts, which were only subdued with tank support, the platoons took Authie. Thereafter, they entrenched on the southern edge of the village, which was under furious artillery and mortar fire. At 1:00 p.m., the North Nova Scotias signalled the capture of Authie to 9th Brigade. Ten minutes later, the brigade informed division that enemy tanks were in place 800 yards east of Authie, but that its position there would hold.[19]

While elements of the Sherbrooke Fusiliers continued on towards Franqueville, further advance for the infantry had become impossible. The entire area was being drenched with heavy German fire.[20] The advance guard was now beyond the range of its own artillery support, the 3rd Canadian Division's 14th Field Regiment, and it would be some time before the regiment's self-propelled 105s could be shifted forward.[21] The Highlanders, moreover, had pushed well past the 3rd British Infantry Division operating on their left, and

---

[18]The 27th Canadian Armored Regiment was one of the three tank regiments of the independent 2nd Canadian Armored Brigade. According to Ellis, each independent Canadian or British armored brigade consisted of some 190 main battle ("cruiser") tanks (mostly Shermans) and 33 light reconnaissance tanks. In contrast, the armored divisions of Dempsey's Second Army possessed about 246 cruiser and 44 light tanks apiece--also organized into one brigade of three tank regiments. Thus, a Canadian or British armored regiment was roughly equivalent in battle tanks to a German Panzer battalion. At midnight, June 7th, the 2nd Canadian Armored Brigade reported to 3rd Canadian Infantry Division 115 cruiser tanks "fit for action," 21 fit within 24 hours and 36 knocked out. PAC. War Diary. 2nd Canadian Armored Brigade. 7 June 1944; PAC. War Diary. North Nova Scotia Highlanders. 7 June 1944; Ellis, *Victory in the West*, pp 534-35, 537; Stacey, *The Victory Campaign*, p 126-27.

[19]PAC. War Diary. North Nova Scotia Highlanders. 7 June 1944; PAC. War Diary. 27th Canadian Armored Regiment. 7 June 1944; Stacey, *The Victory Campaign*, p 128.

[20]The origins of this vigorous German fire are unclear. Evidently, it did not come from the 3rd Artillery Battalion of the 12th SS, which was still under orders from Meyer to hold its fire. Some of the mortar fire most likely emanated from pockets of resistance formed by survivors of the 716th Infantry Division. Artillery of the 21st Panzer Division was also in the area. In his memoirs Kurt Meyer refers to the arrival of a Nebelwerfer (rocket projector) battalion in his sector that morning. Amply furnished with ammunition, the battalion, which was not a unit of the 12th SS, had gone into position near Caen. Meyer, K., *Grenadiere*, p 216.

[21]At this time the field regiments of the 3rd Canadian Infantry Division were all outfitted with the self-propelled 105mm "Priests." According to Stacey, these guns had a range of 10,500 yards. At noon, the 14th Field Regiment had begun to move up from its firing position north of Bény-sur-Mer to a new one southeast of Basly. Authie, some 13,000 yards to the south, was beyond the range of the former gun area. Stacey, *The Victory Campaign*, p 128.

The Victory Campaign, p 128.

with both flanks in the air were seriously exposed. Colonel Petch, therefore, decided to withdraw the troops in Authie and to form a battalion fortress on the rising ground north of the village. "A" Company accordingly dug in southeast of Gruchy. "B" Company, pinned down by shell fire in Buron, could not join in. And before the two platoons of "C" Company could retire from the position covering Authie, they were stunned by a violent counterattack: elements of the 12th SS Hitlerjugend were on the move.[22]

*   *   *

From his tower perch atop the medieval abbey, Meyer carefully monitored the advance of the enemy across the front of his battlegroup. Through his field glasses he followed the stout, olive-green Shermans as they rolled deliberately towards the Caen - Bayeux road, seemingly oblivious to the malevolent German presence:[23]

> Now what is that? Did I see right? An enemy tank pushed through the orchards of St. Contest. Suddenly it stops. The commander opens the hatch and scours the countryside before him. Is the fellow blind? Has he not noticed that he stands barely 200 yards from the grenadiers of my 2nd Battalion, and that the barrels of their anti-tank guns are pointed at him? Apparently not. Leisurely he lights up a cigarette and blinks from the smoke. Not a shot is fired. The battalion has exemplary fire discipline.
>
> Ah! Now everything is clear! The tank is covering their left flank. From Buron enemy tanks are advancing on Authie. My God! What an opportunity! The tanks are moving directly along the front of the 2nd Battalion. Their flank is completely uncovered. I order my battalions, the artillery and the available armor to hold their fire until I give the command.
>
> The commander of our Panzer regiment has his command tank on the abbey grounds. Without delay a telephone line is strung from my observation tower to the tank; the movement of the enemy relayed by radio to the Panzer companies . . . Slowly but steadily the enemy tanks roll into Authie. They drive through the village and advance towards Franqueville.
>
> The attention of the enemy commander appears riveted on the Carpiquet airport, which lies directly before him. He already dominates the place with his weapons. What he does not see is that his destruction lurks nearby. If his tanks cross the Caen - Bayeux road they will run into the waiting company of the Panzer regiment. Only a few hundred yards still separate the steel colossi.

It was now almost exactly 2:00 p.m. Already, four tanks of the 5th Panzer Company had probed northward along the road from Franqueville to Authie.

[22]From Stacey's official history and the war diary of the North Nova Scotia Highlanders, it is clear that the Canadian advance towards Carpiquet had lost its momentum just prior to the counterattack by the 12th SS. PAC. War Diary. North Nova Scotia Highlanders. 7 June 1944; Stacey, The Victory Campaign, p 128.

[23]Meyer, K., Grenadiere, pp 216-17.

ECPA

Willy Kretzschmar's Panzer IV, Nr. 536 (5./II./12.SS-Pz. Rgt.) rolling into attack position on June 7.

They had not gone far before being taken under fire by a group of Shermans concealed in a nearby orchard. In a brief fire fight three of the Panzer IVs were lost.[24]

The counterstroke of the I SS Panzer Corps was not scheduled to begin for two hours, yet the situation demanded prompt action. On his own initiative, Meyer decided to attack at once. He notified the 21st Panzer of this intent and requested support from the division; a dispatch rider informed Witt of the change in plan. Improvising a battle plan,[25] Meyer instructed Wünsche to set the two tank companies west of the abbey in motion. The grenadiers of the 3rd Infantry Battalion, commanded by SS-Obersturmbannführer Karl-Heinz Milius,[26] were to follow closely behind the tanks. From the tower the fair-haired Wünsche relayed the order by telephone to his command vehicle: "Achtung! Panzer marsch!" The command flashed across the radio sets of the concerned tank crews. They secured their steel helmets and slammed armor piercing rounds into the breeches of their guns. Engines whirred. Caterpillar tracks began to jerk and grind. The armor of the 5th and 6th Panzer Companies trundled into battle.[27]

When within range of the enemy, the tanks halted and laid their guns.[28] In short, strident bursts they loosed their salvos. The long-barrel cannon of

---

[24]Fragebogen, Willy Kretzschmar.

[25]The improvised tactical plan called for the regiment to pivot on its right wing. The left (3rd) battalion would attack first, supported by the armor in its sector; subsequently, the entire line would sweep north.

[26]Born on August 19, 1911, Milius entered the Waffen SS in October 1934. From 1934 to 1940 he served with the SS Regiments "Germania" and "Deutschland" and with the SS Division "Wiking." In the West in 1940 he won the Iron Cross first and second class. His promotion to SS-Obersturmbannführer came on November 9, 1943. SS Personalakten, Karl-Heinz Milius.

[27]The Sherbrooke Fusiliers first made contact on their left with the German armor at 2:10 p.m. PAC. War Diary. 27th Canadian Armored Regiment. 7 June 1944.

the Panzer IV possessed a muzzle velocity of 2,461 feet per second; when its 15 pound shell hit solidly home the effect was instantly horrible:[29]

> At best, if the shot lodged but did not penetrate, the blow to the face of the armor detached high-speed fragments from its rear into the interior, which inflicted multiple small wounds on the crew. If the shot penetrated, it would retain some of its velocity but be confined by the armored skin and so ricochet about inside, smashing all it touched, metal or flesh. At worst, it would ignite ammunition and fuel--which first was immaterial, since they burnt together--incinerating whoever could not reach the hatch.

Wünsche's tanks slapped their unsuspecting opponent in the left flank. The Shermans of the Sherbrooke Fusiliers suffered heavy losses. But the Sherman,

Woscidlo

Panzer Regiment commander, Max Wünsche, in the turret of his command Panther, June 7, 1944.

---

[28]Unlike contemporary main battle tanks, which can shoot with great accuracy on the move, the tanks of the Second World War needed to be stationary to fire effectively.

[29]Keegan, *Six Armies in Normandy*, p 198.

which also carried a 75mm gun,[30] was well-matched with its adversary, and immediately the first Panzer IVs erupted in smoke and flame. Others were hit and set ablaze by Canadian anti-tank guns firing incendiary shells (Phosphorgranaten). With barely seconds to escape some of the SS tankmen managed to tumble clear of the flaming hulls; those less fortunate burned in place. The survivors, burned and disfigured, stumbled back towards the rear.[31]

The remaining German armor swept on towards Authie, accompanied by the infantry advancing in a deep, narrow formation through the tall grain.[32] Moving swiftly, the Germans took their first prisoners and dispatched them into captivity. Overhead, clouds of enemy fighter-bombers winged past but did not disturb the attackers, for the aircraft were on their way to contest targets farther inland. While the two lead infantry companies and most of the tanks bypassed Authie on either side, the third company and a handful of Panzer IVs

Grenadiers pulling an ammunition trailer to a gun position. Note the knocked-out Sherman tank at left of photo.

---

[30]A swift, maneuverable tank, the Sherman was well-suited for offensive armored warfare. The tank, however, had its defects, including a high profile that furnished a large target and facilitated detection; when hit, it caught fire too easily, for it was gasoline (petrol) rather than diesel fuelled. Compared to the most modern German designs, the Panther and the Tiger, the Sherman was undergunned. To help remedy the latter concern, roughly one in four was rearmed with the more powerful 17-pounder gun--an activity well underway when the Normandy campaign commenced. Keegan, *Six Armies in Normandy*, pp 197-98.

[31]The tank crews of the 2nd Panzer Battalion wore dark brown leather pants and jackets over their regular uniforms. Max Wünsche had filched the leather clothing from Italian naval stores following the transfer of the Leibstandarte to Italy in the summer of 1943. The leather offered the crews a measure of protection against burns. Interview, Dr. Willi Kändler, April 24, 1983; Interview, Hans Siegel, June 2, 1983; Interview, Heinz Berner, June 1-2, 1983.

[32]The 3rd Battalion advanced with two companies in front and one following in immediate reserve. Record Group 238: Records of Proceedings, p 571.

Tank crew members from the 2nd Panzer Battalion wearing dark brown leather pants and jackets (see Footnote 31).

stormed the village. A Canadian captain, taking the Browning automatics from several knocked-out Shermans, hastily organized its defense. But his small force was rapidly overrun, and no one escaped to record this gallant action. The SS crushed the platoons of the North Nova Scotia Highlanders in and around Authie; with the village secured, they pushed on towards Gruchy and Buron supported by the fire of Bartling's artillery, which roared from every tube.[33]

From the tower Meyer watched his attack go in and could see that it was making good progress. Spotting the 3rd Battalion commander at a road crossing between Authie and Buron, he decided to go to him. Meyer had also detected enemy movements deeper within the attack sector of the battalion, and wanted to inform Milius not to continue the advance beyond Buron. Jumping on a motorcycle, the impetuous SS-Standartenführer raced off towards the fighting. Wounded SS infantry struggled past him on their way to the dressing station at the Abbey Ardenne. Reaching Cussy he noticed fifty Canadian prisoners clustered in an orchard; he ordered them transported to the abbey at once. Moving on at high speed along a secondary road, Meyer was taken under fire by enemy tanks. A near miss wiped out his motorcycle and sent him tumbling into a bomb crater, where he found himself face-to-face with a startled enemy soldier. Canadian artillery fire bracketed the area about them, and both men hugged the earth to avoid the flesh-ripping shell fragments. Briefly shifting a watchful eye from his unwelcome companion, Meyer could see his

[33]Record Group 238: Records of Proceedings, p 571; PAC. War Diary. North Nova Scotia Highlanders. 7 June 1944; Meyer, H., *Kriegsgeschichte*, p 79; Interview, Heinz Berner, June 1-2, 1983.

grenadiers advancing on Buron. The uncomfortable encounter ended when Meyer, braving the shell fire, continued forward on foot. Soon thereafter, a motorcycle messenger recognized his beleaguered commander, scooped him up, and delivered him to Milius. The battalion commander expressed satisfaction with the Kampfgeist of his infantry; losses he reported, had hitherto been negligible. Following the brief conversation, Meyer departed the front of the 3rd Battalion and moved back towards Cussy on foot. In the confusion of battle he was fired upon by his own troops but not injured.[34]

Reeling from the German blow, the North Nova Scotias attempted to regroup late that afternoon and to form a battalion fortress just south of Buron with their surviving forward elements. But "A" Company north of Authie was already surrounded by tanks and infantry; the troops that did reach the new position were soon sprayed by heavy fire from artillery and the always deadly 81mm mortars, with which the 12th SS was lavishly equipped.[35] When the remaining Panzer IVs washed around the flanks of the fortress the position became untenable. Facing imminent encirclement, the Canadians withdrew to the earlier prepared slit trenches directly south of les Buissons and to the rear of "D" Company. Here, the Highlanders settled in and "prepared to hold on to the last."[36]

Continuing the assault the Panzer grenadiers burst into Buron. In house-to-house combat they rapidly cleared enemy stragglers and bagged additional prisoners. But artillery support was once more available to the Canadians in full measure; fountains of shells poured down upon the village, grinding its stone buildings to powder and causing heavy German casualties. From the woods of les Buissons, tanks of the Sherbrooke Fusiliers and some self-propelled guns chimed in, taking aim at the advancing Panzers, while small arms fire from machine guns and Brownings hosed the northern rim of Buron. In almost five years of war Meyer had never witnessed such a murderous fusillade and his thoughts turned instinctively to Verdun, a symbol of annihilation from the First World War. Badly wounded soldiers, among them some Canadians, were placed atop several of the Panzers and transported back towards the abbey. When the tanks arrived in their original staging areas stretcher bearers attended to the wounded. Meyer ordered the tanks to return immediately to the battle.[37]

[34]Record Group 238: Records of Proceedings, pp 573-74; Meyer, K., Grenadiere, pp 218-19.
[35]At full strength, each of the six infantry battalions of the 12th SS Panzer boasted a complement of 12 81mm mortars. One half of the mortars were concentrated in the heavy weapons company of a given battalion; the rest of them distributed evenly between the battalion's remaining three companies. The engineer companies of the division (16./25.SS Pz.Gren.Rgt. and 16./26.SS Pz.Gren.Rgt) also possessed two mortars apiece. Thus, the Panzer grenadier regiments of the 12th SS had between them 70 to 80 of the 81mm mortars. T-354/154/000542. Tagesmeldung. 12.SS-Panz.Div. "Hitlerjugend." I./Pz.Gren.Rgt.25. 2.7.44; Fragebogen, Hubert Meyer.
[36]PAC. War Diary. North Nova Scotia Highlanders. 7 June 1944.
[37]PAC. War Diary. North Nova Scotia Highlanders. 7 June 1944; Stacey, The Victory Campaign, p 132; Meyer, K., Grenadiere, p 219; Meyer, H., Kriegsgeschichte, p 80.

This grenadier advances through a stand of grain and grass to get near Canadian positions.

Disdaining the ferocious gauntlet of fire, the German infantry worked its way through the standing grain and infiltrated the forward slit trenches of "D" Company immediately beyond Buron.[38] The fighting was at close quarters, the grenadiers pitching grenades and pumping machine gun fire into the enemy lines. Two platoons of "D" Company exhausted their ammunition and were forced to surrender. Some of the prisoners, however, managed to escape their captors when the Canadian artillery drove them to ground. About this time one of the "D" Company men reported to battalion headquarters that his unit's forward trenches were overrun, and that support was urgently needed. In response, Colonel Petch snapped up 12 available Shermans, a handful of infantry, and put in a desperate counterattack. Covered by an artillery barrage, the tanks ripped through the freshly won German positions, inflicting many casualties; in some instances they literally ran over the unfortunate defenders. Now too weak to hold their ground, the surviving SS were driven from Buron and withdrew pell-mell to Authie.[39]

Having recaptured Buron the severely lacerated North Nova Scotia Highlanders lacked the strength to consolidate there. At dusk the remnants of the battalion received permission to once again fall back from the village to les Buissons. The 9th Brigade's other battalions--the Stormont, Dundas and Glengarry Highlanders and the Highland Light Infantry of Canada--had already dug in about the place, where, with the surviving tanks of the 27th Armored Regiment, they established a brigade fortress.[40]

*   *   *

At 3:00 p.m., Kurt Meyer had ordered his 1st and 2nd Battalions to join the advance as soon as their left flanks were sufficiently protected by the progress

---

[38]The precise location of "D" Company at the time of the German assault is unclear. However, it must have been entrenched directly north of Buron.

[39]PAC. War Diary. North Nova Scotia Highlanders. 7 June 1944.

[40]PAC. War Diary. North Nova Scotia Highlanders. 7 June 1944; Stacey, *The Victory Campaign*, p 132.

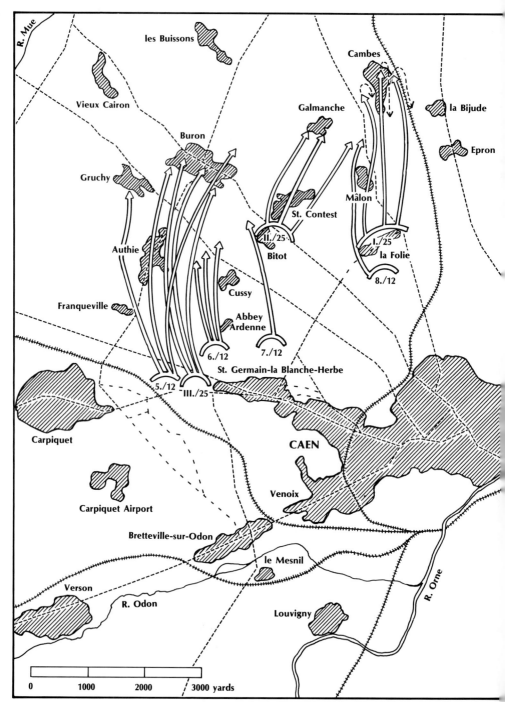

Counterattack of the 25th SS Panzer Grenadier Regiment (June 7, 1944).

of their respective left neighbor. When infantry of the 3rd Battalion and its supporting armor had captured Authie and begun to move on Buron, the 2nd Battalion went forward from its positions about Bitot. The tanks of the 7th Panzer Company followed in wedge formation on the heels of the battalion. The force encountered little opposition (there were no enemy units in the immediate attack sector) and occupied St. Contest forthwith.[41]

The battalion commander, SS-Sturmbannführer Hans Scappini,[42] accompanied the advance at the head of his lead company; he had with him a small staff consisting of his adjutant, the battalion doctor and the company commander, SS-Obersturmführer Heinz Schrott. Together, they halted momentarily to allow the remainder of the infantry to close up. Without warning three Canadian tanks suddenly appeared at a threatening distance. Scappini and his companions scrambled for cover but the tanks had already detected them. A blast of cannon fire followed, and a direct hit removed Scappini's head. At almost the same moment, Meyer pulled up on a motorcycle to check the progress of the battalion. With little fanfare he turned the battalion over to Schrott and briefed him on his new assignment. While the Panzers chased off the three enemy tanks, the grenadiers swept inexorably onward. Discomfited only by desultory artillery fire, they rapidly seized Galmanche and Mâlon.[43]

At 4:15 p.m., the infantry of the 25th Regiment's 1st Battalion finally moved into action. Commanded by SS-Sturmbannführer Hans Waldmüller,[44] the battalion advanced at first without tank support. The initial objective (erstes Angriffsziel) of the formation was an ambitious one: the village of Anguerny more than five miles to the north and halfway to the coastline. Toting machine pistols, bolt-action carbines, and machine guns, Waldmüller's infantry proceeded unmolested to the southern fringe of Cambes.[45] The lead platoons

---

[41]Meyer, H., *Kriegsgeschichte,* p 81.

[42]Few records could be located on Hans Scappini. As a member of the Leibstandarte he participated in the campaigns in France, Greece and in the Soviet Union, first as a platoon leader and later as a company commander. His decorations included the Iron Cross, first and second class. SS Personalakten, Hans Scappini.

[43]Meyer, H., *Kriegsgeschichte,* p 81; Record Group 238: Records of Proceedings, p 577.

[44]The 31-year-old Waldmüller entered the Waffen SS in 1934, serving at first with the SS Verfügungstruppe. In May 1937 he left the Waffen SS and was attached to the SS Security Service (Sicherheitsdienst); in the summer of 1940, he was transferred to the Leibstandarte, and fought from 1941 to 1943 in Russia, where he was wounded on several occasions. His promotion to SS-Sturmbannführer followed on June 21, 1943. Of course, his decorations included the Iron Cross first and second class. For his participation in the Normandy campaign he garnered the Knight's Cross as well. Waldmüller was killed near Basse-Bodeux by Belgian partisans on September 8, 1944. Schneider, *Verleihung Genemigt!* p 406; SS Personalakten, Hans Waldmüller.

[45]The platoon and squad leaders of the division were equipped with rapid fire machine pistols; the ordinary grenadiers were outfitted with the 7.92mm 98K carbine, which weighed nine pounds and had a five round clip. The effective range of the carbine was some 800 yards, and a grenade launcher could be attached to the weapon. *Handbook on German Military Forces.* War Department Technical Manual TM-E 30-451 (United States Government Printing Office, 1945), p VII-5; Interview, Rudolf Grabher-Meyer, May 25, 1983.

pushed on through the village and into the densely wooded area immediately to the north. Then the storm broke. Enemy tanks were suddenly everywhere--in the village, to its left, north of the woods--and bellowed fire. Heavy machine gun and sniper fire whipped and slashed at the advancing grenadiers. Simultaneously, vigorous artillery and mortar fire slammed down on the woods--the murderous effect of the projectiles enhanced by the bursting tree tops. Continuous attack from the air further disrupted the German assault.[46]

The 1st Battalion had come up against the right wing of the 3rd British Infantry Division. Moving up through le Mesnil a battalion of the division, the Royal Ulster Rifles, accompanied by Shermans of the East Riding Yeomanry (independent 27th Armored Brigade), had mounted an attack of its own.

Less than 1000 yards behind the embattled 1st Battalion stood the five available tanks of the 8th Panzer Company. The company commander, SS-Obersturmführer Hans Siegel, watched intently as the SS infantry went to ground and tried to work their way forward by bounds. Large caliber shells dropped among the grenadiers, spewing fountains of dirt violently into the sky. To his right, he could make out tanks of the 21st Panzer Division near Couvre-Chef. The neighboring tank crews sat passively upon their vehicles and observed the nearby pyrotechnics through their field glasses. Siegel guessed correctly that the 21st Panzer had no intention of supporting the advance of the 12th SS.

The intensity of the enemy fire continued to increase, and Siegel thought he could see some of the grenadiers motioning with spades for his armor to come to their relief. Convinced that the attack had bogged down, he decided the moment had come to set his Panzers loose. Advancing in wedge formation, one of the tanks dropped out immediately, the victim of a mechanical failure; the other four skirted the western edge of Mâlon and clattered on towards Cambes. Locating targets to the west of the wooded region, they took them under fire. "I motored forward in the lead tank," Siegel remembers,[47]

> and when our fire halts became increasingly uncomfortable, my tank scurried up to the edge of the wood, which offered some cover. A shell burst in a tree sealed our fate, for the tree top crashed down from a great height and struck us midship in such an unfortunate manner that the leafy branches completely took away our vision and jammed the turret, putting us out of action. We turned every which way but could not shake loose of the thing . . . In the meantime, two of my tanks had already driven past us. During their next fire halt both were hit in rapid succession. One of them lost its tracks, the other continued to shoot back for a time. My final tank (located farther back) slid sideways into a shell crater and became immobilized. Thus, all the tanks were out of action before they could

---

[46]KTB. I./25.SS-Pz.Gren.Rgt. 7.6.44.

[47]Hans Siegel, "Bericht des Kp.-Chefs 8./Pz.Rgt.12 - Ostuf. Hans Siegel aus der Erinnerung niedergeschrieben am 28.2.69."

really enter the battle. The ordeal had lasted no more than a few minutes . . . Still, there were no actual tank losses, for that evening they were salvaged and put back in working order.

Jost W. Schneider

Hans Siegel, here an SS-Hauptsturmführer.

Completing his tour of the battle zone, the ubiquitous Meyer had already reached the front of the 1st Battalion. He suffered an adrenal shock when he discovered that the 21st Panzer had failed to join his attack.[48] His right flank, he realized, was now totally unprotected. Suddenly, several of his infantry lost courage and began to fall back in the direction of Mâlon. Instinctively, Meyer ran towards them and pointed at the enemy. Recognizing their commander, the youths returned at once to their posts. Having steadied the faint of heart, Meyer returned to the abbey.[49]

In and about Cambes the heavy fighting went on without respite. Pressing into the Cambes wood, the Royal Ulster Rifles were greeted by a withering cross-fire from machine guns and forced to withdraw. In the village itself SS troops with recoilless grenade launchers (Panzerfäuste) stalked enemy tanks, destroying several of them at close quarters. The 75mm guns of the PAK platoon finished off at least two more. But the plight of his battalion, as

---

[48]Apparently, Feuchtinger's 21st Panzer had been thrown on the defensive by a British assault on the Lebisey woods. There were, however, other reasons for the division's inactivity. The 21st Panzer, of course, had suffered heavily on D-Day, losing many of its tanks and most of its anti-tank guns. According to Feuchtinger, the British tanks had contested his armor from a distance of some 2000 yards, while the Panzer IVs, he asserts, were only effective up to 600 yards. Thus, it is not inconceivable that Feuchtinger was too intimidated to join the attack of the 12th SS on June 7th. Wilmont, *The Struggle for Europe,* p 296; Feuchtinger, B-441, pp 22, 28.

[49]Meyer, K., *Grenadiere,* p 219.

Woscidlo

This grenadier holding a Panzerfaust klein 30 "Gretchen" is standing next to a knocked-out Sherman tank.

Waldmüller assessed it, was not a pleasant one. He no longer had any tank support, and his right flank was open; the friendly artillery covering his front had ceased firing, for the forward artillery observer had been killed and his radio set destroyed. Under these circumstances Waldmüller decided to break off the assault, and to pull back to the southern rim of Cambes. The withdrawal was not contested by the enemy, and the companies of the 1st Battalion entrenched directly below the village.[50]

*   *   *

Meyer's battlegroup had been locked in combat since early afternoon, and the hour was rapidly approaching 6:00 p.m. The casualties had continued to mount and the orchards of the Abbey Ardenne were now overflowing with wounded grenadiers. In the abbey courtyard more than 100 Canadian prisoners passively awaited an uncertain fate. Meyer chatted briefly with several captured officers, then, in an exercise that had become a reflex, he again scrambled atop his observation tower. Pointing his binoculars westward he could see great flags of dust rising ominously beyond the Mue. The cause of the disturbance was readily apparent: enemy tanks in large numbers were advancing steadily towards Bretteville-l'Orgueilleuse,[51] and there were no Ger-

---

[50]Norman Scarfe, *Assault Division. A History of the 3rd Division from the Invasion of Normandy to the Surrender of Germany* (London: 1947), pp 97-98; KTB. I./25.SS-Pz.Gren.Rgt. 7.6.44.

[51]The tanks belonged to the 6th Canadian Armored Regiment (1st Hussars); elements of the Regina Rifles, a battalion of the Canadian 7th Brigade, had been in place at Bretteville-l'Orgueilleuse since midday.

man troops in the area to stop them. Meyer's 1st Battalion had already halted its attack, and enemy tanks were counterattacking Buron (see page 139); with both his flanks now in serious danger, he decided to suspend the advance temporarily and to dig in along the line he had gained.[52]

Throughout the day Allied warships had tossed their shells in and about Caen in support of their troops on the ground; early that evening, they loosed a staggering cannonade across the forward line of the 12th SS. The massive projectiles approached their targets with a perfectly infernal roar and ripped huge craters in the earth. To those on the receiving end it must have seemed as if a giant were shaking the universe. The bombardment caused additional casualties, and its psychological effect on the young soldiers was, no doubt, considerable.[53]

But both sides had suffered terribly in their initial encounter. Among the Allies the North Nova Scotia Highlanders had endured the worst losses. The Canadian official history states that the battalion lost 242 men, including 84 dead.[54] The 27th Armored Regiment had some 60 personnel casualties, of which 26 were fatal; the tank unit also had 21 battle tanks knocked out and seven more damaged.[55] The sacrifice of the 12th SS Hitlerjugend was equally severe. The three battalions of the 25th Regiment alone suffered close to 300 dead, wounded and missing; the tank companies of Prinz' battalion 22 dead and 21 wounded. A dozen Panzer IVs were a total loss, and others had been damaged.[56]

Despite his losses, Meyer could review the results of the battle with some satisfaction. On the right flank, he had held the British in check; on the left,

---

[52]Following the recapture of Buron that evening, the front of the 25th SS Panzer Grenadier Regiment ran roughly in an arc from the rail line Caen - Luc-sur-Mer due west of la Bijude, via Galmanche - St. Contest - Buron - Gruchy - Authie to Franqueville, near the Caen - Bayeux road. KTB. I./25.SS-Pz.Gren.Rgt. 7.6.44; Meyer, K., *Grenadiere,* pp 220-21; Meyer, H., *Kriegsgeschichte,* pp 83-84.

[53]Among the Allied warships operating within range of the 12th SS was the battleship H.M.S. "Rodney," with 9 16" and 12 6" guns. Between 6:30 and 8:30 p.m., the battleship fired nearly 200 rounds from its 16" guns and 100 rounds from its 6" guns at several targets around Caen. At least a portion of this fire was in support of elements of the 3rd British Division not engaged against the 12th SS. Whether the "Rodney" also hit positions of the 12th SS could not be ascertained. Apparently another battleship, the H.M.S. "Warspite," was also in action off the British beachhead on June 7th. Public Record Office (London). Battle Log. H.M.S. "Rodney." 7 June 1944; Kenneth Thompson, *H.M.S. "Rodney" at War* (London: Hollis and Carter, 1946), pp 147-48; Meyer, H., P-164, p 23.

[54]The war diary of the Highlanders lists 11 dead, 30 wounded and 204 missing--the majority of the latter, no doubt, either killed or made prisoner. PAC. War Diary. North Nova Scotia Highlanders. 7 June 1944; Stacey. *The Victory Campaign.* p 132.

[55]At 2:00 a.m., June 8th, the 27th Canadian Armored Regiment reported to its superiors 24 cruiser tanks fit for action; another seven would be combat-ready within 24 hours. PAC. War Diary. 27th Canadian Armored Regiment. 7 June 1944; PAC. War Diary. 2nd Canadian Armored Brigade. 8 June 1944.

[56]The losses of Meyer's regiment broke down as follows: 1st Battalion, 15 dead, 87 wounded, 10 missing; 2nd Battalion, 21 dead, 38 wounded, 5 missing; 3rd Battalion, 28 dead, 70 wounded, 12 missing. Losses in weapons and equipment, however, appear to have been light. Meyer, H., *Kriegsgeschichte,* pp 84-85; KTB. I./25.SS-Pz.Gren.Rgt. 7.6.44.

his battlegroup had caught the Canadian advance guard off balance and defeated it in detail. The German blow was well-coordinated, the infantry, armor and artillery playing their parts in close cooperation with one another. For the Canadians the engagement signified a serious local reverse. At a time when the 9th Brigade's lead elements were within sight of their objective, the Carpiquet airport, they were hurled back more than two miles; the lost ground would not be recovered for a full month. "These events," concludes the official Canadian historian, ". . . helped to ensure that Caen would remain in German hands and the eastern flank of the Allied bridgehead would be much more constricted than had been planned."[57] Yet the counterattack of the 12th SS Panzer had only gone forward as far as the line Cambes - Buron, still six to seven miles from the coast. More fundamentally, the operation was not conducted with sufficient strength to have much effect upon the bridgehead battle as a whole.

* * *

Gradually, the night's enveloping blackness settled over the apocalyptic landscape. At the Abbey Ardenne, Meyer dictated to his adjutant an entry for the regimental war diary, and perused a map of the battle area. Thereafter, he received a situation report from divisional headquarters. The report made evident that Fritz Witt was still concerned about the belated arrival of Mohnke's 26th SS Panzer Grenadier Regiment at the front; its battalions were only beginning to reach their jump off positions north and northwest of Grainville-sur-Odon.[58] The fact that the Panzer Lehr had yet to reach its staging areas south of Bayeux, covering the left flank of the 12th SS, caused additional anxiety.[59]

Upon the battlefield activity did not cease with darkness. The infantry of the 25th Regiment improved their positions and awaited the inevitable resumption of the enemy advance on Caen. While harassing artillery fire fingered the line of the regiment, its patrols probed cautiously into no-man's-land to fix the positions of the enemy.[60] Grenadiers of the 3rd Battalion, supported by tanks, counterattacked Buron; finding its ruins evacuated, the SS troops occupied

---

[57]Stacey, *The Victory Campaign,* p 133.

[58]Reaching Grainville-sur-Odon late in the afternoon, Mohnke's 1st Battalion had continued on to Cheux. The 2nd Battalion assembled in the area about le Mesnil-Patry during the night of June 7-8. The 3rd Battalion had reached Fontenay-le-Pesnel by midnight; leaving its armored personnel carriers behind, it then proceeded on foot to Cristot. Meyer, H., *Kriegsgeschichte,* pp 88, 92, 95; Meyer, H., P-164, p 25.

[59]For reasons that remain unclear, the Panzer Lehr was apparently at first assigned to the same sector--St. Manvieu - Cristot - Fontenay-le-Pesnel - Cheux-- as the 26th SS Panzer Grenadier Regiment; by the early morning of June 8th, elements of the division had begun to arrive in this sector on the heels of Mohnke's infantry. Most likely the Panzer Lehr was to support the attack of the 26th Regiment as a second wave (zweites Treffen). However, because the British had captured Bayeux, and had begun to push southward beyond the village, the I SS Panzer Corps ordered Bayerlein to regroup his forces, shift them to the west--astride the road from Bayeux to Tilly-- and recapture Bayeux the next day. Record Group 238: Records of Proceedings, p 579; Ritgen, *Die Geschichte der Panzer-Lehr-Division im Westen,* pp 107-12.

[60]KTB. I./25.SS-Pz.Gren.Rgt. 7.6.44; Record Group 238: Records of Proceedings, p 579.

them. In a quiet moment, those crews of the 5th Panzer Company fortunate enough to have "liberated" rations from wrecked Canadian tanks within their lines enthusiastically devoured their find, which included chocolate, corned beef and peanuts.[61] The youngsters of the 12th SS had fought with skill and determination, as had their opponent. Yet for those marooned upon the killing ground, the days and weeks ahead would bring new trials as terrible as the one that had just clawed its shattering impressions into their brains.

* * * * *

Woscidlo

This dazed and wounded youthful grenadier is probably pondering the hell of combat just experienced.

[61]The soldiers of the 12th SS were generally well-fed during the Normandy campaign. Normandy was rich in dairy products and livestock, enabling the division to live partly off the land. Normal rations included bread, margarine, marmalade, sausage, dried vegetables and soup; the standard iron ration was a chocolate concoction laced with caffeine and called Schoka-Kola. Because of the threat from Allied fighter-bombers, the division was revictualled during the hours of darkness. Interview, Dr. Willi Kändler, April 24, 1983; Fragebogen, Rudolf Grabher-Meyer; Fragebogen, Günther Gurowski; Fragebogen, Rudolf Klein; letter to the author from Frank Kucklach, June 25, 1981.

Chapter 8
THE DEFENSE OF CAEN: JUNE 8-10, 1944

In large-scale operations with thousands of bombers and fighter-bombers the enemy air forces smothered our tank attacks and inflicted heavy losses upon the Panzer divisions. Any reliable calculation of time and space concerning the movements of our forces is rendered impossible by the enemy air forces, which even operate deep in the interior . . . Unremitting shellfire from heavy naval guns, which is hardly contested by our land and air forces, continued throughout the day, and, in combined action with aerial carpet bombing, caused heavy losses in men, materiel, ammunition and fuel.

(War Diary of Army Group B, June 8, 1944)

Early on the morning of June 8, 1944, Field Marshal Bernard Montgomery, the commander of Allied ground forces for the Normandy invasion, set foot ashore in France and occupied his tactical headquarters in the gardens of the château at Creully, a small village east of Bayeux. Although his forces had failed to capture Caen, which, perhaps unrealistically, he had hoped to seize on D-Day, Montgomery could feel satisfied with the broad results of the first two days of the invasion battle. By nightfall, June 7th, the Second British Army held a solid bridgehead 22 miles in length and five to ten miles in depth; before dawn the next day British commandos had captured Port-en-Bessin, thereby establishing firm contact with V U.S. Corps and giving the Allies a continuous stretch of coastline some 35 miles wide. To the west the Americans had also gained ground. Pushing southward, the 1st U.S. Division of V Corps had established a foothold across the Aure River, while VII U.S. Corps was making good progress over difficult terrain on the Cotentin Peninsula.[1]

Montgomery could draw further encouragement from the fact that his grand strategy was working nicely. The Caen sector of the Normandy front was of

---

[1]Advancing across marshy, flooded terrain and close bocage country, elements of VII Corps held a bridgehead eight miles deep and nine miles wide by dark on June 7th. As yet, however, there was no link between the two American corps. To forge the link, General Omar N. Bradley, the commander of the American forces, decided that Carentan would have to be taken before he could proceed with his principal mission--the capture of Cherbourg. Paratroopers of the 101st U.S. Airborne Division would capture Carentan on June 12th, providing the Allies with one continuous front in Normandy. Wilmont, *The Struggle for Europe*, pp 297-99, 307.

crucial significance to the opening phase of the Allied operational plan. By exerting sustained pressure in that area, he hoped to attract the bulk of the German mobile reserves onto the front of the Second British Army, thereby facilitating the breakout of the American forces on the western flank and the eventual drive towards the Seine. The Allied diversion was effective, for the threat to Caen was a thoroughly credible one: a breakthrough into the good tank country south of the city would open the road to Argentan, Le Mans, and the Loire, thus unhinging the entire German front south of the Seine. Montgomery's plan, in fact, only confirmed the contours of German strategic thinking, for all along the Germans were convinced that the main Allied effort would come on the eastern flank, opposite Caen; as the British Field Marshal had hoped, the Panzer divisions were already being drawn towards Caen like a magnet.[2]

Field Marshal Bernard Montgomery (center), Lt. Gen. Omar N. Bradley (left) and Lt. Gen. M.C. Dempsey, commander of the Second British Army, in Normandy.

In contrast to Montgomery's satisfaction, German commanders in the West were growing increasingly impatient. While the Allies pumped fresh troops, equipment and supplies to their beachhead, repeated attack from the air disrupted and delayed the movements of German reinforcements towards the invasion front.[3] The few available Panzer divisions were coming into battle

---

[2]Field Marshal Viscount Montgomery, *The Memoirs of Field-Marshal The Viscount Montgomery of Alamein, K.G.* (New York: The World Publishing Company, 1958), pp 227-28.

[3]On D-Day the German High Command had ordered the movement to Normandy of the 2nd SS Panzer Division from Toulouse, the 17th SS Panzer Grenadier Division from the Loire Valley, the 77th Infantry Division from St. Malo, the 3rd Parachute Division from the area near Brest and several regimental battlegroups from

in piecemeal fashion and had yet to assemble for a concentrated counterattack. Rommel himself, despite visits to both Dietrich and Geyr, had been unable to prod his tank commanders into meaningful action. At 8:10 a.m., June 8th, the frustrated Field Marshal ordered Seventh Army to commit all three tank divisions of the I SS Panzer Corps at once, with their main weight on the left; if necessary, they were to attack with advance elements (Vorausabteilungen).[4]

If Rommel's directive sounded simple enough, the grim realities that confronted Dietrich's Panzer Corps did not permit its execution. Feuchtinger's 21st Panzer was now pinned firmly on the defensive; by dusk, June 8th, the division had but 55 operational tanks and had suffered severe infantry losses in battle with British paratroopers.[5] The battalions of Kurt Meyer's SS battlegroup were also firmly in place and could not easily be regrouped for offensive action; Bayerlein's Panzer Lehr was only beginning to reach the front, and would soon have its hands full trying to blunt the methodical British push southward from Bayeux. In addition to the losses in troops and weaponry, large quantities of ammunition and fuel had been eliminated through Allied air and naval attacks. Shortages of ammunition and fuel were already beginning to appear, and what remained of both could only be brought forward during the few hours of darkness, when the enemy air forces were less active.[6]

A further consequence of Allied air superiority was the near total disruption--both active and passive--of German radio communications. By the evening of the 8th, Geyr had lost three quarters of his radio trucks; Dietrich had only four operational sets out of twenty.[7] Moreover, the mere threat of attack from the air meant that German reinforcements destined for Normandy maintained strict radio silence during the approach march; as a result, con-

other formations stationed in Brittany. Only the SS formations, however, were adequately motorized, while the infantry often travelled by bicycle or on foot. All units suffered at the hands of the Allied tactical air forces. To provide additional firepower for the I SS Panzer Corps, the III Flak Corps and the 7th Werfer Brigade were also dispatched to Normandy. According to its commander, the III Flak Corps lost approximately 100 dead, 200 wounded and 100 vehicles during the approach march, while shooting down some 35 enemy aircraft. Despite its losses, by June 10th the Corps' 88m Flak was moving into position west and southwest of Caen, from where it hoped to support Geyr's counterattack. Wilmont, *The Struggle for Europe,* pp 304-5; General Wolfgang Pickert, B-597. "III. Flak Korps." pp 9-11; T-84/281/000769. KTB Heeresgruppe B.

[4]T-84/281/000789. KTB Heeresgruppe B; T-312/1568/000958. Telephone Log. Seventh Army.

[5]T-84/281/000798. KTB Heeresgruppe B.

[6]Shortly before the beginning of the Normandy invasion, the staff of Dietrich's Panzer Corps learned that large quantities of ammunition had been stored openly since 1940 in the forests south and west of Caen and entrusted in part to the care of French civilian personnel. The predictable result of such carelessness was that the French underground was soon well informed over the locations, types and quantities of the ammunition. From June 6th on the Allied air forces systematically obliterated these stores; the resulting shortages were soon felt by the Germans. Major-General Walter Staudinger, B-832. "Artillerie in Normandie." p 12.

[7]T-84/281/000798. KTB Heeresgruppe B.

cerned commanders were often poorly informed of the whereabouts of units on the march.[8]

The cumulative effect of such concerns was that the Germans were unable to launch a major counterstroke in the critical few days from June 8-10, when the Allied bridgehead was still relatively small and vulnerable; in its place, the I SS Panzer Corps managed but a series of limited and largely uncoordinated attacks of purely local significance. The 12th SS Panzer was in action throughout this period, once again opposite the 3rd Canadian Infantry Division, and experienced some of the most furious fighting of the entire Normandy campaign; yet it was unable to repeat the success of its initial effort on June 7th. The opposition proved formidable, lavishly equipped and tenacious in the defense. Witt, Wünsche, Meyer and other veterans of the Leibstandarte soon discovered that the Blitz style tactics that had worked so well in earlier campaigns were much less effective in Normandy, and their attacks were often beaten back by the sheer volume of enemy firepower. The two dozen 105mm guns of the 12th Canadian Field Regiment alone fired some 1,500 shells apiece from June 7-9 in support of the Canadian infantry, contributing in no small measure to the failures of the 12th SS.[9] By June 10th, the front had

Kurt Meyer, Fritz Witt and Max Wünsche at the Abbey Ardenne, early June 1944.

[8]For example, the Seventh Army Chief of Staff, General Pemsel, informed Rommel at 4:00 a.m., June 7th, that all three Panzer divisions of the I SS Panzer Corps had reached their staging areas and were about to attack. At the time, of course, elements of the 12th SS were only beginning to reach the front, while the Panzer Lehr was still a day's march away. T-312/1569/000009. KTB Seventh Army.

[9]Questionnaire, John Shearer. Special thanks to Mr. Shearer for providing excerpts from the records of the 12th Field Regiment, Royal Canadian Artillery.

become virtually static, the formations of the Panzer Corps locked in a grinding battle of attrition—a Materialschlacht, the Germans called it, in which sheer weight of numbers of tanks, artillery, and aircraft determined victory or defeat. And as the Germans recognized, the calculus of such a battle clearly favored their opponent.

*   *   *

During the early morning hours of June 8th, the battalions of Mohnke's 26th SS Panzer Grenadier Regiment completed their assembly in the assigned sector west of Meyer's battlegroup. The line of the regiment stretched from Cheux northwest to le Mesnil-Patry and Cristot.[10] The arrival of Mohnke's infantry partially closed a gap more than six miles wide in the front of the 12th SS—a gap that extended from the left wing of the 25th SS Panzer Grenadier Regiment at Buron[11] westward to Audrieu (six miles southeast of Bayeux), where the reconnaissance battalion was now in position covering the open flank of the division.[12] Beyond Audrieu, the front of the I SS Panzer Corps had yet to come into being,[13] and physical contact with the neighboring LXXXIV Army Corps did not exist.[14] The staff of the Panzer Corps evinced real concern over these openings in the line, through which the enemy could move at any time and destroy elements of the 12th SS and the Panzer Lehr in their assembly areas.[15]

Already on the evening of June 7th, Witt had ordered Mohnke to attack early the next day, and to capture the villages of Norrey-en-Bessin, Bretteville-l'Orgueilleuse, Putot-en-Bessin and Brouay.[16] The clearing of these villages, which lay astride or near the Caen - Bayeux road, would help to furnish the I SS Panzer Corps with better jump-off positions for the big push to the sea. Another consideration was that the two heavily fortified Luftwaffe radar stations west of Douvres-la-Délivrande, though cut off, were still holding out;

---

[10]According to Kurt Meyer, the 26th SS Panzer Grenadier Regiment established its main headquarters in a wooded area north of Grainville-sur-Odon. Record Group 218: Supplementary Report SHAEF Court of Inquiry. Exhibit 8. p 27.

[11]On the morning of June 8th, the front of Kurt Meyer's three infantry battalions stretched from the Caen - Luc-sur-Mer rail line to the western rim of Buron; in position from Gruchy southward to Franqueville were his Flak and reconnaissance companies and a platoon from the engineer company, supported by two batteries of 88mm guns from the division's Flak battalion. Record Group 238: Records of Proceedings, p 588; Meyer, H., *Kriegsgeschichte*. p 99.

[12]Aggressively screened by patrols of both the 12th SS and the Panzer Lehr, the Canadians had failed to exploit this vulnerable sector.

[13]The Panzer Lehr would not be in position astride the road from Tilly-sur-Seulles to Bayeux until the following morning, June 9th. See Ritgen, *Die Geschichte der Panzer-Lehr-Division im Westen*, pp 111-112.

[14]Technically, the boundary between the I SS Panzer Corps and the LXXXIV Army Corps was that of the 716th and 352nd Infantry Divisions; it ran north from Fontenay-le-Pesnel to the coast at Asnelles. Of course, the 716th Infantry Division was largely destroyed during the D-Day fighting, as were elements of the 352nd Infantry Division. The formations of Dietrich's Panzer Corps were endeavoring to fill the vacuum.

[15]See for example, Kraemer, C-024, p 23.

[16]This sector, with the exception of Brouay, was held by elements of the 7th Brigade, 3rd Canadian Infantry Division.

their relief was urgently required.[17] The attack was to go in under cover of darkness; tanks and artillery were to support the advance.[18]

In contrast to the open and nearly level terrain directly north and northwest of Caen, the sector assigned to Mohnke's Panzer grenadier regiment was generally less open and more severely undulating, varying in height from about 180 to 300 feet above sea level. West of the axis St. Manvieu - Bretteville-l'Orgueilleuse and into the area about le Mesnil-Patry, wide, hedgeless fields of wheat, turnips and clover blanketed the ground; only along the Mue were there thickets of trees and bush. Around le Mesnil-Patry itself hedges and clumps of trees somewhat limited visibility. South of Brouay the country was typical bocage. Its dominant feature was the hedgerow--a bank several feet high with a ditch on either side and crowned by a line of trees or thorny bushes with deep roots. The hedgerows enclosed a maze of meadows and ploughed fields, providing secure cover for the defender. Sturdy, high stone walls encased the ubiquitous orchards and numerous individual farmsteads, and wove their way through the villages, creating additional obstacles for the attacker. The villages, moreover, with their stout stone buildings and narrow thoroughfares, represented formidable strongholds in the hands of a determined defender. Finally, the Caen - Cherbourg rail line ran south of the Route National 13, skirting Putot-en-Bessin and cutting directly through Brouay; with its many high embankments the rail line posed an additional obstacle, particularly to armor.[19]

A conference in a bocage area of Normandy.

---

[17]Surrounded by barbed-wire and mines, the radar stations were protected by 238 Luftwaffe ground personnel equipped with six 50mm guns, 16 machine guns and three heavy mortars. They held out for 11 days. Stacey, *The Victory Campaign*, pp 70, 134.

[18]Meyer, H., P-164, p 23; Meyer, H., *Kriegsgeschichte*, pp 91-92.

[19]The author visited this battlefield in March 1981, and again in June 1983.

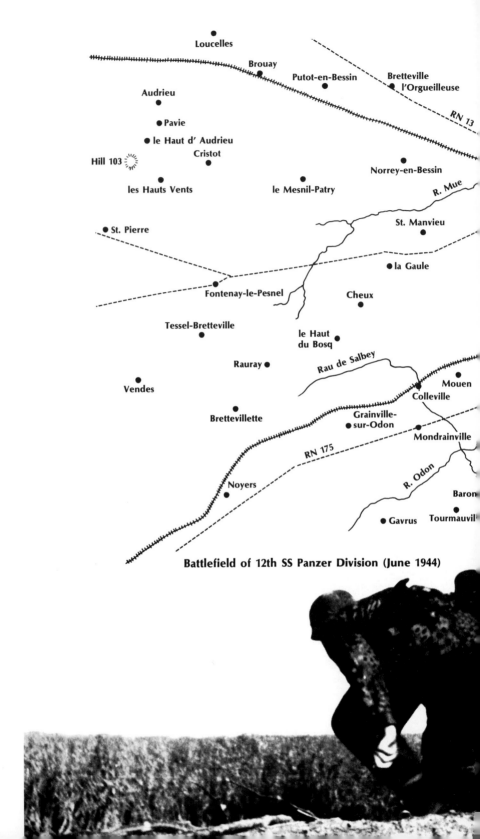

Loucelles

Brouay

Putot-en-Bessin

Bretteville
l'Orgueilleuse

Audrieu

Pavie

le Haut d' Audrieu

Cristot

Hill 103

Norrey-en-Bessin

les Hauts Vents

le Mesnil-Patry

R. Mue

St. Pierre

St. Manvieu

la Gaule

Fontenay-le-Pesnel

Cheux

Tessel-Bretteville

le Haut
du Bosq

Rau de Salbey

Mouen

Rauray

Colleville

Vendes

Grainville-
sur-Odon

Brettevillette

Mondrainville

RN 175

R. Odon

Baron

Noyers

Gavrus

Tourmauvil

Battlefield of 12th SS Panzer Division (June 1944)

RN 13

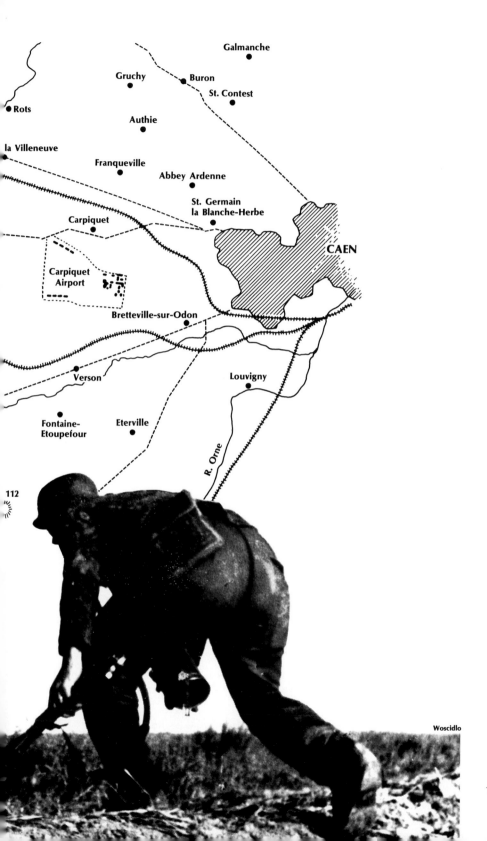

Galmanche

Gruchy
Buron
St. Contest

Rots

Authie

la Villeneuve

Franqueville
Abbey Ardenne

St. Germain
la Blanche-Herbe

CAEN

Carpiquet

Carpiquet
Airport

Bretteville-sur-Odon

Verson
Louvigny

Fontaine-
Etoupefour
Eterville

R. Orne

112

Woscidlo

155

At 3:00 a.m., June 8th, the companies of Mohnke's 1st Battalion debouched from their positions covering Cheux and advanced on Norrey-en-Bessin. The 3rd Company was on the right, the 2nd on the left; the 1st Company followed on the far right and echeloned to the rear to cover the open flank of the battalion. The attack went in without the anticipated tank support, for the Panthers of Wünsche's 1st Battalion had yet to reach the battlefield. Defending Norrey were "B" and "C" Companies of the 1st Battalion The Regina Rifle Regiment.

Passing St. Manvieu, a straggling village nearly hidden in the bed of the Mue, the 3rd Company came under fire from a small enemy covering force, which soon withdrew. Crossing the Mue the attackers were subjected to heavy Canadian artillery fire that drove them to cover on the rising ground before Norrey. The 2nd Company managed somewhat better progress, reaching the rail line northwest of Norrey and clearing a group of buildings there (Cardenville). However, with both the 1st and 3rd Companies pinned down, the battalion commander, SS-Sturmbannführer Bernhard Krause,[20] had no choice but to suspend the advance.[21] The battalion dug in but was granted no respite, for throughout the day enemy artillery and mortar fire pummeled its positions, paralyzing all movement.

Jost W. Schneider

SS-Sturmbann-
führer Bernhard
Krause.

[20]Krause entered the Waffen SS on January 1, 1934, assigned initially to the Regiment "Deutschland." As an SS-Hauptsturmführer he came to the Leibstandarte on November 1, 1939. With the LAH he participated in the Balkan and Russian campaigns, earning the Iron Cross first and second class. Promoted to SS-Sturmbannführer on September 1, 1941, Krause played an important role in the recapture of Kharkov in March 1943 as the commander of the Flak battalion of the LAH. For his soldierly virtues Krause received the German Cross in Gold on August 7, 1944; several months later he was awarded the Knight's Cross to the Iron Cross. He was killed in Hungary on February 19, 1945, fighting with Army Group South in the Gran bridgehead. SS Personalakten, Bernhard Krause; Schneider, Verleihung Genehmigt!, p 196.

The 2nd Battalion of the 26th Regiment had reached the battlefront too late to go forward together with the 1st; commanded by SS-Sturmbannführer Bernhard Siebken,[22] it attacked from its positions in and about le Mesnil-Patry shortly after dawn. Although hammered by enemy artillery and machine gun fire, the grenadiers of the 2nd Battalion pressed their assault with vigor, infiltrating into Putot-en-Bessin and taking many prisoners.[23] Assisted by numerous snipers in Putot, the German infantry brought the defenders, the Royal Winnipeg Rifles, under steadily increasing pressure; by noon, more grenadiers had worked their way into the town and around the Canadian light machine gun posts and slit trenches, which were now under direct German artillery and mortar fire. By 1:30 p.m., "A," "B" and "C" Companies of the Winnipegs were completely surrounded, with most of their automatic weapons knocked out and ammunition running low; immediate tank support was not available. The beleaguered companies attempted to pull back under cover of artificial smoke, but few men escaped to battalion headquarters, located due east of Putot, where the nearly intact "D" Company established a defensive position.[24]

Having lost Putot the commander of the Canadian 7th Brigade, Brigadier H.W. Foster, set about to get it back. Foster, as soon as he became aware that things were going badly for the Winnipegs, had warned the commander of the 1st Battalion The Canadian Scottish Regiment to be ready for action; at 8:30 p.m., the battalion mounted a violent counterattack supported by a squadron of tanks from the 6th Armored Regiment and a portion of the Cameron Highlanders of Ottawa (medium machine guns). The assault went in behind a creeping barrage laid down by the 12th and 13th Field Regiments. The SS defenders resisted furiously, but were unable to maintain their positions in the face of a numerically superior opponent. Siebken's companies had already suffered heavy losses, and they lacked anti-tank weapons in sufficient numbers with which to contest the enemy armor. By 9:30 p.m., Putot was once again in Canadian hands, the Germans having retired to the rail line on the southern fringe of the village. Later that night, Siebken pulled back his infantry an additional 200-300 yards to gain a more effective field of fire and dug in. The Canadian Scottish took over the defense of Putot, while the remnants of the Winnipegs were moved into brigade reserve.[25]

[21]A laconic entry in the war diary of the Regina Rifles merely acknowledges that the German attack was "repulsed." PAC. War Diary. Regina Rifle Regiment. 8 June 1944; Meyer, H., *Kriegsgeschichte*, p 92; Meyer, H., P-164, p 24; Meyer, K., *Grenadiere*, p 222.

[22]Like Fritz Witt and Wilhelm Mohnke, the 34-year-old Siebken was one of the original 120 members of the Leibstandarte. With the LAH he had taken part in all of the major campaigns of the war. SS Personalakten, Bernhard Siebken.

[23]According to a Canadian participant, the attackers came on inexorably, taking little evasive action despite the heavy fire that greeted them. Questionnaire, George Lacouvee; Fragebogen, Helmut Sallach.

[24]PAC. War Diary. Royal Winnipeg Rifles. 8 June 1944; Stacey, *The Victory Campaign*, p 135.

[25]PAC. War Diary. The Canadian Scottish Regiment. 8 June 1944; Stacey, *The Victory Campaign*, pp 135-36; Meyer, H., *Kriegsgeschichte*, p 94; Meyer, K., *Grenadiere*, p 222.

Mohnke's 3rd Battalion, meanwhile, had been the last of his infantry to move into action that morning. Commanded by SS-Sturmbannführer Erich Olboeter,[26] the battalion had reached Fontenay-le-Pesnel by midnight, June 7th; from there, it had proceeded on foot, reaching Cristot at first light. Canadian artillery fire dropped in and about the village, and, during a briefing in a nearby wooded area, the commanders of the battalion's 10th and 11th Companies were badly wounded.[27]

Jost W. Schneider

SS-Sturmbannführer
Erich Olboeter.

Following the replacement of the disabled officers, the battalion put in its attack at about 8:00 a.m. The 11th Company advanced on the right, the 10th on the left, while the remainder of the battalion initially stayed behind in Cristot. The objectives were two-fold: to seize Brouay and to close the gap between the regiment's 2nd Battalion and the reconnaissance battalion. Traversing a tall wheat field, the lead platoon of the 11th Company soon came under fire from a single machine gun. But the firing ceased abruptly as the grenadiers worked their way forward individually, reaching a fork in the road 150 yards south of Brouay. From there, they could make out soldiers on the northwest rim of the village. Because it was uncertain if these soldiers were friend or foe, the company commander resolved to seize Brouay in a lightning assault (Sturmangriff). Without firing a shot, the SS troopers stormed into the village, where, to the astonishment of all, they discovered a covering force of the Panzer Lehr in place along the rail embankment. The force consisted of

---

[26]The 26-year-old Olboeter joined the Waffen SS in September 1934. As a soldier with the Leibstandarte he saw action on all the major battlefields of Europe, serving as a company commander in the French, Balkan and Russian campaigns. Repeatedly wounded, he had earned the Iron Cross first and second class, and, for his contribution to the recapture of Kharkov, the German Cross in Gold. On July 27, 1944 he received the Knight's Cross. Olboeter was killed on September 2, 1944, near Hirson, France. SS Personalakten, Erich Olboeter; Schneider, *Verleihung Genehmigt!* p 260.

[27]Meyer, H., P-164, p 25.

several machine gun positions and believed itself to be cut off from the rest of the division.[28]

Meanwhile the 10th Company, although discomfited by light enemy artillery fire (Störungsfeuer), reached the woods southwest of Brouay about midday. What confronted them there was a picture of utter devastation: advanced elements of the Panzer Lehr obliterated by the formidable firepower of the Allied invasion fleet. The shattered remains of dead soldiers littered the ground, their body parts hanging from the trees. Destroyed equipment and vehicles were everywhere, including armored personnel carriers ripped apart like tin cans. In sepulchral silence the young SS troopers contemplated the destruction around them. For these boys, "the war had shown its claws and torn off its pleasant mask."[29]

Continuing the advance the platoons of the 10th Company pushed on into Brouay as far as the rail embankment. Here, they settled in along with the 11th Company to defend the line they had gained, subjected to the unremitting harassing fire of the enemy artillery. Patrols of the battalion probed the flanks, establishing contact with the neighboring 2nd Battalion on the right and with Bremer's reconnaissance battalion on the left.[30]

Grenadiers of the 26th SS Pz. Gren. Rgt. resting in the hedge rows of Normandy. Note full camouflage uniforms.

---

[28]Meyer, H., P-164, p 25; Meyer, H., *Kriegsgeschichte,* p 95.
[29]The words are Ernst Jünger's.
[30]Meyer, H., P-164, p 25.

Thus ended the baptism of fire for the 26th SS Panzer Grenadier Regiment. The sacrifice on both sides had been great. The Royal Winnipeg Rifles alone had suffered 256 casualties, including 105 dead, in their unsuccessful defense of Putot.[31] German losses totaled 137 personnel, of which at least 30 were fatalities;[32] and while the cost had been high, the results were meager. Mohnke's battalions had attacked piecemeal and without tank support; except for the short-lived success at Putot and the capture of Brouay, which was undefended by the enemy,[33] they had failed to reach their objectives.

During the afternoon and evening of June 8th, the 12th SS had experienced growing pressure on its extreme left flank. Here, the 12th SS Reconnaissance Battalion, commanded by SS-Sturmbannführer Gerhard Bremer, had formed a loose chain of strongpoints extending from la Rue, across Audrieu and Pavie, to the area west of Hill 103 (southwest of le Haut d'Audrieu) by the evening of June 7th. About midday, June 8th, the staff and headquarters company of the battalion arrived at the Château d'Audrieu, near Pavie, and established themselves on the château grounds. The battalion command post was under a large spreading sycamore tree behind the château.[34]

That morning, on instructions from the British 50th Northumbrian Division, the 8th Armored Brigade Group had concentrated in the sector St. Gabriel - Brécy - Martragny. The brigade group was to push southward through Audrieu and to occupy the high ground above Villers-Bocage, 15 miles south of Bayeux.[35] The possession of this area, it was felt, would serve to interdict the flow of German reinforcements to the Normandy battlefield; it would also outflank the still tenuous front of the I SS Panzer Corps.

The advance guard of the 8th Armored Brigade Group consisted of the 61st Reconnaissance Regiment on the right, and the 24th Lancers (an armored regiment) on the left. At 2:00 p.m., the reconnaissance regiment began to advance towards le Bas d'Audrieu; reaching the rail line just north of the village, it was turned back by spirited opposition from Bremer's battalion, and retired to the high ground northwest of Loucelles. The tanks of the 24th Lancers fared no better; apparently drawn by accident into the fighting around Putot, they were repulsed by heavy and accurate German artillery fire.[36] Meanwhile the

---

[31]The Canadian Scottish reported its losses for June 8th and 9th as 125, including 45 dead. According to C.P. Stacey, however, "it is evident that most of the casualties suffered in the counterattack on the evening of the 8th were recorded under the date of the 9th." Stacey, *The Victory Campaign*, p 136.

[32]The losses of the 26th SS Panzer Grenadier Regiment were as follows: 1st Battalion, 5 dead, 20 wounded; 2nd Battalion 19 dead, 58 wounded and 21 missing; 3rd Battalion 6 dead and 8 wounded.

[33]The extreme right flank of the Canadian 7th Brigade was located in Putot. West of Putot, and north of Brouay, began the front of the neighboring British 50th Northumbrian Division.

[34]Meyer, H., *Kriegsgeschichte*, p 88; Record Group 218: Supplementary Report SHAEF Court of Inquiry. p I:3; MacDonald, B.J.S., *The Trial of Kurt Meyer*, pp 17-18.

[35]Ellis, L.F., *Victory in the West*, p 230.

[36]At 7:00 a.m., the 24th Lancers had assembled in the area about Martragny. Moving east down the Caen - Bayeux road their lead elements were soon "heavily engaged" by anti-tank guns, which destroyed a Stuart tank. Late that afternoon the

SS-Sturmbannführer Gerd Bremer (right) and his adjutant, Kurt Buchheim (left), under a knocked-out Sherman tank in Cristot.

Sherwood Rangers Yeomanry, another British tank regiment, had received orders to thrust southward--west of the axis Loucelles - Audrieu--and to seize Hill 103. The regiment's advance took it through dense hedgerow country and along, though sufficiently removed from, the line of the 12th SS Reconnaissance Battalion. Encountering little opposition, the Sherwood Rangers were upon their objective by late afternoon.[37]

While British tanks explored the gap in the German line, British artillery hammered Audrieu and Cristot. At 8:00 p.m., a murderous cannonade laid

Lancers attacked a "particularly active enemy position" at Putot-en-Bessin: "the position was found to be strongly held by three battalions [an overstatement] of a Panzer Grenadier Regiment in the Hitler Jugend Division, numbers of which had hidden themselves in the long grass in the orchards west of Putot and also at the tops of trees, whence tank commanders were continually sniped." Public Record Office Index Number WO 171/849. War Diary. 24th Lancers. 8 June 1944.

[37]According to its war diary, the regiment "moved with remarkable speed and in spite of minor enemy opposition from anti-tank guns positioned itself on [Hill] 103 at approximately 4:00 p.m. [Hill] 103 held a commanding view [of] the villages of St. Pierre and Fontenay. On arrival, Captain Douglas and Lieutenant Bethell-Fox went on a patrol into the village of St. Pierre. It was only with the greatest difficulty that they managed to contact civilians who were hiding in cellars, [and] who told them that there were approximately 20 Germans in the village. Douglas and Fox continued their patrol on foot and suddenly around a corner came face to face with a German Patrol [perhaps from the reconnaissance battalion of the Panzer Lehr] consisting of one officer and 8 men. Both [patrols] were so surprised that they turned about and made with maximum speed for their respective bases. In the evening some anti-tank guns joined us and also some machine guns. We were all rather pleased to see them as we felt somewhat lonely." Public Record Office Index Number WO 171/861. War Diary. Sherwood Rangers Yeomanry. 8 June 1944.

down by ground and naval artillery began to pound Audrieu into the earth; within an hour, the village was a ruin. About 9:00 p.m., the shell fire shifted southward to the Château d'Audrieu, smashing Bremer's headquarters group. This second barrage also continued for about an hour, then ceased abruptly, apparently to entice the Germans from their hiding places to care for the wounded. Minutes later, another Feuerschlag slammed down on the château grounds; it lasted for 20 minutes and caused the greatest number of casualties, in addition to knocking out a number of armored personnel carriers and scout vehicles. Because of its high losses and the pressure exerted by the enemy armored force along its front, the reconnaissance battalion had little choice but to pull back. Its new position stretched from a point southwest of Brouay, across Cristot and les Hauts Vents, and into the countryside 500 yards northeast of St. Pierre. Battalion headquarters was concealed in the close country south of Cristot. Wounded in the shoulder, Bremer temporarily relinquished command to SS-Hauptsturmführer Gerd von Reitzenstein, hitherto commander of the headquarters company.[38]

* * *

On the front of the 25th SS Panzer Grenadier Regiment, the 8th of June would not bring a renewal of the Canadian drive towards Caen.[39] At first light, the commander of the regiment, SS-Standartenführer Kurt Meyer, was again ensconced atop his observation tower at the Abbey Ardenne. Looking northwest, Meyer detected an enemy concentration in the area north of Cairon, but after observing the hostile force for some time, he correctly concluded that it was not intent upon immediate offensive action. With his own front momentarily quiet, Meyer decided to assist his division via a "thrust towards Bayeux."[40] If successful, such a course of action would relieve the Canadian pressure on Mohnke's 1st Battalion; in addition, it would close an opening approximately four miles in length that still separated the inner flanks of the division's two Panzer grenadier regiments.[41] Finally, a successful incursion down the Caen - Bayeux highway would outflank the positions of the Regina Rifles in Norrey and threaten them with encirclement.

Early that afternoon, Meyer discussed his plan in detail with the commander of the 12th SS Panzer Regiment, Max Wünsche. The immediate objective was the village of Bretteville-l'Orgueilleuse, five miles northwest of Caen. To

---

[38]The losses of the 12th SS Reconnaissance Battalion on June 8th were 18 dead, 48 wounded and 14 missing. To reinforce the battalion, the 2nd Panzer Company (Panthers) moved up to Fontenay-le-Pesnel during the night of June 8-9. Meyer, H., *Kriegsgeschichte,* pp 98, 111; Record Group 218: Supplementary Report SHAEF Court of Inquiry. p IV: 20-21.

[39]The Canadians, in fact, would not launch another major operation in the sector north of Caen until the second week of July 1944.

[40]During his trial, Meyer provided an exhaustive account of his thinking and activities on June 8th. The plan to attack down the Caen - Bayeux road was apparently his own. Record Group 238: Records of Proceedings, pp 586-87, 593-94.

[41]The gap extended west from Buron, where Meyer's 3rd Battalion was in place, to the extreme right flank of the 26th SS Panzer Grenadier Regiment at St. Manvieu. Directly north of la Villeneuve a small battlegroup from the divisional escort company (a heavy machine gun squad and a motorcycle squad) was in position. BAMA. Tagebuch Divisions-Begleit-Kompanie. 7.6.1944.

gain surprise, and to avoid the attention of the Allied air forces, the attack was to go in under cover of darkness. A battlegroup composed of the available companies of the Panther battalion[42] and of the motorcycle riflemen (Kradschützen) of Meyer's own reconnaissance company[43] was to conduct the assault, supported by a battery of 105mm self-propelled artillery.[44] The 1st Battalion of the 26th Regiment was also to lend support by attacking from its positions about St. Manvieu.

Following the discussion at the abbey tower, Meyer briefed SS-Obersturmführer Meitzel, a staff officer from divisional headquarters, so that he could put Fritz Witt in the picture. After lunching together, Wünsche returned to his tanks to ready them for combat, while Meyer slept momentarily.[45]

At dusk (shortly before 10:00 p.m.) the SS battlegroup began to roll west from its staging area southwest of Franqueville. Meyer led the advance in a sidecar motorcycle--piloted by his friend and soldierly companion since 1939, SS-Oberscharführer Helmut Belke--making good on a promise he had made to accompany his reconnaissance troops during their baptism of fire.[46] Close behind followed a squad of motorcyclists and the vehicle of the artillery observer. Then came the main body of the force: the Panthers of the 4th and the 1st Panzer Companies advancing right and left of the Caen - Bayeux road, respectively, with the majority of the reconnaissance company mounted on the tanks.[47]

Skirting the emplacements of an 88mm Flak battery, the battlegroup rapidly picked up speed. In wedge formation the Panthers moved swiftly across the

---

[42]The 1st and 4th Panzer Companies were the first to reach the front. From Canadian records it appears that they had assembled near Franqueville by late morning. At 8:58 a.m., the Regina Rifles detected the presence of enemy tanks at Hill 69 due west of Franqueville. At 11:00 a.m., "D" Company of the Reginas, situated on the extreme left flank of the battalion at la Villeneuve, reported German tanks "in considerable strength" just 1000 yards before its front. At 5:00 p.m., the company withdrew to Cardenville, located athwart the rail line south of Bretteville, to improve the battalion fortress. Cardenville had been captured that morning by infantry of the 26th SS Panzer Grenadier Regiment, but must have been abandoned by the Germans shortly thereafter. PAC. War Diary. The Regina Rifles. 8 June 1944.

[43]All three of Meyer's infantry battalions were now firmly in line and could not be extricated; the solution was to free up the reconnaissance company by relieving it with his engineer company, hitherto in position on the right flank of the regiment and subordinated to the 1st Battalion. According to Meyer, the battalion commander, SS-Sturmbannführer Hans Waldmüller, was reluctant to let go of the engineer company; after some arm twisting, however, he acquiesced. Record Group 238: Records of Proceedings, p 587.

[44]The 105mm "Wespe," or wasp, was the most common self-propelled version of the standard German light field howitzer; mounted upon a modified Panzer II tank chassis it had a maximum range of 13,500 yards. Handbook on German Military Forces, p VII: 65-67.

[45]Record Group 238: Records of Proceedings, pp 593-94.

[46]Meyer, an experienced motorcycle and recee soldier, felt a special attachment to his reconnaissance company. Acutely aware of the critical role that it played in his battle leadership, he had instilled a special sense of eliteness in the young soldiers of the company. During the training period at Beverloo in the summer of 1943 Meyer had promised to accompany them during their baptism of fire. Ibid., pp 555-56.

[47]Meyer, K., Grenadiere, p 224; Meyer, H., Kriegsgeschichte, p 100.

Woscidlo

105mm "Wespe" from the 1st Btn. of the 12th SS Pz. Art. Rgt.

open, level terrain, the infantry ducking behind the thickly armored turrets for shelter. Atop his motorcycle Meyer raced on to the outskirts of le Bourg, a hamlet directly south of Rots. Minutes later the tanks rolled up. The lead squad of riflemen dismounted and swept forward on foot: le Bourg was free of the enemy; the little bridge over the Mue intact. In single-file the 45 ton behemoths rumbled across the bridge, then they reverted to the original wedge formation. The tanks of the 4th Company were now straddling the highway, with those of the 1st Company advancing south of it.[48]

When clear of le Bourg, Meyer let the lead Panthers push on ahead of him. Racing on towards Bretteville they soon disappeared in the enveloping darkness, betrayed only by the fiery tongues of flame disgorged from their exhaust pipes. The battlegroup bored on towards its destination, the tension steadily mounting, for contact with the enemy was but moments away. Descending a gentle forward slope barely 300 yards from Bretteville, the attackers struck a wall of anti-tank and machine gun fire. The tanks of both companies halted; with their powerful 75mm guns they hosed the entrance to the village with high explosive shells, supported by the battery of 105mm self-propelled artillery. The Panthers of the 4th Company then made a wild dash towards their objective.

The battle that followed was utterly murderous, and, at times, dominated by indescribable confusion; it would last through the early morning hours. Racing forward to the eastern fringe of Bretteville, the 4th Company was again sprayed by vicious enemy anti-tank fire. The Panther of the company commander received a direct hit and burst into flames. The SS riflemen, exposed to a furious mélange of small arms fire from infantry of the Regina Rifles ("A" Company) entrenched about the village, dismounted and attempted to work their way forward.[49]

---

[48]Ibid.

164   [49]Ibid.

In the first shock of the German assault parts of the Canadian position were overrun. Some of the Panthers managed to push to within some 300 yards of the Reginas' battalion headquarters, situated near the church in the center of Bretteville; here they stopped, shelling and machine gunning the village for a considerable time. About midnight, two Panthers entered the village. One of them actually pulled up before the headquarters, but was quickly disposed of by three successive hits with PIAT bombs.[50]

Motorcycles and Panthers of the division move on Bretteville on the evening of June 8.

Throughout the night the armor of Meyer's battlegroup was all about Bretteville, orbiting the Reginas' headquarters and blasting away at the enemy infantry in their slit trenches. The whole sky was aglow from gunfire, blazing buildings, and the dazzling light of the Canadian parachute flares, which illuminated the Panzers for the defenders' anti-tank guns and blinded the German tank crews. In the confusion at least some of the SS appeared at times convinced that all opposition had ceased:[51]

> A fool-hardy German dispatch rider rode down the main street of Bretteville on a captured Canadian motorcycle only to be brought down by the commanding officer's Sten gun. Some time later a German officer rolled up in his Volkswagen to BHQ (battalion headquarters), dismounted and gazed around for a few seconds until a PIAT gunner let fly a bomb which hit him directly. He disappeared. Despite the confusion and the odds against the Battalion everyone was in high spirits and never considered the situation

---

[50]PAC. War Diary. The Regina Rifles. 8-9 June 1944; Stacey, *The Victory Campaign,* pp 136-37.

[51]The quote is from a history of the Regina Rifles published sometime after the war. The author is unknown. PAC. War Diary. The Regina Rifles. 9 June 1944.

desperate. Our confidence in ourselves and our weapons increased. The dreaded Panther tank was not invincible and could be knocked out by infantry who knew how to use their weapons.

The losses of the 12th SS were indeed severe. The platoons of Meyer's reconnaissance company suffered terrible lacerations as they tried unsuccessfully to storm the village.[52] The company commander, SS-Hauptsturmführer Horst von Büttner, was one of the casualties--fatally wounded in the stomach early in the battle. Meyer's driver, Belke, was also killed. Meyer himself got into a scrape with an enemy machine gun, whose fire punctured the fuel tank of his motorcycle, enveloping him in flames. Happily, a group of friendly infantry were close by; they wrestled their commander to the ground and extinguished the flames. Meyer suffered only minor burns.[53]

The grave of SS-Oberscharführer Helmut Belke, Kurt Meyer's driver who was killed during the attack on Bretteville.

---

[52]The remnants of one platoon, seven men in all, reached the church in the center of Bretteville after furious fighting. Once there, they fired off flares--a prearranged signal for the tanks to follow up their advance. But the tanks never came. When Meyer's battlegroup withdrew, the seven remained behind in the interior of the church, completely cut off from friendly forces. On the morning of the 9th, a group of Canadian infantry flushed the Germans from the church, taking two of them prisoner. The other five men eluded capture and took cover in a bush covered depression in the nearby cemetery. Here they would remain for six days, exhausted and hungry but relatively unmolested by the Canadians, who no doubt believed the Germans would eventually give themselves up. Throughout the daylight hours, the surrounded SS could hear the Canadian artillery observer directing fire from the church tower. Eventually, they managed to bore a small hole through the stone wall bordering the cemetery with a bayonet; through this opening three of the soldiers finally made their escape under cover of darkness to the German lines. By then too weak to move, the other two elected to remain behind. Meyer, H., *Kriegsgeschichte*, pp 100-101; 103-104.

Faced with stiffening Canadian resistance, the German attack along the Route Nationale 13 sputtered. To get it moving again, Wünsche ordered his 1st Panzer Company to bypass Bretteville to the south, wheel to the north, and attack the place from the southwest. But this attempt to outflank the enemy soon ended in fiasco; in rapid succession several more Panthers received lethal hits from Canadian anti-tank weapons. One tank, hit in the motor room, burned like a torch; another was smashed through the turret, blinding and badly wounding the loader; still another was struck beneath the cupola, removing it along with the head of the tank commander. The 1st Panzer Company broke off its attack.[54]

Despite initial success, the SS battlegroup had failed to break the enemy resistance. The Regina Rifles, buttressed by the 6-pounders of the 3rd Anti-Tank Regiment, had "stood off the attack." Conversely, the grenadiers of Mohnke's 1st Battalion had failed to provide urgently needed support, although a company of the battalion had managed to capture Rots against weak enemy resistance. Short of infantry and confronted by a vigilant and well-equipped adversary, Meyer and Wünsche resolved to call off their attack.[55]

As the glimmer of dawn showed towards Bayeux, the remaining Panthers rode away from the burning ruins and pulled back behind the Mue, to the high ground in the vicinity of Rots.[56] Meeting his tanks as they returned, Wünsche was slightly wounded by shell fragments (splinter wounds and a slight concussion) when one of the Panzers was hit on its frontal armor.

Max Wünsche with bandaged head, shortly after being wounded.

[53]Meyer, K., *Grenadiere*, pp 227-28; Record Group 238: Records of Proceedings, p 595; Meyer, H., P-164, p 24.
[54]Meyer, H., *Kriegsgeschichte*, pp 101-102.
[55]Meyer, K., *Grenadiere*, p 228; Stacey, *The Victory Campaign*, p 137.

As the diarist of the Regina Rifles penned appropriately, it had been "a very hectic night."[57] And it had ended in stinging defeat for the 12th SS. The Panzer regiment alone had sustained 12 dead and 30 wounded; the platoons of Meyer's reconnaissance company 19 dead, 16 wounded and 9 missing. At least six tanks were a total loss. The SS infantry covering Rots (1st Company, 26th Regiment) also suffered heavy casualties when saturated by enemy tank and artillery fire.[58]

After the war Kurt Meyer attributed the failure of his attack to the shortage of infantry and to the firm Canadian hold on Norrey-en-Bessin, which had prevented cooperation between his forces and the right wing of Mohnke's regiment. Yet in assessing the countermoves of both Meyer's battlegroup and of the 26th SS Panzer Grenadier Regiment on June 8, 1944, it is hard to avoid the judgements of the official Canadian historian:[59]

> The German operations at this stage leave the impression of rather hasty and ineffective improvisation. The attacks were pressed with courage and determination but with no particular tactical skill. Brigadier Foster remarked that no use was made of the fact that the Reginas' flanks were exposed; instead, 'the enemy flung himself straight against the strongest points and utterly failed to exploit the undoubted weakness of his opponent's position.' The operations seem to have been locally conceived and control even on the divisional level was ineffective. The two major enterprises of 8 June, the attacks against Putot and Bretteville, were apparently independent and uncoordinated. The Germans threw in their troops piecemeal as the battalions arrived on the ground.

Although the fighting had gone badly for the 12th SS, it had been a wonderful day for divisional intelligence. A scouring of the battlefield between Authie and Franqueville that morning had yielded a copy of enemy radio procedures and codes–filched from a knocked-out Canadian tank. That evening, two Canadian armored cars motoring across a mined bridge on the eastern rim of Brouay were put out of action by an anti-tank gun of the 3rd Battalion of the 26th Regiment. While one of the vehicles burned up, incinerating its crew, the other remained virtually intact, although both the driver and his companion, a first lieutenant, were killed. From the second armored car the Germans salvaged a special code map of their own defenses in the Caen sector prior to D-Day. The two discoveries proved complementary and facilitated the monitoring and evaluation of enemy radio traffic by the radio intercept unit (Nachrichtennahaufklärungszug) of the 12th SS Panzer. "When we came to look at the map," recalls Hubert Meyer, the division's operations officer,[60]

[56]Record Group 238: Records of Proceedings, p 595.
[57]PAC. War Diary. The Regina Rifles. 9 June 1944.
[58]Meyer, H., Kriegsgeschichte, p 103.
[59]Stacey, The Victory Campaign, p 137.
[60]Meyer, K., Grenadiere, p 223; Alexander McKee, Last Round Against Rommel: Battle of the Normandy Beachhead (New York: The New American Library, Inc., 1966), pp 76-77.

we were astounded at the accuracy with which all the German fortifications were marked in, even the weapons, right down to light machine guns and mortars, were listed. And we were disgusted that our own intelligence had not been able to stop this sort of spying. We found out, later on, that a Frenchman had been arrested who admitted that he had spied for years in the Orne sector, appearing every day with his green grocer's van on the coastal road. We could clearly see on this map the result of his activities, and that of other spies also. What was useful for us, now, was that all the place names had been substituted, for instance, the Orne was marked as 'Orinoco,' and that the enemy continued to use these cover names in his radio transmissions for quite a while afterwards . . . Taken together with the radio codes also captured, we were able to understand much of the enemy's radio traffic, which helped partly to make up for the advantages he enjoyed . . . In effect it was espionage by radio.

*   *   *

On the evening of June 8th, General Geyr von Schweppenburg and his Panzer Group West staff finally assumed operational control of the Panzer divisions anchoring the eastern flank of the Seventh Army front.[61] Geyr's task, it will be remembered, was to plan and to execute the decisive counterstroke against the Allied beachhead. As he analyzed the situation confronting him, Geyr concluded that a major enemy offensive north of Caen was not imminent; Montgomery, always deliberate, would not budge before he had completed his meticulous preparations. Yet to await a resumption of the British offensive would be to forfeit the initiative once and for all. Thus, Geyr was determined to attack and to do so at once, before his opponent could act. From General Dollmann, the commander of Seventh Army, Geyr requested and was granted complete control of the operation.[62]

Geyr's plan was, perforce, a simple one, for the modest forces at his disposal (three Panzer divisions) as well as incipient shortages of fuel and ammunition rendered impractical a more ambitious design.[63] He would assemble his armor astride and to the west of the Caen - Luc-sur-Mer rail line; from there, the concentrated armored fist would advance directly north over gently falling terrain to the Channel coast, splitting the British - Canadian beachhead in twain. Because support from the Luftwaffe was not available, the attack would have to begin under cover of darkness. X-Hour was the night of June 10-11.[64]

---

[61]By Geyr's own account, he had intentionally not intervened earlier so as not to disrupt operations of the I SS Panzer Corps already in progress. Geyr, B-466, p 25.

[62]Ibid., pp 25-27.

[63]"From a theoretical standpoint," writes Geyr, "it was a tempting thought to push immediately into the British beachhead, deliver a blow there, and, screening that flank, to then turn against the eastern flank of the Americans with all available forces." But this, he notes, would have been a "textbook solution" (Hörsaallösung) with little prospect of success, for the Panzer Group lacked the resources for such a strategy. Thus, Geyr had no choice but to elect a more "ordinary" plan of action. Ibid., pp 27-28

[64]Ibid., pp 29-30

The next day (June 9th) Geyr drove out to the Abbey Ardenne, where, accompanied by Kurt Meyer, he climbed one of the abbey towers to reconnoiter the terrain for his big offensive.[65] The immediate area was well-known to the General from September 1940, when he had participated there in the abortive preparations for Operation Sealion--the proposed invasion of England. On Geyr's request, Meyer briefed his superior on the conditions at the front, and voiced his concern that the next few days would determine the outcome of the war. The latter remark elicited a clipped response: "My dear Meyer," Geyr said, "the war can only now be won through political means."[66] The General then outlined his plan of attack, pointing out his intent to insert the Panzer Lehr Division into the sector now occupied by the 26th Regiment (St. Manvieu - Putot - Brouay); the latter formation would be shifted to positions east of the Mue, between the left flank of Meyer's 25th Regiment and the little stream. Such a deployment, Geyr reasoned, would enable the left wing of his Panzer Group to lay its assault across the good tank country astride the Mue and the lower reaches of the Seulles, to its mouth at Courseulles.[67]

While still in the tower, Geyr looked on as tanks of the 12th SS moved up for a local counterattack. No sooner had they left the cover of a western suburb of Caen than a large group of enemy bombers appeared and showered them with bombs. The incident reinforced the General's conviction that only a night offensive offered any probability of success.[68]

What Geyr had observed was the armor of the Panzer regiment's 3rd Company preparing to attack Norrey-en-Bessin. For the Germans, the failure of the 12th SS to dislodge the enemy from the village the previous day was a cause for growing concern. The Canadian position there formed a salient in the division's line, threatening the right flank of the 2nd Battalion of the 26th Regiment. Elimination of the salient would remove this threat, and, more importantly, provide Panzer Group West with a superior staging area for its big

---

[65]According to Geyr, his visit to the abbey occurred early on June 10th. However, the tank movements of the 12th SS he witnessed there took place on the early afternoon of the 9th. In his memoirs, Kurt Meyer also places Geyr's visit on the 9th of June. Meyer, K., *Grenadiere*, p 229.

[66]When interrogated by the Canadians in August 1945, Meyer mentioned his meeting with the commander of Panzer Group West. According to Meyer, he and Geyr resolved to inform the High Command "in the strongest terms" that further resistance in Normandy against the overwhelming superiority of the enemy on land, at sea, and in the air was futile; furthermore, they would advise that steps be taken to pull back to the Seine, using the Panzer divisions as a screen to cover the withdrawal of the less mobile infantry units. Whether this advice was proffered to the High Command is unknown. Meyer, K., *Grenadiere*, p 229: PAC. Special Interrogation Report, Kurt Meyer, p 4.

[67]Geyr's plan, however, had already been overtaken by events, for the Panzer Lehr was moving into action north of Tilly and could not be pulled from the line. See Ritgen, *Die Geschichte der Panzer-Lehr-Division im Westen*, pp 111-112; Meyer, K., *Grenadiere*, p 229.

[68]It is unknown what losses, if any, were caused by this bombing attack. The incident is not mentioned in the in-house history of the tank company, *Die 3. Kompanie*. Geyr, B-466, p 30-31.

offensive, which now appeared imminent. Thus, the enemy hold on Norrey would have to be broken at once.

The author of the operation against Norrey on June 9th cannot be determined with certainty. Max Wünsche was still at the division's main dressing station recovering from his wounds; the staff of the Panther battalion had yet to reach the front. Most likely it was the always aggressive Kurt Meyer who conceived of the attack. In any case, the plan was to overrun the companies of the Regina Rifles defending the village by means of an armored thrust south of the Caen - Cherbourg rail line. The Panthers of the 3rd Panzer Company were to conduct the assault.[69]

ECPA

A camouflaged Panzer IV in position near Caen.

---

[69]The following account of this operation is gleaned largely from information provided the author by former members of the tank company. Particularly useful were two reports written after the war by Alois Morawetz. See also, *Die 3. Kompanie,* pp 36-40.

Crossing the Orne at Thury-Harcourt, the 3rd Panzer Company had arrived in the area west of Caen on June 8th, but not in time to participate in the attack on Bretteville-l'Orgueilleuse. To avoid the Allied fighter-bombers the tanks had moved mainly at night; shortages of fuel and the requirement for periodic maintenance had caused additional delays. From Thury-Harcourt the company had continued on via Carpiquet to Franqueville, passing through countryside littered with shot up Canadian tanks--the remains of the violent engagement less than 24 hours before. On instructions from Meyer the company then moved up to Authie, where it occupied a covering position on a forward slope near the Château de St. Louet, located due west of the village.

Later that day (June 8th), the interim company commander, Captain Lüdemann,[70] assembled his tank commanders for a briefing, which took place behind Lüdemann's command tank. While the conference was underway, Allied naval artillery unleashed a furious bombardment, which continued for perhaps half-an-hour. "Suddenly shells whistled in over our heads," remembers SS-Unterscharführer Alois Morawetz, at 19 the youngest tank commander in the 3rd Company:[71]

> They struck the entrance to the village behind us. To this day I remember precisely how, at the first sound of the approaching projectiles, we hurled ourselves to the ground. Following the initial salvo we all ran back to our tanks, climbed through the hatches and waited, come what may. It wasn't long until the shell fire screamed down again, striking a point some 100 yards in front of us . . . The next salvo hit about 40 yards from my tank. I looked about and gained the impression that the enemy fire was concentrated on my own vehicle. Nevertheless, I resolved not to be the first who abandoned his position. Then the earth heaved up once more, this time barely 15 yards behind me. I was now convinced that the enemy artillery observer was well-positioned and aiming his fire directly upon my tank. Earlier, I had seen a small vehicle disappear into a group of bushes about 800 yards away. A high explosive shell dispatched thither would have been the appropriate response, but we had orders not to shoot because of the supply situation. We fired up the motor and waited for the order to withdraw. Instead, the ground shook again and dirt poured in through our open turret. As we determined later, this shell landed just one or two yards to the right of the tank, causing damage to a wheel. If the enemy artillery men were skilled at their job, the next salvo would have to be a direct hit. Now I had to act. Suddenly I thought of history with all its dead heroes and that made my decision easier. My platoon leader, whose tank stood next to mine, had also

[70]No first name could be ascertained for Lüdemann. An experienced tank officer, he apparently had been transferred from the regular army to the Waffen SS. *Die 3. Kompanie.* p 36.

[71]Alois Morawetz, "Bericht über meine Zeit in der SS Panzerdivision 'Hitlerjugend' von März 1943 bis zum Beginn der Invasion im Juni 1944;" letter to the author from Alois Morawetz, October 25, 1981.

started his motor and begun to pull back. At once I ordered my driver to do the same. We did so just in time, for no sooner had we moved back some 15 yards than a shell struck the exact spot where we had been. It would have been a direct hit . . . Sometime later the shell fire ceased. When the quiet had continued for a while we climbed out and (inspected the damage, which proved to be minor) . . . Standing behind our tank we looked at one another and savored our good fortune.

Astonishingly, the bombardment caused no casualties, the tanks withdrawing to a less vulnerable position on a reverse slope immediately west of Authie. Following this unsettling experience the night passed peacefully along the company's front. To the west, however, the tank crews could make out the fearsome cacophony of battle, punctuated by the violent thud of tank fire. As they later learned, the engagement involved Meyer's battlegroup attempting to storm Bretteville-l'Orgueilleuse.

About 9:00 a.m. the next morning, a company of Panzer IVs rolled up and relieved the 3rd Company, which then motored west towards Rots. The Panthers had hardly begun to move when the enemy shell fire resumed, pulverizing the positions they had just vacated. Morawetz, travelling at the rear of his company, looked back and watched as the first Panzer IV exploded in flames. At Rots the tanks wheeled to the left and advanced south, crossing the Caen - Bayeux road at la Villeneuve. At the road crossing stood an unexpected, albeit dearly welcome visitor: SS-Obersturmführer von Ribbentrop. Von Ribbentrop had commanded the 3rd Panzer Company until wounded by an enemy fighter-bomber only days before the Normandy invasion. Without authorization, he had bolted from the military hospital in Bernay and returned to his

Charles W. Zvarich

SS-Obersturmführer Rudolf v. Ribbentrop.

company. However, with his arm still in a sling he was not yet ready to resume his command.[72]

Earlier, the company tank commanders had finally received their battle orders in the vicinity of la Villeneuve. The objective was Norrey–presumed to be held by strong enemy forces; the time of attack, 1:00 p.m. Infantry of the 26th Regiment was to furnish support by assaulting the village from the south.

Roughly 500 yards south of the Route Nationale 13, the road from la Villeneuve intersected the Caen - Cherbourg rail line. Rolling through the railroad underpass the tanks deployed in a line abreast at a right angle to the rail line. The three platoons (Züge) of the company were now facing west, tucked behind a reverse slope for concealment. Forming the right wing, the 3rd Platoon was flush against the high rail embankment.

It was nearly 12:30 p.m., and relatively quiet. As was customary for this time of day, few enemy fighter-bombers were in the sky.[73] A short time later the tanks lurched forward to attack. Traversing the gentle slope before them, they were soon crossing open, level ground dotted with fields and meadows. Swift, dangerously armed, and thickly armored,[74] the sahara-brown Panthers swept forward at high speed. Norrey lay to the southwest. At first all went well, the tanks advancing unmolested. One young tankman, his eyes riveted anxiously to the protective armored walls of his vehicle, would later recall that he felt safe so long as he could see no holes in them![75]

When the left wing had nearly reached the village, the line of tanks began to wheel southward. With the change in course, the 3rd Platoon left behind the protection of the rail embankment, uncovering its right flank. Well-hidden behind some hedgerows a group of enemy anti-tank guns were waiting, and

---

[72]Meyer, H., *Kriegsgeschichte,* p 106.

[73]Numerous German accounts of the Normandy battle confirm that the Allied fighter-bombers were mostly absent from the sky from about noontime until roughly 2:00 p.m. Perhaps this was due to refueling and rearming patterns, or maybe it was simply a rest period. See, for example, Kraemer, C-024, p 32.

[74]The Panther was arguably the best tank developed by the Germans during the Second World War. Its 75mm L/70 gun was longer and possessed a greater muzzle velocity (3,068 feet per second) than that of the Panzer IV. Highly maneuverable, the Panther had a maximum speed of about 30 miles per hour. The Panther(G), which equipped the 1st Battalion of the 12th SS Panzer Regiment, was the final production version of the tank. In comparison to the Panzer IV, however, the Panther did suffer some disadvantages. For example, the newer and more technically complex Panther suffered a greater incidence of mechanical breakdown. According to a former member of the 1st Panzer Battalion's maintenance echelon (Instandsetzungsstaffel), the motor of the Panther was particularly prone to problems. But under favorable conditions a new motor could be installed in four to five hour's time. Because it had a higher profile than the Panzer IV, the Panther was not as easy to conceal behind a bush or a hedgerow; when hit, it also caught fire with frightening regularity--a problem apparently attributable to the hydraulic fluid used in the Panther's steering mechanism. *Handbook on German Military Forces,* pp VII: 80-82; *Die 3. Kompanie,* p 38; Interview, Hellmuth Poch, June 4, 1983; Interview, Wolfgang Lincke, June 21, 1983; Interview, Heinz Berner, June 1-2 1983; Interview, Willy Kretzschmar, June 2, 1983; Interview, Willi Kändler, April 24, 1983.

[75]Fragebogen, Heinz Korte.

they loosed a withering broadside.[76] One after the other the five Panthers of the platoon burst into flames. One tank erupted so violently its turret lifted off. Many of the tankmen perished in their vehicles. The dazed survivors, almost without exception badly burned, struggled to work their way back to the relative security of the rail embankment; despite enemy machine gun and artillery fire that blanketed the area, some of them managed eventually to reach the rail underpass. Disdaining the intense Canadian fire, the company's medical orderly (Sanitätsdienstgrad), Siegfried Goose, scoured the battlefield in a sidecar motorcycle, gathering up the more seriously wounded. Goose's heroics came to a tragic end when enemy machine gun fire cut him down.[77]

Firing furiously, the remaining Panthers broke off the attack and jerked back in defeat. Max Wünsche, returning from the division's main dressing station, arrived just in time to see the company shot to pieces. "I could have screamed from rage and grief," he would later write.[78] Indeed, of the 12 tanks that had participated in the attack, seven had been destroyed; some 18 men were dead and about an equal number wounded.[79] Captain Lüdemann suffered a nervous breakdown and had to be relieved. Despite his wounds, von Ribbentrop again took command of the company.[80]

A distraught v. Ribbentrop (left) and Wünsche (right) leave the field for unit headquarters after watching the destruction of their armor on June 9th.

---

[76]Although German accounts mention the presence, and devastating effect, of the hostile anti-tank guns, it is also possible that tanks participated in the Canadian defense.

[77]*Die 3. Kompanie,* pp 37-38; letter to author from Wilhelm Fischer, February 17, 1982; Alois Morawetz, "Bericht über meine Zeit in der SS Panzerdivision 'Hitlerjugend;'" letter to author from Alois Morawetz, October 25, 1981.

[78]Meyer, H., *Kriegsgeschichte,* p 107.

[79]Most of the wounded had suffered second and third degree burns on the hands and face. *Die 3. Kompanie,* p 38; letter to author from Alois Morawetz, October 25, 1981; letter to author from Wilhelm Fischer, February 17, 1982.

[80]*Die 3. Kompanie,* p 38.

Some time later, several survivors of the 3rd Panzer Company were decorated with the Iron Cross for their participation in the assault. But medals offered little consolation for what had been a devastating setback. The company had fallen into a trap and suffered defeat before it could even get into action; again, the 1st Battalion of the 26th Regiment had failed to provide assistance. "The attack," concedes Hubert Meyer, "was without doubt an unfortunate undertaking from the start. Once again it had turned out that (in Normandy) Blitz tactics (Handstreiche) held scant prospect of success."[81]

* * *

On the morning of June 10th, the 12th SS would undertake a final attempt to crack the Canadian stranglehold on Norrey-en-Bessin.[82] This time the assign-

Woscidlo

This grenadier dashes across an open field dragging ammunition cans.

---

[81]The remnants of the 3rd Panzer Company were inserted on the left flank of the 12th SS at Fontenay-le-Pesnel. Here they fought for several days, and, by June 14th, had but four operational tanks. At that time, these were handed over to another company of the Panther Battalion. The survivors of the 3rd Company returned to Harcourt (a small village near Le Neubourg) from where, on June 6th, they had so confidently commenced their journey to the front. In remembrance of their fallen comrades, the company erected a large, carved wooden cross, into which were burned the names of the dead--an ironically appropriate memorial.

While in Harcourt the company was reorganized and rebuilt; receiving 17 replacement tanks, it would return to action in early July. It is noteworthy that, of the 250 German tanks destroyed in the first six weeks of the Normandy fighting, only 17 were replaced. The replacements must have been those received by the 3rd Company. Perhaps this was more than coincidence: the commander of the company, Rudolf von Ribbentrop, was the son of the German foreign minister. *Die 3. Kompanie,* pp 39-40; Wilmont, *The Struggle for Europe,* p 386.

[82]The German preoccupation with Norrey was such that, on the 9th, they had attempted to destroy the tower of the village's medieval church, from where the Canadian artillery observers had an excellent view deep into the sector of the 26th Regiment. An 88mm Flak gun was hustled into position near Carpiquet and took the tower under fire; despite several hits, the tower could not be completely destroyed. Meyer, H., P-164, p 28.

ment fell to the 12th SS Engineer Battalion, the only battalion of the division not yet committed to the line, and hence available for offensive action. Commanded by SS-Sturmbannführer Siegfried Müller,[83] the battalion received instructions to conduct a frontal assault on the village before dawn. To gain surprise, the operation was to begin without a preliminary bombardment, although both artillery and mortars were to furnish fire support in the final phase of the attack.

SS-Sturmbannführer
Siegfried Müller.

In the attenuating darkness the companies of the engineer battalion completed their final preparations. At 5:00 a.m.,[84] they began to advance from their jump-off positions directly behind the line of Mohnke's 1st Battalion. The assault troops went forward without firing a shot, crossing the coverless landscape that rose gently towards Norrey from the Mue. They had not gone far when intercepted by a furious enemy artillery and mortar barrage. In a spirited surge, some of the attackers contrived to evade the deadly gauntlet of fire and to push to within 100 yards of the Canadian entrenchments covering the village. Sprayed by small arms fire, they then sought cover in a sunken road (Hohlweg), from where they attempted to shoot back.

Some ten minutes later, the Canadian response slackened momentarily. Grasping the opportunity the battalion's 1st Company, commanded by First-Lieutenant and Knight's Cross holder Otto Toll, attempted to carry the enemy positions in a coup-de-main. Struck by violent gusts of machine gun fire the attack was quickly broken off, the survivors falling back to the sunken road, which was soon filled with badly wounded soldiers. Among the wounded lay

---

[83]The 29-year-old Müller entered the Waffen SS in October 1935. His father had been killed at Verdun in May 1916. During the war, Müller had fought with the SS "Totenkopf" Division in France and Russia before his transfer to the 12th SS. His decorations included the Iron Cross first and second class. Later, for his participation in the Ardennes offensive in December 1944, he would receive the Knight's Cross. SS Personalakten, Siegfried Müller.

[84]BAMA. Tagebuch Divisions-Begleit-Kompanie. 10.6.1944.

Woscidlo

Oberleutnant Otto Toll, who was attached to the 12th SS Panzer Engineer Battalion.

Otto Toll, who, despite the frantic efforts of the battalion doctor to save him, bled to death.

According to the war diary of the divisional escort company, the attack of the engineer battalion had completely collapsed by 10:00 a.m.--beaten back by the artillery, tanks, mortars and machine guns of an abundantly equipped opponent. By evening, the badly mutilated battalion (28 dead, 42 wounded and 10 missing) had withdrawn to its original assembly area.[85] For the 12th SS,[86]

> four attempts to capture Norrey, a cornerstone (Eckpfeiler) of the Canadian defense, had failed. Together with Bretteville, the village formed a blocking position (in the path of the planned offensive of Panzer Group West). Therefore, repeated efforts were made via different approaches to take these positions. They failed because of insufficient forces, insufficient preparation due to real or imagined time pressures, and, not least of all, because of the bravery of the defenders . . . who were well-entrenched and effectively supported by strong artillery, anti-tank defense and tanks.

*　　*　　*

Throughout the opening days of the Normandy campaign, Field Marshal Rommel had tirelessly toured the front to keep his finger firmly on the pulse of the battle. Early on June 10th he once more departed his headquarters at la Roche-Guyon and headed for the killing zone. The sky above him soon teemed

---

[85]Meyer, H., *Kriegsgeschichte,* pp 109-10; Meyer, H., P-164, p 28; BAMA. Tagebuch Divisions-Begleit-Kompanie. 10.6.1944.
[86]Meyer, H., *Kriegsgeschichte,* p 110.

with enemy fighter-bombers. Forced to abandon his vehicle and dive for cover some 30 times, he never did make it to the commander of the I SS Panzer Corps, Sepp Dietrich. That afternoon, however, he contrived to reach Geyr at Panzer Group West headquarters, nestled in an orchard at la Caine (12 miles southwest of Caen).

Together they studied the maps spread out in Geyr's headquarters bus and discussed the counterattack that now seemed so urgently necessary. It was not a happy exchange. In the presence of his operations staff, Geyr talked at some length on the situation that confronted him. Gasoline and ammunition, he told Rommel, were in short supply; the Nebelwerfer brigade and the anti-aircraft corps promised him had yet to reach the battlefield. Meanwhile, the enemy pressure across his front was increasing steadily, while the Panzer Group, he said, was being thrown onto the defensive. The Allied air forces dominated the skies deep into the interior of France, blasting bridges, taking out rail lines, and strafing roadways with almost no regard for French civilians. The results of the conference were predictable–the attack had to be postponed.[87]

Rommel at the Normandy front.

Leo Frhr. Geyr v. Schweppenburg, here a Colonel.

[87]BAMA. 63181/1. KTB Panzer-Armeeoberkommando 5. 10.6.1944; T-84/281/000824. KTB Heeresgruppe B; Geyr, B-466, pp 31-32; Irving, *The Trail of the Fox,* pp 379-80.

Barely an hour after Rommel's departure, formations of the Allied Second Tactical Air Force virtually annihilated Geyr's headquarters. Four squadrons of rocket firing Typhoons, 40 aircraft in all, opened the attack, followed by 71 Mitchell light bombers with a Spitfire escort. Between 9:19 and 9:21 p.m., the bombers saturated the target area with 436 500-pound bombs, leaving in their wake large volumes of smoke and flame.[88] The entire operations staff was wiped out; all told, at least 32 men perished in the air strike, including Geyr's Chief of Staff, Brigadier-General Edler von Dawans.[89] Geyr himself escaped with minor wounds, but was badly shaken. The devastating attack was clearly the result of Ultra–the spectacular Allied code-breaking success of the Second World War–which, by the morning of the 10th, had twice reported the location of Panzer Group headquarters to concerned Allied commanders, the second time with pinpoint accuracy.[90]

The dead soldiers "were buried in one of the bomb craters over which the Germans were to raise a huge cross of polished oak, emblazoned with eagle and swastika."[91] On June 13th, Geyr and his shattered headquarters group withdrew to Paris to recuperate; they would be back in action within a fortnight.[92]

* * * * *

SS-Hauptsturmführer Wilhelm Beck, serving as liaison between I SS Panzer Corps and Geyr's headquarters, was killed during the June 10 Allied air attack at la Caine.

---

[88]Geyr, B-466, p 32; Michael J.F. Bowyer, *2 Group R.A.F.--A Complete History, 1936-1954* (London: Faber and Faber), pp 373-74.

[89]The operations staff suffered 17 dead and one missing; the signal detachment (Pz.Gr.Nachr.Abt. 676) 12 dead; the guard company three dead. Among the fatalities was the liaison officer from the I SS Panzer Corps, SS-Hauptsturmführer Wilhelm Beck. A Knight's Cross holder, Beck had commanded the 2nd Panzer Company of the 12th SS for a period before the Normandy invasion. BAMA. KTB Panzer-Armeeoberkommando 5. 10.6.1944.

[90]The time of transmission of the second Ultra signal was 4:39 a.m., June 10th; the signal identified la Caine as the headquarters of Panzer Group West as of the evening of June 9th. Information provided by Ultra was based on decryptments of intercepted German radio communications. For a detailed history of the role of Ultra in Normandy see, Ralph Bennett, *Ultra in the West--The Normandy Campaign, 1944-45* (London: Hutchinson & Co., Ltd., 1979); Public Record Office. Ultra Signal 7225.

[91]Wilmont, *The Struggle for Europe*, p 303.

[92]BAMA. KTB Panzer-Armeeoberkommando 5. 13.6.1944, 27.6.1944.

Chapter 9
OF FRIGHT AND FURY
The Murder of Canadian Prisoners
by the 12th SS Panzer Division (June 7-17, 1944)

As a result of the investigations made by the Special Inquiries
Section G-1, SHAEF, covering the period following the Allied
landings in Normandy, it was found that the conduct of the 12th
SS Panzer Division (Hitler-Jugend) presented a consistent pattern
of brutality and ruthlessness.

(Supplementary Report, SHAEF Court of Inquiry)

I have a clear conscience.

(Kurt Meyer)

On the morning of June 8, 1944, SS-Sturmmann Jan Jesionek, a driver and
dispatch rider in the reconnaissance company of the 25th SS Panzer Grenadier
Regiment, was on patrol near Caen. Suddenly one of the vehicles in the patrol
blew up, seriously injuring its occupants, who were evacuated to the regimental aid post. Afterwards a Wehrmacht sentry emerged from some bushes and
informed the SS soldiers that they had stumbled into a friendly minefield. The
commander of the patrol, SS-Untersturmführer Fehling, severely upbraided
the sentry and accused him of falling asleep; to replace the destroyed vehicle,
Fehling dispatched Jesionek to the nearby Abbey Ardenne to pick up a motorcycle.

Reaching his destination Jesionek found the motorcycle out of order, and
for the time being could do nothing. A short time later he looked on as seven
Canadian prisoners, guarded by two soldiers of the 25th Regiment, were escor-
ted by them onto the Abbey grounds and hustled into a stable off an adjoining
courtyard. One of the guards asked the 17-year-old Jesionek if he knew where
they might find the regimental commander. Only minutes before the prisoners
were brought in, low-flying aircraft had attacked the abbey, prompting Kurt
Meyer to order that all staff vehicles and motorcycles be concealed at once
within the protective walls of the chapel. Thinking that Meyer was probably at
the chapel, Jesionek suggested the guard follow him there.

The two men walked over to the chapel, where Meyer was standing. The
guard approached his commander and reported the arrival of the captured
Canadians. Visibly angered, Meyer replied, "Why do you bring prisoners to

the rear? They only eat up our rations." Meyer spoke briefly with a nearby officer, but in a low tone of voice that could not be heard by Jesionek, and then, so that all present could hear, said, "In the future no more prisoners are to be taken!"

Following the discussion with Meyer, the officer left with the guard and walked towards the stable where the prisoners were. Jesionek, meanwhile, had retrieved a towel and some soap from one of the vehicles and followed to the courtyard, where he hoped to wash at a water pump close to a concrete pool and an archway leading into a garden. Directed away from the pump, he went instead to wash at the pool.

From there he could see the officer to whom Meyer had just spoken interrogating the prisoners one at a time in English:[1]

> One of the prisoners had tears in his eyes, and the officer laughed at him in a sneering manner. The officer seemed to be enjoying himself and frequently burst out laughing as he spoke to the prisoners. He took their papers from them and returned to the chapel.
>
> The guard who had spoken to Meyer took up a position at the (archway) leading to the garden or park. Each of the seven prisoners was then called by name and in turn had to walk from the stable entrance to where the guard was at the (archway). They were then directed up some steps and into the garden. Here each made a left turn, and as he did so an Unterscharführer, who had previously gone into the garden and was awaiting the prisoners, shot him in the back of the head.
>
> As each of the prisoners came out of the stable, he shook hands with the others before walking into the garden. They all seemed to know what was about to happen, and the sound of the shots and occasionally a scream could be clearly heard.

When the shooting was over, Jesionek walked to the pump by the archway, where he saw the SS-Unterscharführer reload his pistol as he emerged from the garden. Jesionek went into the garden and observed the dead bodies of the seven Canadian soldiers, which were lying in a large pool of blood. Wounded that evening during Meyer's assault on Bretteville-l'Orgueilleuse and hospitalized, he did not know what was done with the bodies.[2]

*　　*　　*

---

[1]MacDonald, B.J.S., *The Trial of Kurt Meyer*, p 110.

[2]The Allies first learned of the murders on April 22, 1945, when, during a routine screening of German prisoners at the POW camp in Chartres, France, Technical Sergeant Siegmund Stern of the U.S. Military Police interrogated Jesionek, then a prisoner in the camp. A subsequent Canadian investigation of the incident not only confirmed Jesionek's story in most of its details but revealed that a total of 20 Canadian soldiers had been murdered and buried at the Abbey Ardenne following their capture and interrogation. Eighteen of the murders occurred on June 7th and 8th; the final two on June 17th. Prior to the arrival of the Canadian investigative team at the abbey, the bodies had been removed to a military cemetery. According to MacDonald, a member of the team and later the prosecutor at Kurt Meyer's trial, the bodies were then exhumed and "identified by discs which were still on them . . . The pathologist stated that the head wounds were produced by single bullets fired into the base of the

The murders at the Abbey Ardenne were not an isolated event, rather they were typical of behavior all too common to the 12th SS Panzer Division during the initial days of the Normandy campaign. In fact, SHAEF (Supreme Headquarters Allied Expeditionary Force) Court of Inquiry[3] and Canadian investigations established that, from June 7-17, 1944,[4] members of the division murdered at least 134 Canadian prisoners of war in separate incidents involving the 25th and 26th SS Panzer Grenadier Regiments, the 12th SS Reconnaissance Battalion and the 12th SS Engineer Battalion.[5] The normal method of execution in individual shootings was a single aimed pistol shot fired into the base of the skull; executions by firing squads were carried out with Schmeisser machine pistols.

The majority of the killings took place following the first flush of combat. On June 7th, soldiers of the 3rd Battalion (Milius) of the 25th Regiment murdered in and about the villages of Authie and Buron some 23 Canadians after their capture. Most of the victims belonged to the North Nova Scotia Highlanders and the Sherbrooke Fusiliers; some of them had already been wounded and disabled. The bodies were left unburied, and in some cases moved deliberately into roadways where passing tanks and other vehicles crushed them. The supplementary report of the SHAEF Court of Inquiry provides a detailed record of these murders, which included the following:[6]

> A prisoner, while lying unarmed and helpless owing to a serious wound, was bayoneted and shot to death by a number of soldiers of (the 12th SS), one of whom is believed to have been an officer.

---

skull, by multiple bullet wounds, or by the application of a blunt instrument such as a club or rifle butt." Macdonald, B.J.S., *The Trial of Kurt Meyer*, pp 64, 109-111; Record Group 238: Records of Proceedings. Exhibit B2. Statement of Jan Jesionek. April 22, 1945.

[3]Soon after the invasion of Normandy reports of suspected killings of unarmed Allied prisoners began to reach British and Canadian headquarters. Most of these reports emanated from the sector defended by the 12th SS Panzer Division, and they prompted Montgomery to appoint a Special Court of Inquiry to investigate them. The initial investigations concerned alleged atrocities at the Château d'Audrieu (12th SS Reconnaissance Battalion) and at Mouen (12th SS Engineer Battalion). Gradually, reports of additional shootings began to reach the Court, and on August 20, 1944, a Standing Court of Inquiry was appointed to examine them. Major-General R.W. Barker (U.S. Army), Assistant Chief of Staff, G-1 Division at SHAEF, headed the Court. Record Group 218: Supplementary Report SHAEF Court of Inquiry. p III: 8.

[4]Few murders are recorded after mid-June. By that time, the 3rd Canadian and 12th SS Divisions had experienced a lull in the fighting and few prisoners were taken by either side. It must have also been apparent to the perpetrators that the battle was going badly for them; to continue to shoot unarmed Allied prisoners would only invite retaliation should they themselves be captured. Allied planes, moreover, had dropped leaflets telling of the murder of Canadian POWs and promising punishment after the war for those responsible.

[5]Several British soldiers and at least one American pilot were also shot following capture by the 12th SS. Three additional American prisoners, also pilots, were killed near the Caen - Falaise road just north of Argentan on June 7th. From available evidence, it appears that soldiers of the 12th SS were responsible for the latter murders as well. Record Group 218: Supplementary Report SHAEF Court of Inquiry. pp IV: 22-23, 28.

[6]Ibid.; pp IV: 18-20.

A prisoner, while unarmed and with hands up in token of surrender, was denied quarter and shot to death.

A prisoner, while being searched and otherwise unarmed, was found to have on his person a grenade which he had evidently had no opportunity to discard. He was thereupon shot by one of his guards. While lying on the road dying, he was kicked and some 15 minutes later dispatched by shots fired into the head . . .

A prisoner, while standing in line with other prisoners some distance behind the battlefront, unarmed and with both hands above the head, was shot in the stomach for turning his head and died two days later at Caen . . .

Eight prisoners after capture were marched behind the lines and were sitting under guard at the side of a street in the village of Authie. They were told to remove their helmets, and the guards then stepped into the street and with automatic weapons shot all the prisoners dead . . .

A large number of Allied Prisoners of War were being marched in column along a road in the vicinity of Caen, when a passing German truck was intentionally and at high speed driven into the column. Two of the prisoners were killed and another seriously injured.

The 26th Regiment did not get into action until the morning of June 8th. During the assault on Putot-en-Bessin the 5th and 7th Companies of the regiment's 2nd Battalion took between 25-30 Canadian prisoners, mostly, no doubt, from the Royal Winnipeg Rifles. The captives were evacuated by their guards through 2nd Battalion headquarters at le Mesnil-Patry, where another group of prisoners joined them, making a total of forty all ranks.

That evening the Germans marched their prisoners south, towards the Caen - Fontenay-le-Pesnel road. The guards were the same and were commanded by an SS-Oberscharführer (NCO). Along the way, they encountered an officer in a camouflaged vehicle. The party then halted while the SS-Oberscharführer apparently asked for instructions. Annoyed, the officer motioned in a southerly direction, giving some of the prisoners the impression that he had ordered their execution.

They continued to march until within 100 yards of the Caen road. At that point the SS guards directed the prisoners into a field, instructing them to sit close together--with the wounded in the center--and to face east. After an armored column had passed on the road, a half-track vehicle turned into the field, disgorging a number of soldiers toting Schmeisser machine pistols. Among the newcomers were two officers. There was a consultation with the guards, who then also equipped themselves with Schmeissers. Forming a line, the Germans advanced menacingly towards the prisoners, who were still seated and resting, and opened fire. Thirty-five of the Canadians died in the ensuing massacre. Five of the prisoners, however, managed to escape. Their suspicions aroused by what they had seen and heard, they had resolved to make a run for it should their estimate of the guards' intentions prove correct. When the shooting started the five men bolted into a wheat field and were eventually recaptured by other German troops, who evacuated the men to prisoner of war camps, where they remained until the end of the war.[7]

Between 2:00 and 5:00 p.m., June 8th, 19 more Canadian POWs were shot to death, this time by members of the 12th SS Reconnaissance Battalion. The shootings took place near battalion headquarters at the Château d'Audrieu–two groups of three prisoners each gunned down in an adjacent wood, and a third group (13 men of the 9th Platoon, "A" Company, Royal Winnipeg Rifles) murdered by their escort within 100 yards of the battalion command post. Bremer's driver, SS-Oberscharführer Leopold Stun, commanded some of the firing squads, which consisted of motorcycle dispatch riders attached to the headquarters.[8]

*　　*　　*

If it is the responsibility of the historian to record such unhappy events, it is perhaps better left to men of greater wisdom and deeper understanding of the human heart to interpret them. Still, a brief analysis of the battlefield atrocities of the 12th SS can offer a measure of insight into their origins. Prior to his sentencing by a Canadian military court, Kurt Meyer had this to say about the murders committed by his division:[9]

> I have here during these proceedings been given an insight into things which, in the aggregate, were unknown to me up to now. I wish to state to the Court here that these deeds were not committed by the young soldier. I am convinced of it, that in the Division there were elements, who, due to the year-long battles, due to five years of war, had in a certain respect become brutalized.

Meyer's words are plausible enough, and they place responsibility for the murders where it principally belongs--with former members of the Leibstandarte SS Adolf Hitler (LAH) serving in the 12th SS. Because of the many killings, in which officers and NCOs participated, the SHAEF Court reached the "irresistible" conclusion that a policy of denying quarter or executing prisoners after interrogation, if not actually ordered, was at least tolerated by regimental and divisional commanders of the 12th SS.[10] The Court recommended that Kurt Meyer, Wilhelm Mohnke, Karl-Heinz Milius, Gerhard Bremer,

---

[7]MacDonald, B.J.S., *The Trial of Kurt Meyer*, pp 20-22.

[8]According to German witnesses, SS-Hauptsturmführer Reitzenstein ordered at least some of the killings in retaliation for the wounding of the battalion commander, Bremer, by artillery fire. But the Court of Inquiry concluded that Bremer was most likely still at the château and had not yet been wounded when the murders took place. One French witness recalled that the German commander wore the Knight's Cross about his neck. This could only have been Bremer. Other civilian witnesses pointed out that there was no artillery fire in the vicinity of the château until about 6:30 p.m., by which time the executions were completed. MacDonald, B.J.S., *The Trial of Kurt Meyer*, pp 17-19; Record Group 218: Supplementary Report SHAEF Court of Inquiry. pp IV: 20-22.

[9]MacDonald, B.J.S., *The Trial of Kurt Meyer*, p 193.

[10]From records of the Court, it is also evident that the impression was widespread within the 12th SS that British and Canadian forces would take no SS prisoners--an impression promoted by some officers and NCOs of the division. See for example, Record Group 218: Supplementary Report SHAEF Court of Inquiry. Exhibit 5. Testimony of Friedrich Torbanisch.

Siegfried Müller, and Heinz Prinz be brought to trial for failure to comply with the "laws and usages of war" and the terms of the Geneva Conventions of 1929.[11] Witt,[12] Meyer, Mohnke and Bremer, of course, as well as many other officers and NCOs in the 12th SS, were veterans of the LAH. In Mohnke's case the evidence is persuasive that, on at least one occasion, he personally ordered the shooting of Canadian prisoners of war and then watched while the order was carried out.[13] Although less unequivocal, Meyer's behavior at the Abbey Ardenne on the morning of June 8th points to the conclusion that he, too, most likely ordered similar shootings. Moreover, witnesses to murders in the Authie area noted the Adolf Hitler insignia worn on the left arm of the perpetrators-- an insignia worn within the 12th SS only by veterans of the Leibstandarte.

Another explanation is that the murders took place simply because the 12th SS was an elite formation of the Waffen SS, with an aggressive style of combat and an uncompromising attitude vis-à-vis its opponents. The battlefield atrocities of the Waffen SS are well catalogued,[14] yet with the possible exception of Russia, where Hitler acted out his fantasy of an ideological Vernichtungskrieg, and where such atrocities were commonplace on both sides, it is not clear that the soldiers of the Waffen SS were more prone to criminal behavior than those of the Wehrmacht, or of the Anglo-American armies for that matter.[15]

---

[11]Of these six men, it appears that only Kurt Meyer ever stood trial. Prinz was killed in August 1944; Mohnke ended up in Russian captivity, where he remained until October 1955. For reasons unknown, Bremer, Milius and Müller never went to trial. The British, however, placed the commander of the 2nd Battalion of the 26th Regiment, Bernhard Siebken, on trial in Hamburg in 1948 for the murder of several Canadian prisoners at le Mesnil-Patry; despite protests from the historian Liddell Hart against such war crimes trials, they executed Siebken on January 20, 1949. Record Group 218: Supplementary Report SHAEF Court of Inquiry. p III: 16; Meyer, H., *Kriegsgeschichte*, Bd. II, pp 558-60.

[12]Fritz Witt was killed at his headquarters in Venoix on June 14, 1944. See Chapter Ten, p 205.

[13]The incident occurred on June 11, 1944, in the vicinity of Mohnke's headquarters. After Mohnke had interrogated the three prisoners (shouting and gesticulating in an angry manner) he had them shot at the edge of a deep bomb crater, where the Allies later discovered them. MacDonald, B.J.S., *The Trial of Kurt Meyer*, pp 27-28.

[14]Most of the atrocities committed by the Waffen SS occurred on the eastern front. Notable cases in the western theater include La Paradis, France, where, in 1940, the 3rd SS Division "Totenkopf" (Death Head) massacred some 100 British prisoners. On June 10, 1944, soldiers of the 2nd SS Division "Das Reich" killed all 642 inhabitants of the French village of Oradour-sur-Glâne, near Limoges, in retaliation for the fatal shooting of one of their officers by a French resistance fighter. Most of the unfortunate villagers, including women and children, were burned alive in the village church. Of course, from the American point of view, the worse Waffen SS war crime took place near Malmédy, Belgium, where, in December 1944, elements of the Leibstandarte Panzer Division killed some 90 American prisoners. For an overview of these and other examples of Waffen SS atrocities see Stein, *The Waffen SS*, pp 250-81.

[15]Only a small fraction of the nearly 1,000,000 men who served with the Waffen SS were involved in any known war crimes: "All officers and noncommissioned officers of the Waffen SS were kept in prison camps for as long as four years after the war. After their release, these men were haled before German de-Nazification courts; 99 percent were found to be free of personal guilt." Ibid., pp 251, 281.

Woscidlo

The absolute exhaustion of these young dispatch riders is clearly evident. Exhaustion, plus frustration and rage from seeing comrades killed by air attacks and naval bombardment, probably caused much of the retaliation.

At a more fundamental level, the significance of pure frustration and rage as a cause of the murders must not be overlooked. After the war Kurt Meyer admitted openly that the fighting in Normandy was the most difficult he had ever experienced.[16] From the beginning the German soldiers there faced unprecedented challenges. Harried by the enemy air forces, blasted by the heavy guns of the invasion fleet and grappling on the ground with a determined and numerically superior opponent, it is not surprising that some Germans retaliated against Allied prisoners. Such behavior, writes Alexander McKee,[17]

> (is) rooted in the twin springs of fright and fury. In shock, and horror, and revulsion, and the overwhelming impulse to hit back; to assert the naked human personality in the screaming wilderness of bombardment. And once so asserted, the pent-up nerves are momentarily eased and relaxed. In these circumstances killing becomes an act of macabre pleasure, having no moral, and certainly no political, significance. It is so very easy, with all restraint removed.

For the veterans of the LAH, their fighting techniques honed in the crucible of the eastern front, the shooting of prisoners of war signified nothing out of the ordinary. Yet despite the murders committed by the 12th SS, the great majority of its soldiers fought with dignity and within the rules of war throughout

---

[16]PAC. Special Interrogation Report, Kurt Meyer, p 10.
[17]McKee, *Last Round Against Rommel,* p 188.

the Normandy campaign. In some instances, officers from the division intervened to prevent the killing of prisoners; on occasion, soldiers of the 12th SS even treated their opponent in a chivalrous manner.[18]

War crimes, of course, are not the exclusive province of any one nation, army, or organization. Many Canadian soldiers admit freely that their own forces were also guilty of shooting enemy prisoners in Normandy.[19] Allied aircraft often attacked clearly marked German Red Cross vehicles or military field hospitals;[20] on occasion, they even strafed columns of French civilians attempting to flee the battle zones.[21]

*   *   *

For Kurt Meyer the war came to an abrupt end on September 7, 1944, when American troops captured him near Liège, Belgium.[22] Later interrogated at

---

[18]For example, following the bitter engagement at le Mesnil-Patry on June 11th, soldiers of the 12th SS did not interfere with Canadian ambulances and Red Cross personnel as they collected their wounded from the battlefield. Hans Siegel, "Die zweite Schlacht um Caen, 11.-16. Juni 1944."

[19]Questionnaires completed for the author by veterans of the 3rd Canadian Infantry Division confirm that German prisoners, particularly those from the Waffen SS, were sometimes shot. In his memoir Kurt Meyer states that on June 9th he discovered a group of dead German soldiers (four or five men), who apparently had not died in battle, on the rail line south of Rots. The soldiers, he asserts, belonged to the 21st Panzer Division and to the staff of the 12th SS; they had all been shot through the head.

One incident well-documented by German sources concerned the Panzer Lehr Division. On June 8th, a group of soldiers belonging to the staff of the Panzer Lehr's artillery regiment were conducting a reconnaissance on a small height (probably Hill 102) just south of Cristot. The group consisted of the regimental commander, Colonel Luxenburger; one of his battalion commanders, Major Zeissler; the regimental adjutant, Captain Count Clary-Aldringen, and some six other personnel. Without warning, two British patrols (armored cars) surprised the Germans and took them captive. The patrols belonged to "C" Squadron of the Inns of Court Regiment (I British Corps), and had orders to advance far behind enemy lines to destroy bridges across the Orne. Thereafter, two British officers beat Luxenburger unconscious and bound him to the front of a scout car for use as a target butt (Kugelfang). When the British scout cars attempted to make their way back through German lines, an anti-tank gun destroyed them. Luxenburger, who had already lost an arm during the First World War, suffered fatal wounds and died several days later at a German field hospital. The fate of the remainder of his group remains unclear. According to Hubert Meyer, the British gunned down the Germans, killing them all with the exception of Captain Clary, who, although badly wounded, managed to crawl to safety, where soldiers of the 12th SS (2nd Battalion, 26th Regiment) found him and administered first aid. Unfortunately, Ritgen, the most recent chronicler of the Panzer Lehr, sheds little light on the incident, although he does mention that Luxenburger was "struck down" (niederschlagen). The other men, he states, managed to escape. Meyer, K., *Grenadiere*, p 230; Meyer, H., *Kriegsgeschichte*, pp 96-97; Meyer, H., P-164, p 26; Kurowski, *Die Panzer Lehr Division*, pp 44-45; Ritgen, *Die Geschichte der Panzer-Lehr-Division*, p 109.

[20]Veterans of the 12th SS told the author that such attacks were quite frequent. According to Kurt Meyer, the division went so far as to paint its ambulances (Sankas) snow white--a measure that had no deterrent effect. Meyer, K., *Grenadiere*, p 221.

[21]See for example, Heinrich von Lüttwitz, B-257. "2. Panzer Division in Normandie." pp 23-24; Pickert, B-597, pp 37-38.

[22]For a dramatic account of Meyer's initial capture by Belgian partisans on September 6th, and seizure the next day by the Americans, see Meyer, K., *Grenadiere*, pp 313-21.

length by the SHAEF Court of Inquiry, Meyer at first denied all knowledge of the murders committed by the 12th SS, and expressed shock and bewilderment over them:[23]

Question: Now do you say that you had no knowledge whatever of any of these atrocities at the time?

Answer: I did not know anything of it at the time; I have only just heard about it . . .

Question: I show you these volumes (President indicates 5 bound reports of Court of Inquiry) which contain evidence given by men of your own division, civilians and escaped prisoners who saw these things, evidence of medical experts who have examined the bodies, and there can be no doubt what we have found actually occurred.

Answer: From my division? In what sector can these things have taken place? I find it impossible to believe . . .

Question: You appreciate that someone has to be responsible for what we know was done . . . Now where does the responsibility lie?

Answer: If these things did occur, the senior officers knew nothing about them.

Question: You may take it that they did occur. Now who were the responsible persons?

Answer: I can only repeat what I said before. The Court must judge (for) itself. I have a clear conscience.

Suddenly, on October 26, 1945, shortly before his trial was to begin, Meyer changed his mind and decided to make a new statement at once.[24] In his new statement he first corrected some tactical information he had provided his captors.[25] He had, he said, discussed the information with Max Wünsche, who was also a prisoner, and wanted to make it more accurate. But Meyer was more concerned about his answer to a question during an interrogation on October 15th:[26]

Question: Was it reported to you by anyone that Allied prisoners had died at your Headquarters and that it was necessary to bury them there?

Answer: No.

He now stated that, on June 10th or 11th, while at the Abbey Ardenne, two of his officers had come to see him. They were SS-Sturmbannführer Dr. Erich

---

[23]Record Group 218: Supplementary Report SHAEF Court of Inquiry. Exhibit 8, p 47; Exhibit 9, pp 33-34.

[24]On October 15th, Meyer had been informed in detail of Jan Jesionek's evidence against him, and advised that he would be put on trial. At the time, however, Meyer had still denied any knowledge of the murders committed at the Abbey Ardenne. MacDonald, B.J.S., *The Trial of Kurt Meyer*, p 141.

[25]Meyer, it seems, could talk endlessly about his military exploits, and he accompanied the Court on numerous tours of the Caen battlefields, providing expositions on his activities there. "This," admits MacDonald, "while interesting at first, eventually became rather tiresome." Ibid., p 141.

[26]Ibid., pp 66-67

Gatternig, the regimental doctor, and SS-Obersturmführer Dr. Stift, Meyer's dental officer and steady companion. The officers, he said, reported to him the presence of some 18 or 19 unburied bodies of Canadian soldiers in the little garden on the abbey grounds; the soldiers appeared to have died from head wounds. Meyer was at first incredulous and ordered his adjutant, SS-Obersturmführer Schümann, to investigate. Schümann quickly confirmed the report, and Meyer then made a personal inspection. After viewing the bodies he ordered them buried, and directed his adjutant and SS-Hauptsturmführer Dr. Tiray, the legal officer, to conduct an investigation of the killings. Meyer also reprimanded Schümann,[27] reminding him that he, as the regimental adjutant, was responsible for everything that went on at the headquarters, and that he would be relieved of his post. Finally, Meyer reported the entire affair to Fritz Witt, who was extremely angry and ordered his subordinate to determine who was responsible. Such was Meyer's story.[28]

At 10:30 a.m., December 10, 1945, Meyer's trial by Canadian Military Court got underway at the former German naval barracks in Aurich, Germany. The reconstructed conference room of the barracks, "with its beautiful panelling, pictures and chandeliers compared favorably in the dignity of its appointments with court rooms anywhere." In an ironic twist, Major-General H.W. Foster, who had commanded the Canadian 7th Brigade in Normandy, served as president of the court. Lieutenant-Colonel B.J.S. MacDonald was the prosecutor, while Lieutenant-Colonel Maurice W. Andrew was appointed Meyer's defense counsel.[29] The judge advocate arraigned the accused and the first charge sheet was read to Meyer, who through an interpreter pleaded not guilty to all charges:[30]

First Charge Sheet

The accused, Brigadeführer Kurt Meyer,[31] an officer in the former Waffen SS, then a part of the Armed Forces of the German Reich, now in the charge of 4 Battalion, Royal Winnipeg Rifles, Canadian Army Occupation Force, Canadian Army Overseas, is charged with:

---

[27]Schümann, no doubt, was the staff officer (referred to by Jesionek) who had received instructions from Meyer and then interrogated the seven Canadian prisoners shot at the abbey on June 8th.

[28]Meyer repeated this story during the trial. Record Group 238: Records of Proceedings, pp 602-604.

[29]A native of Nova Scotia, Lieutenant-Colonel MacDonald had practiced law in Windsor, Ontario before the war. In 1939 he volunteered for active military service and rose rapidly through the ranks; in 1944 he commanded an infantry battalion in Normandy. His appointment as chief prosecutor of war criminals for the Canadian forces followed in early 1945. Lieutenant-Colonel Andrew, who would conduct an admirable defense of Kurt Meyer, was the commander of the Perth Regiment and a lawyer in civilian life. Tony Foster, *Meeting of Generals* (Toronto: Methuen, 1986) pp xxii, 456.

[30]There was a second charge sheet that the prosecution did not proceed with; it concerned Meyer's responsibility for the execution of seven Canadian POWs at Mouen on June 17th, after he had become division commander. His responsibility here "was more remote, and the convening officer authorized the prosecution to nolle pros this charge." MacDonald, B.J.S., *The Trial of Kurt Meyer*, pp 89-90.

[31]Meyer had been promoted to SS-Brigadeführer on September 1, 1944.

First Charge: Committing a war crime, in that he in the Kingdom of Belgium and Republic of France during the year 1943 and prior to the 7th day of June 1944, when Commander of 25 SS Panzer Grenadier Regiment, in violation of the laws and usages of war, incited and counselled troops under his command to deny quarter to Allied troops.

Second Charge: Committing a war crime, in that he in the Province of Normandy and Republic of France on or about the 7th day of June 1944, as Commander of 25 SS Panzer Grenadier Regiment, was responsible for the killing of prisoners of war, in violation of the laws and usages of war, when troops under his command killed twenty-three Canadian prisoners of war at or near the villages of Buron and Authie.

Third Charge: Committing a war crime, in that he at his Headquarters at (the Abbey Ardenne) in the Province of Normandy and Republic of France on or about the 8th day of June 1944, when Commander of 25 SS Panzer Grenadier Regiment, in violation of the laws and usages of war gave orders to troops under his command to kill seven prisoners of war, and as a result of such orders the said prisoners of war were thereupon shot and killed.

Fourth Charge: (Alternative to Third Charge) Committing a war crime, in that he in the Province of Normandy and Republic of France on or about the 8th day of June 1944, as Commander of 25 SS Panzer Grenadier Regiment, was responsible for the killing of prisoners of war in violation of the laws and usages of war, when troops under his command shot and killed seven Canadian prisoners of war at his Headquarters at (the Abbey Ardenne).

Fifth Charge: Committing a war crime, in that he in the Province of Normandy and Republic of France on or about the 7th day of June 1944, as Commander of 25 SS Panzer Grenadier Regiment, was responsible for the killing of prisoners of war in violation of the laws and usages of war, when troops under his command killed eleven Canadian prisoners of war (other than those referred to in the Third and Fourth Charges) at his Headquarters at (the Abbey Ardenne).

During the trial, the testimony of Daniel Lachèvre, a French teenager who had lived at the abbey until mid-June, proved particularly damaging to Meyer's cause. Lachèvre and some other boys had been allowed to move about the premises quite freely; they had gone to the garden at about 8:00 p.m., June 8th, to play on the horizontal bars and swings there. The boys played for about three-quarters of an hour, and returned to play on the 9th and 10th. Questioned by the Court, the witness said that the ground in the garden was bare; no dead bodies were there on any of the three days, and had they been there the boys certainly would have seen them.[32] "This evidence," writes

---

[32]Clearly, the Germans had buried the dead prisoners (in carefully concealed, unmarked graves) before the evening of the 8th.

MacDonald, "supported as it was by that of the next witness, was one of the decisive turning points in the trial. It disproved completely, if it ever had been believed, Meyer's last minute explanation of the discovery of the bodies by him (on or about) June 11th . . ."[33]

On the afternoon of December 27, 1945, the Court reached a verdict. The Court found Meyer not guilty of the second and third charges. This meant that it had acquitted Meyer of responsibility for the murder of the 23 Canadians at Authie and Buron, and of the charge of ordering the execution of the seven prisoners at the Abbey Ardenne on the morning of June 8th. Yet it also signified that the Court found him guilty of inciting and counselling his troops to deny quarter,[34] and held him responsible for the shooting of the 18 prisoners at the abbey on June 7th and 8th, as laid out in the first, fourth and fifth charges.[35]

At 11:45 the next morning, the Court reassembled for sentencing:[36]

> In the breathless hush that settled on the packed room the accused was brought before the Court. The President, sternly concealing his emotion, for this was for him a difficult task, in a gruff voice, pronounced judgment and sentence:
>
> 'Brigadeführer Kurt Meyer, the Court has found you guilty of the First, Fourth and Fifth Charges in the First Charge Sheet.
>
> The sentence of the Court is that you suffer death by being shot.
>
> The findings of Guilty and the sentence are subject to confirmation.
>
> The proceedings are now closed.'
>
> Meyer, erect, flushed as the words were interpreted to him; with a grim tightening of the jaw, but with no other show of emotion, he bowed low, and was marched from the court room.
>
> The trial was over.

*   *   *   *   *

---

[33]MacDonald, B.J.S., *The Trial of Kurt Meyer,* p 153.

[34]According to Jesionek, Meyer, during an address to the troops of his reconnaissance company at Le Sap, France, shortly before D-Day had told them to retaliate against enemy troops for the aerial bombing of German cities and the killing of innocent women and children. Jesionek and others in the company had taken Meyer's utterance to mean that they were to shoot their prisoners. In any case, it seems that Meyer on more than one occasion counselled troops under his command to take no prisoners. MacDonald, B.J.S., *The Trial of Kurt Meyer,* pp 108, 113-114; Record Group 238: Records of Proceedings. Exhibit 4. Testimony of Alfred Helzel.

[35]The Court, like a grand jury, gave no reasons for its findings.

[36]During the trial Meyer's behavior had been, for the most part, "polite, restrained and poised;" his accusers "had come to admire this German general for his qualities and proficiency as a soldier [and to respect] his courage and his dignity throughout the trial . . ." On January 13, 1946, Major-General Chris Vokes, the commander of the Canadian Army Occupation Force in Germany, commuted Meyer's sentence to life imprisonment. In his memoirs Vokes writes: "When I studied the

Kurt Meyer at the time of his sentencing.

evidence against Meyer . . . I found it to be a mass of circumstantial evidence. It did indeed deal with the murder of a number of Canadian soldiers quite close to where Meyer had his headquarters; there was certainly the inference to be drawn that he had given the order to have Canadian soldiers executed. But nowhere in the evidence could I find that order to be proved. Not to my satisfaction. There was hearsay evidence. There was nothing direct . . . So I ordered the execution stayed." Apparently, a guilty conscience played a part in Vokes' decision, for the general openly admits that his own troops had killed German prisoners in Italy and northwest Europe.

Following the trial, Meyer was hustled to Canada in great secrecy and lodged in the Dorchester Penitentiary in New Brunswick; there he remained for more than five years, "as a common convict along with Canada's most undesirable citizens. He was employed mostly in the library during this time and learned to speak English. For the most part he made a favorable impression on his jailers, the chaplain and others with whom he came in contact." Still obsessed with the Soviet military threat, Meyer "prepared pages of unsolicited tactical recommendations for the Canadian army based on his experience fighting the Russians. From memory he drew detailed maps of various campaigns, citing the errors and omissions on both sides. Everything he produced was turned over to . . . National Defense HQ in Ottawa. Before long NDHQ staff officers began arriving at Dorchester for private discussions with [Meyer.] They left marvelling at his talents. For three years this bizarre state of affairs continued." In recognition of Meyer's tactical acumen, the Canadians eventually used him briefly (and quite secretly) as a military advisor while he was a prisoner in New Brunswick.

In October 1951, the Canadian Government transferred Meyer to the British (solitary confinement) prison for convicted war criminals at Werl, West Germany, ten miles east of Dortmund; here, he joined other imprisoned German military leaders, including Field Marshal Kesselring and Generals Mackensen and Falkenhorst. The many years of hardship had taken their toll, and Meyer's health was already deteriorating; he suffered from arthritis, bad kidneys and high blood pressure. In the summer of 1952, Meyer was hospitalized with ailments culminating in a tonsillectomy that nearly killed him; shortly thereafter, he suffered a mild heart attack.

In June 1953, Meyer received a visit from the West German Chancellor, Dr. Konrad Adenauer--an indication of Meyer's still considerable popularity. Adenauer publicly shook the former SS general's hand and promised to do all that he could to end the imprisonment. On the early morning of September 7, 1954 (ten years to the day that American forces had captured him) Meyer was released from captivity.

Meyer went to work for a local brewery (Andreas Brewery) in Hagen in January 1955, "in charge of the 27 sales drivers who covered the district. Typically, he gave the job everything he had. His reputation provided immediate access to owners of every watering hole and family inn throughout the region, and he managed to introduce the delights of Andreas bottled beer to the messes of the Canadian armed forces serving in Europe."

Although courted by union leaders and politicians of the right and center, the only organization Meyer openly supported was the HIAG--a veterans organization assisting former members of the Waffen SS; by 1956 he had become one of the HIAG's principal spokesmen, seeking in vain legislation from the Bonn government that would entitle veterans of the Waffen SS to pensions on an equal basis with veterans of the Wehrmacht.

In July 1961, Meyer suffered a mild stroke, followed by two more strokes in November. On the evening of December 23, 1961, he died of a heart attack. It was his birthday. He was 51 years old. He was survived by his wife, Kate, four daughters and a son.

Meyer "had the largest funeral in Hagen's history. Thousands of condolences poured in. Extra staff were hired by the post office to handle the telegrams, letters and telephone calls. Adenauer and Strauss [Dr. Franz-Joseph Strauss, the West German Defense Minister] sent their sympathies. Relatives, family friends and Waffen SS comrades arrived in droves from all over Europe. Newspaper accounts placed the attendance at 5,000." Hubert Meyer read the eulogy: "You did not build yourself a monument of stone but erected a shining example in the hearts of your comrades. You worked a lifetime for a Fatherland, happy and free. We will love it as you did. Wherever we are, privately, publicly, at home or abroad we will say with pride: 'I . . . was a comrade of Panzermeyer!' " Foster, *Meeting of Generals*, pp 487-89; 499-515; MacDonald, B.J.S., *The Trial of Kurt Meyer*, pp 195-201; Schneider, *Verleihung Genehmigt!*, pp 241-43; Major-General Chris Vokes (with John P. Maclean), *Vokes, My Story* (Ottawa: Gallery Books), p 205.

Chapter 10
STALINGRAD REVISITED:
THE DESTRUCTION OF THE HITLER YOUTH DIVISION

> Two hours after dawn on [June 26th] the 15th Scottish Division, with the 31st [Tank] Brigade, moved into their first battle under a leaden and threatening sky. Ahead of them the barrage rolled across sodden [fields of grain] and dripping hedges. A minefield checked the tanks but the infantry tramped stolidly on across the Caen - Tilly road and fought their way into the string of hamlets around Cheux . . . The troops of the 12th SS, who were holding this sector, fought with a tenacity and a ferocity seldom equalled and never excelled during the whole campaign.
>
> (Chester Wilmont)
>
> We are not beaten . . . we are simply crushed and driven back by overwhelming superior forces.
>
> (Erich Maria Remarque)

Following the destruction of Panzer Group West headquarters, control of German operations in the Caen sector reverted to the commander of the I SS Panzer Corps, Sepp Dietrich, who immediately shelved Geyr's aggressive plan of attack. Dietrich's decision was the proper one, for even without the loss of the Panzer Group staff it is difficult to see how Geyr could have ever carried out his intent. By June 10th, all three of Dietrich's armored divisions were pinned firmly on the defensive. Forming the right wing of the Panzer Corps, the 21st Panzer was in position from just east of the Orne to the Caen - Luc-sur-Mer rail line; under Feuchtinger's uninspired leadership, the division had already sacrificed the majority of its armor, as well as large numbers of infantry. In the center, the 12th SS Panzer, which had also suffered heavy losses in men and equipment, held a front approximately ten miles in length, stretching westward from the rail line (near la Bijude) to les Hauts Vents, one-half mile southwest of Cristot. On the left flank, the Panzer Lehr had finally moved into battle on June 9th,[1] and was now firmly ensconced in the dense bocage country south of Bayeux, its line extending from the southern rim of St. Pierre

---

[1] A battlegroup led by Major Prinz Schönburg-Waldenburg, the commander of the Panzer Lehr's Panzer IV battalion (2nd Battalion, Panzer Lehr Regiment 130), had attacked late that morning from its staging area near Tilly-sur-Seulles. Advancing northwest, it captured Ellon (several miles northwest of Tilly) apparently without resistance; emerging from the village, however, the Germans detected enemy tanks

across Tilly-sur-Seulles - Lingèvres - la Sanaudière to the headwaters of the Aure, some five miles west of Tilly. But beyond the Aure a dangerous gap existed between the inner flanks of the Panzer Corps and the neighboring LXXXIV Army Corps, causing grave concern at even the highest level of command (i.e., Hitler).[2] The Panzer Corps, moreover, lacked any meaningful reserves, and most of its remaining tanks were now distributed across its front in small groups to provide mobile anti-tank protection for the infantry.[3]

At 11:00 p.m., June 11th, Field Marshal Rommel dispatched a teleprinter signal to OKW that offered a blunt estimate of the situation confronting his Army Group B:[4]

> . . . Because of the enemy's air superiority it has not been possible to bring up in timely fashion the forces intended for the counterattack between the Orne and the Vire. The I SS Panzer Corps has been forced onto the defensive. For the present, the Army Group must be content with forming a connected front . . . The Army Group is endeavoring to replace the Panzer units with infantry divisions, and (to reform mobile reserves with them).

Clearly, the Panzer divisions needed to be extricated from the front and concentrated as mobile reserves if they were to perform the intended offensive tasks. To accomplish their relief, the infantry divisions of the powerful Fifteenth Army north of the Seine were most readily available, yet in a rare display of unanimity, the Germans refused to move them. For once, it seems, Hitler, Rundstedt, and Rommel were in complete agreement: the invasion of Normandy was merely a diversion to entice German reserves west of the Seine as a prelude to the main enemy attack in the Pas-de-Calais.[5] Thus they were

---

to the northeast. In response to this sudden threat the battlegroup suspended the advance and pulled back to its original start line. Thus ended the "only classical tank attack" that the Panzer Lehr would undertake during the entire Normandy campaign. Major Schönburg was killed two days later in the fighting for Hill 103. Ritgen, *Geschichte der Panzer-Lehr-Division*, pp 112, 134.

[2]Entries in the war diary of Army Group B on June 12th clearly show German anxieties concerning the gap between the two corps. The opening, which Allied forces had already begun to exploit, extended westward from the Panzer Lehr into the area about Balleroy, a village six miles northwest of Caumont; to close it, Hitler ordered that Army Group B use any means at its disposal, including the 2nd Panzer Division. Consequently, Rommel ordered the division to advance at once to the vulnerable sector, and even dispatched a staff officer to hurry it along. Commanded by General Heinrich von Lüttwitz, the 2nd Panzer had already begun to move west towards the invasion front on June 9th from its positions astride the Somme (Abbeville - Amiens). The lead elements of the division would move into action at Villers-Bocage on the afternoon of the 13th, helping to close the gap between the two corps. T-84/281/000845-46, 000855, 000867. KTB Heeresgruppe B; Schramm, *KTB OKW* (Wehrmachtführungsstab), Band IV, p 313; Kraemer, C-024, p 38.

[3]According to Fritz Kraemer, Chief of Staff to the I SS Panzer Corps, the bulk of the armor of all three Panzer divisions was now committed to the forwardmost line, mostly in separate groupings of 5-9 tanks. Kraemer, C-024, p 27.

[4]Schramm, *KTB OKW* (Wehrmachtführungsstab), Band IV, p 314.

[5]Rommel's concern for a second Allied invasion focused on the mouth of the Somme; Hitler's anxieties were less discriminating, and stretched all the way from

determined to keep the Fifteenth Army intact to protect the V-weapon (Vergeltungswaffen) rocket sites and the short route into the Ruhr. Consequently, the Fifteenth Army's tactical reserves (including five infantry divisions) were to remain where they were, "idle and useless."[6]

For the next five weeks German fears of a second Allied landing on the Channel coast would bedevil their strategy and undermine their defense of the Normandy front. What the Germans did not know was that their anxiety was largely the product of an elaborate enemy deception, code-named Fortitude, and of treason within their own intelligence community. As part of the Fortitude plan the Allies had invented the First U.S. Army Group, purportedly under the command of the mercurial General George S. Patton. This "Army Group" existed only on paper, yet Colonel Freiherr Alexis von Roenne, the Chief of German Army intelligence in the West, was only too eager to accept it as genuine. For months he had purposely and consistently exaggerated the strength of Allied forces massing in England for the invasion; by June 6th, D-Day, he had tacked on Patton's spurious Army Group to his estimates, complete with 25 battleworthy divisions. These divisions, he maintained, were being held in readiness for a second invasion. The aristocratic von Roenne was a member of the anti-Hitler resistance and was later executed by the Nazis.[7]

If such intrigues were far removed from the immediate concerns of the 12th SS Panzer, they still greatly affected the division's deployment in battle. With no relief forthcoming, it would remain constantly in the line, successfully anchoring the German defense of Caen until its capture by the Allies in early July. Thereafter, the 12th SS would be withdrawn into reserve, only to be back in action within days. In the weeks that followed the division's young soldiers would play a major part in the grim defensive struggle between Caen and Falaise, at times standing between the enemy and the total collapse of the German front; with fatalistic resignation, the survivors would fight a skillful delaying action during the final days of the campaign, helping large numbers of German troops to escape encirclement and certain destruction. In this manner the 12th SS Hitlerjugend, which had had its genesis in the Stalingrad disaster of 1942-43, experienced its own Stalingrad on the fertile plains of Normandy, where by mid-August 1944 the fighting had reduced the division to a small fragment of its original combat strength.

*   *   *

Oostende (in Belgium) to Dieppe. T-84/281/000823, 000847. KTB Heeresgruppe B; Wilmont, *The Struggle for Europe*, p 294.

[6]One infantry division from the Fifteenth Army, however, the 346th, had already been dispatched to the battlefront. The division had begun to cross the Seine on D-Day; by June 9th, it was in position between the Orne and the Dives. T-84/281/000800. KTB Heeresgruppe B; Wilmont, *The Struggle for Europe*, p 294.

[7]On June 26th, for example, under the influence of von Roenne's falsified data, Army Group B estimated the number of enemy divisions in England at 67, of which 57 were considered fit for action in France. In fact, there were only 15 divisions in England at the time awaiting transport to Normandy. BAMA. RH 19/IX/8. Wochenmeldung Heeresgruppe B. 19.-26.6.44; see also Anton Staubwasser, B-782. "Das Feindbild beim O.dHg.B. 6.6.-24.7.44;" Irving, *The Trail of the Fox*, pp 363-64, 377.

After the fighting on June 7th, the front of Kurt Meyer's 25th SS Panzer Grenadier Regiment had remained virtually static. On the 8th, two companies of British infantry supported by tanks struck the seam between the regiment's 1st and 2nd Battalions, but were turned back in cooperation with the 8th Panzer Company, which destroyed two of the hostile tanks.[8] The next day, the Royal Ulster Rifles (3rd British Infantry Division) renewed their attack on Cambes;[9] in a spirited assault, they captured the village and its adjacent wood despite severe losses from intense German artillery, mortar and machine gun fire.[10] The fighting on June 8-9 cost the 1st Battalion 5 dead and 20 wounded. On June 10th, the battalion commander, SS-Sturmbannführer Waldmüller, distributed 30 Iron Crosses second class to deserving members of his unit.[11]

Three young soldiers of the division after being awarded the Iron Cross, second class.

Intense entrenching (Stellungsbau) characterized the days that followed, as the soldiers of the 25th Regiment bored deeper into the ground seeking protection from the violents gusts of artillery and mortar fire that swept their line. Working day and night, the grenadiers soon transformed their shallow foxholes into regular bunkers.[12] To inflict maximum casualties on their opponent,

[8]KTB I./25.SS-Pz.Gren.Rgt. 8.6.44.

[9]Neither the 12th SS nor the British had occupied the village after the battle there on June 7th.

[10]The attack of the Royal Ulster Rifles began at 3:15 p.m., supported by its divisional artillery as well as fire from a British cruiser. According to Scarfe, the intensity of the German artillery and mortar fire in the Cambes wood from about 4:00 p.m. until dusk "was as withering as anything experinced [by the 3rd British Infantry Division] during the whole campaign." Scarfe, *Assault Division*, pp 98-100.

[11]KTB I./25.SS-Pz.Gren.Rgt. 10.6.44.

[12]The regiment's 1st Battalion cannibalized railroad ties from the nearby Caen - Luc-sur-Mer rail line, and used them to brace the inner walls of its bunkers. Meyer, H., *Kriegsgeschichte*, p 113.

they also cut fields of fire through the tall grain for their machine guns and planted Teller mines along suspected enemy approaches.

To furnish added firepower, the 12th SS was heavily reinforced with artillery. By June 12th, the three batteries of the I SS Panzer Corps' medium artillery battalion (schwere SS-Artillerie-Abteilung 101/501) had moved up from Beauvais and into position southwest of Caen, from where they could cover the entire line of the division. The battalion's 1st Battery consisted of 210mm howitzers with a range of 10 miles; the 2nd and 3rd Batteries both comprised 170mm cannon with a range of nearly 20 miles.[13] In addition to the artillery, the 12th SS also received a Nebelwerfer battalion. With its deadly fragmentation effect and rapid rate of fire, the Nebelwerfer (christened "moaning minnie" by those on the receiving end because of the infernal scream of its projectiles) would become one of the weapons most feared by the Allies in Normandy.[14]

*   *   *

Since its stinging defeat on June 7th, the 3rd Canadian Infantry Division had made no further attempt to renew its advance. On the 10th, the division began to plan an operation for the 2nd Canadian Armored Brigade. The plan called for the brigade's 6th Armored Regiment (the 1st Hussars) and the Queen's Own Rifles of Canada (an infantry battalion) to advance from Norrey-en-Bessin, and, via a right hook through le Mesnil-Patry, to seize the high ground south of Cheux. The enterprise was scheduled for June 12th. As a preliminary move, the British 46th Royal Marine Commando, under the command of the 8th Canadian Infantry Brigade and supported by tanks, was to clear the wooded banks of the Mue between Cairon and Rots on June 11th. The Canadians, however, to better coordinate their activities with those of the neighboring XXX British Corps, hastily advanced the date of the Cheux operation,[15] thus both their projects were carried out on the same day, June 11th. As a result, the main blow was inadequately prepared, with no time allowed for reconnaissance and no artillery preparation provided.[16]

Shortly after 2:30 p.m., on a beautiful clear day, the 6th Canadian Armored Regiment debouched from Norrey-en-Bessin. "B" Squadron tanks led the

---

[13]Subordinated to Kurt Meyer's 25th Regiment, the howitzer battery established a forward observation post in one of the turrets of the Abbey Ardenne. According to Meyer, the 12th SS also received a Flak regiment (88mm) about this time. PAC. Special Interrogation Report. p 4; KTB I./25.SS-Pz.Gren.Rgt. 11.6.44; Meyer, *Kriegsgeschichte,* pp 115-16.

[14]The Nebelwerfer battalion was also subordinated to the 25th Regiment. The battalion belonged to the 83rd Werfer Regiment, a component of the 7th Werfer Brigade. KTB I./25.SS-Pz.Gren.Rgt. 12.6.44.

[15]XXX Corps was attempting with its armor to push through to Villers-Bocage. The Canadian venture was meant to cover the left flank of the British attack. The 3rd Canadian Division was still a part of the I British Corps.

[16]In the opinion of one Canadian company commander, the entire plan was "conceived in sin and born in iniquity." The 12th SS, moreover, through intercepts of its adversary's radio traffic, became privy to the danger just as the Canadians were assembling to attack. Lieutenant-Colonel W.T. Barnard, *The Queen's Own Rifles of Canada 1860-1960* (Ontario: Ontario Publishing Company Limited, 1960); Stacey, *The Victory Campaign,* pp 138-39; Meyer, H., *Kriegsgeschichte,* p 121.

way--the men of "D" Company of the Queen's Own Rifles riding on their backs. Le Mesnil-Patry was 1,200 yards away; the intervening terrain dominated by flat fields of tall grain. Despite heavy mortar fire, the attackers rapidly infiltrated the positions of the 12th SS Engineer Battalion.[17] The defenders, well-concealed in foxholes hidden among the grain, loosed devastating small arms fire upon the enemy infantry, still riding upon the tanks. While the Canadian infantry dismounted and engaged their opponent at close range, the Shermans of the 1st Hussars moved on at high speed towards le Mesnil-Patry, spraying machine gun fire in every direction. Well equipped for anti-tank defense, the SS engineers battled the hostile tanks with grenade launchers and magnetic hollow charges (Hafthohlladungen). Grenadiers of Mohnke's 26th Regiment defending in the area were also drawn into the fighting.[18]

Two knocked-out Shermans at the Normandy Front.

That very morning the 12th SS had shifted its Panzer regiment's 2nd Battalion (SS-Sturmbannführer Prinz) into the area south of le Mesnil-Patry.[19] Alerted by the growing din of battle, elements of the battalion now intervened decisively, destroying one enemy tank after the other.[20] The engineer bat-

---

[17]Following its unsuccessful assault on Norrey-en-Bessin (June 10th), the engineer battalion had been inserted into the line between the 1st and 2nd Battalions of the 26th SS Panzer Grenadier Regiment to provide additional infantry.

[18]Stacey, *The Victory Campaign*, p 140; Barnard, *The Queen's Own Rifles of Canada*, pp 201-2; Meyer, H., *Kriegsgeschichte*, p 121.

[19]According to Hans Siegel, commander of the 8th Panzer Company, the tanks of the 2nd Panzer Battalion had moved into positions stretching from St. Manvieu to Cristot during the early morning hours of June 11th, perhaps in anticipation of a major Canadian thrust in that sector. The battalion, it will be recalled, had hitherto been deployed behind the front of Kurt Meyer's 25th Regiment. Siegel, "Die zweite Schlacht um Caen 11.-16. Juni 1944."

[20]Siegel was the first to intervene--with several tanks of his company closest to the fighting. Apparently he did so on his own initiative without awaiting orders from Prinz. Siegel, "Die zweite Schlacht um Caen 11.-16. Juni 1944."

SS-Sturmbannführer Karl-Heinz Prinz, commander of the Panzer regiment's 2nd Battalion.

D. Rose

talion's 1st Company put in a counterattack of its own, throwing back the enemy infantry or taking them prisoner. Although some of the Hussars' tanks and a party of infantry had managed to fight their way into the village, the vigorous German response compelled the commander of the Canadian advance group to order his force to pull back to the start line. Further misfortune struck the Canadians when,[21]

> The Germans managed to get into our artillery wireless net and put in a call for defensive fire on The Queen's Own area and on The Regina Rifles at Norrey-en-Bessin. It was a clever move on the part of the enemy. Immediately heavy fire poured down; some twenty minutes elapsed before Brigade H.Q. could get it stopped. The havoc wrought was dreadful. Not only did The Queen's Own suffer. The forward company of the Regina Rifles was badly shot up; the battalion's reserve ammunition was destroyed, and the 1st Hussars lost many of their reserve tanks positioned in Norrey-en-Bessin.

"B" Squadron, apparently, never received the order to withdraw and was virtually annihilated; only two of its 21 tanks returned.[22] "C" Squadron, attempting to come to "B" Squadron's relief, was also shot to pieces by Prinz' Panzer IVs. All told, the 6th Canadian Armored Regiment lost 37 tanks in the debacle; its personnel losses amounted to 80, included 59 dead.[23] The Queen's

---

[21]Barnard, *The Queen's Own Rifles of Canada*, p 202.

[22]The two surviving tanks and their fortunate crews had experienced mechanical problems and withdrawn before the fighting had started. PAC. War Diary. 2nd Canadian Armored Brigade. 11 June 1944; *A History of the First Hussars Regiment 1856-1945* (London: Hunter Printing, 1951), p 75.

[23]The personnel losses of the 1st Hussars on this "black day" equalled roughly one-third of their entire losses for the European campaign 1944-45. On the night of June 16-17, the Canadians would occupy le Mesnil-Patry without opposition; one of

Own Rifles suffered 99 casualties, of which 55 were fatal.[24] The sacrifice of the 12th SS was also great: some 150 casualties, including 48 dead and 11 missing. The Panzer regiment, however, lost only four tanks--three from the 8th and one from the 9th Panzer Companies.[25]

The costly failure at le Mesnil-Patry was the last major Canadian operation during the month of June 1944. The respite was a welcome one indeed. In the first six days of Operation "Overlord" the battle casualties of the 3rd Canadian Infantry Division and attached troops had totaled 196 officers and 2635 other ranks; more than 1000 of them had lost their lives.[26] These were brutal losses, and morale within some Canadian units was correspondingly low.

There remained, however, the task of clearing the Germans from the Mue valley. Positioned in and about Rots was the 1st Company of the 26th SS Panzer Grenadier Regiment, supported by the divisional escort company, the 4th Panzer Company (Panthers), a platoon of engineers (16th Company, 26th Regiment) and two 75mm anti-tank guns. Although not a large force, its forward location threatened the flank of Canadian forces in Norrey-en-Bessin and Bretteville-l'Orgueilleuse, hence it had to be eliminated.

Accompanied by a squadron of Shermans (10th Canadian Armored Regiment), the 46th Royal Marine Commando advanced down the valley from the vicinity of Thaon. The elite British unit[27] cleared the villages of Cairon, Lasson and Rosel in swift succession, encountering little opposition;[28] by early evening, the Commando and its tank support had burst into Rots and the fighting turned furious. The Marines and SS infantry battled hand-to-hand with rifle butts, bayonets and grenades, or shot each other at point blank range. Despite heavy losses, the British quickly captured the northern half of the village, crushing the platoon of the 1st Company defending there. The divisional escort company, commanded by SS-Obersturmführer Fritz Guntrum, then counterattacked with two squads of infantry and several Panthers and hurled the enemy from Rots, destroying six Shermans and taking many

the survivors of the 1st Hussars and the regiment's chaplain were then able to get out to the tanks lost on June 11th to identify the dead: "In some cases the bodies were indistinguishable from one another, simply a mass of cooked flesh welded together in the great heat; we had to sift through this for identity tags. Each tank told the same story--broken legs, broken arms, open-chest wounds, and so on, had trapped many, so that they had burnt alive. The screams I thought I had heard during the action had not been imaginary after all." A History of the First Hussars Regiment, p 77; Mckee, Last Round Against Rommel, p 90.

[24]All but three of these casualties belonged to "D" Company of the Queen's Own. PAC. War Diary. The Queen's Own Rifles of Canada. 11 June 1944; Stacey, The Victory Campaign, p 140.

[25]One of the 8th Company's shot up Panzer IVs was later salvaged from the battlefield and repaired. Siegel, "Die zweite Schlacht um Caen 11.-16. Juni 1944;" Fragebogen, Ernst Haase; Meyer, H., P-164, p 29; Meyer, H., Kriegsgeschichte, p 123.

[26]Stacey, The Victory Campaign, p 140.

[27]This commando belonged to the 4th Special Services Brigade. Each commando consisted of 24 officers and 440 other ranks, organized into troops of three officers and 60 men each. The men were lightly armed and equipped, and possessed minimum wheeled transport. Ellis, Victory in the West, p 539.

[28]Whether there were any German troops in these villages is unknown.

prisoners. Yet the victory was short-lived, for the Marines regrouped and came on again; with the help of eight Shermans, they once more broke through the thin German line.[29]

Throughout the night and into the early morning hours of June 12th, the fighting raged on through the streets and battered stone buildings of the little village. Exhausted and overwhelmed, the remaining SS then withdrew permanently, establishing a new main battle line some 1000 yards south of Rots.[30] The battered Marines were relieved by a battalion of the 8th Canadian Infantry Brigade, Le Régiment de la Chaudière, which took over the defense of the village. Moving into Rots that morning, the battalion observed first hand the results of the struggle that had preceded them:[31]

> . . . The dead lay corpse by corpse. We searched every house, every courtyard, to avoid ambush. And here is the confirmation of how ferocious last night's battle must have been. The Commandos lie dead in rows beside the dead SS. Grenades are scattered all over the road and in the porches of houses. Here we see a Commando and an SS-man, literally dead in each other's arms, having slaughtered each other. There, a German and a Canadian tank have engaged each other to destruction, and are still smouldering, and from each blackened turret hangs the charred corpse of a machinegunner. Over here, are a group who ran towards a wall for shelter, and were shot down before they got there . . .

The night's work had cost the Commando 17 dead, 9 wounded and 35 missing. The 12th SS lost another 67 of its soldiers: 22 dead, 30 wounded and 15 missing. Among the German dead was SS-Hauptsturmführer Hans Pfeiffer, the commander of the 4th Panzer Company. The 10th Canadian Armored Regiment lost roughly a dozen of its Shermans; the 12th SS lost at least one Panther.[32]

*   *   *

The two weeks that followed the engagements on June 11th were relatively quiet along the front of the 12th SS, as the focus of Allied strategy in the Caen sector temporarily shifted elsewhere.[33] During the initial days of the Nor-

[29]BAMA. Tagebuch Divisions-Begleit-Kompanie. 11.6.44.

[30]On June 12th, the divisional escort company reestablished itself south of the village. The new positions of the 1st Company (26th Regiment) and of the 4th Panzer Company could not be ascertained. Several days later, the escort company was removed from the line and dispatched to the hard-pressed Panzer Lehr, with which it would serve through the end of June. Ibid., 12.6.1944, 16.6.1944.

[31]McKee, *Last Round Against Rommel*, pp 87-88.

[32]Stacey, *The Victory Campaign*, p 139; Meyer, H., P-164, p 29; Meyer, H., *Kriegsgeschichte*, p 127.

[33]On June 13th, elements of the I SS Panzer Corps' 101st SS Heavy Tank Battalion (Tiger tanks), supported by tanks from the Panzer Lehr and infantry from the 2nd Panzer Division, thwarted a British flanking maneuver at Villers-Bocage, saving Caen from envelopment. Other historians have exhaustively covered this spectacular German victory, thus it need not be reexamined here. For a colorful account of the engagement see, Keegan, *Six Armies in Normandy*, pp 153-154.

Jost W. Schneider

Kurt Meyer drives his division commander, Fritz Witt, on a motorcycle to a battalion HQ of the 25th regiment, approximately June 8. The regimental medical officer, SS-Sturmbannführer Dr. Erich Gatternig, climbs into the pillion seat.

mandy campaign, the division commander, **SS-Brigadeführer**[34] Fritz Witt, had visited the battlefront each morning to confer with his subordinates and to inspect the defenses of his troops. Despite the vigorous pace, Witt found a moment on June 10th to pen a letter to his wife in Germany. Perhaps to allay her fears he wrote confidently of the battle along the invasion front--a battle, he fully realized, that was growing more unequal with each passing day. His division had too much ground to defend and too few resources; no replacements had arrived for infantry and armor already lost, and few, if any, were expected. Reserves were virtually non-existent.[35]

---

[34]Witt had been promoted to SS-Brigadeführer on April 20, 1944. SS Personalakten, Fritz Witt.

[35]On June 11th, the 12th SS had just 74 tanks fit for action, 42 Panzer IVs and 32 Panthers. Apparently, the division (or a Luftwaffe liaison?) reported this information to its superiors by radio--a signal intercepted by Allied listening posts, decoded by Ultra, and passed on to concerned Allied commanders at 1:05 p.m., June 13th. Public Record Office. Ultra Signal KV7853.

There survives a photograph of Witt, taken at his headquarters in Venoix on June 13th or 14th. It shows him on the château grounds, sitting at a small table adorned with a white tablecloth. Beside him sits Max Wünsche, his head still bandaged from the wound suffered on June 9th, and Kurt Meyer, attired as he always was in his SS camouflage uniform. The mood of all three men appears somber, and the strain of battle shows clearly on Witt's face. Within hours Fritz Witt was dead, killed at his headquarters by a salvo from the 16" guns of a British battleship.[36] On orders from Dietrich's Panzer Corps, Kurt Meyer took command of the 12th SS the next day, June 15th. At 33, Meyer became the youngest division commander in the German armed forces. At once he

T. Pooler

[36]Witt was killed about midday, June 14th. The initial salvo had missed his headquarters and plunged into the Odon valley, where several hundred yards to the southeast a battery of the division's 100mm artillery was in position. Witt, who had observed the hostile shellfire with staff officer Meitzel, at first believed the artillery battery to be the object of the enemy barrage. But as the shelling continued, it soon became apparent that the enemy was attempting to take out division headquarters. Witt then ordered his staff to take cover at once in the slit trenches located directly behind the château, beneath some tall shade trees. After seeing to the safety of his men, Witt also sought cover in the trenches. At that very moment, a 16" shell exploded in the trees above him, killing him instantly. The naval gun fire, which only lasted for several minutes, also killed three others and wounded nine. The château itself was unscathed; had Witt remained inside the château, where he was when the shelling began, he would have survived.

Among the Ultra messages transmitted on the morning of June 12th is one pinpointing the location of the 12th SS' headquarters in Venoix. Although entirely possible that this message led to the shelling of Witt's headquarters, one must be careful in linking specific Ultra information directly to Allied action, for Ultra does *not* tell us how concerned Allied commanders used that information, or even if they believed it. The author examined thousands of Ultra messages, finding many that provided the Allies with significant insights into the intentions, activities, and combat strength of the 12th SS Panzer Division. Meyer, H., *Kriegsgeschichte,* pp 133-34; Public Record Office. Ultra Signal KV7648; Interview, Peter Witt (son of Fritz Witt), June 8, 1981; Interview, Hubert Meyer (in Venoix), June 4, 1983.

moved division headquarters to Verson, a village some 2½ miles southwest of Venoix and astride the highway from Caen to Villers-Bocage.[37]

The loss of Fritz Witt was deeply felt by the entire division. A decent and caring soldier, Witt had always taken a special interest in the well-being of his young troops--a responsibility that had only grown more burdensome as he led them in the crucible of combat. "The news of our division commander's death," reflects an officer in the 26th Regiment,[38]

> upset everyone greatly. Never in the following days and weeks--be it after great losses, the failure of an attack, or during the continuous retreats--did I see all comrades more depressed. Many of us could not conceal unsoldierly tears. Still, we all grit our teeth. In spite of everything we'd do it now! Our deeds would honor him and his work. Those were our thoughts and the topics of our conversations. All others were forgotten. Only why Witt, why him?

One of the last photographs taken of Fritz Witt.

Kurt Meyer, shortly after taking over as division commander.

Woscidlo

---

[37]Meyer turned over his 25th Regiment to SS-Obersturmbannführer Milius, hitherto commander of the regiment's 3rd Battalion. Meyer K., *Grenadiere*, p 237.
[38]Meyer, H., P-164, p 32.

The new commander of the 12th SS, Kurt Meyer, began at once to reorganize the division's defenses in preparation for the inevitable resumption of the Allied offensive. To shorten the left flank, the 26th Regiment withdrew from its exposed positions north of Cristot and le Mesnil-Patry to a more defensible front below the two villages.[39] The withdrawal took place on the night of June 15-16, and was not contested by the enemy. The regiment's new line followed the course of the Mue (south of the stream) from the Caen - Cherbourg rail line, across St. Manvieu, to the stream's intersection with the road from Carpiquet to Fontenay-le-Pesnel; from there, the line continued westward, directly north of the road, to the Parc de Boislonde, one-half mile north of Fontenay. The 12th SS Engineer[40] and Reconnaissance Battalions had also participated in the retrograde movement, the latter formation falling back to Brettevillette and Missy to provide a small reserve of infantry. To furnish anti-tank defense, the tanks of the 2nd Panzer Battalion were dug in and well-camouflaged along a broad front behind the 26th Regiment. The companies of the Panther Battalion were pulled completely from the line and assembled around Noyers as an operational armored reserve.[41]

The infantry battalions of the 26th Regiment immediately entrenched along the new main battle line, carefully camouflaging their positions and covering them with mines and barbed-wire entanglements. No sooner had this activity begun than the 49th British (West Riding) Infantry Division, supported by tanks of the 8th Armored Brigade, struck the extreme left flank of the regiment at the Parc de Boislonde. For the next two days, June 17-18, the regiment's 3rd Battalion experienced bitter fighting at close quarters in densely wooded terrain. Smashed by the enemy's artillery and overrun by his tanks, the Panzer grenadiers endured heavy losses. The survivors retired to Fontenay-le-Pesnel and dug in.[42]

Along the front of the 25th Regiment north and northwest of Caen the fighting was less vigorous, as both sides appeared content to probe their adversary's line with patrols. The grenadiers of the 25th Regiment continued to strengthen their positions, sowing more mines, and, at least in the sector of the 1st Battalion, undertaking the development of an interconnected trench system. Positions for the heavy infantry weapons were carefully selected and prepared for close combat (Nahverteidigung). Artillery and mortar fire, however, along with naval bombardments and fighter-bomber attacks, con-

---

[39]The 2nd and 3rd Battalions of the regiment, in position since June 8th south of Putot-en-Bessin and at Brouay, respectively, projected a salient into the enemy line that the 12th SS knew it could not hold against a major attack.

[40]Müller's engineer battalion, still subordinated to the 26th Regiment, occupied the portion of the new line directly north of Cheux.

[41]From the distribution of its armor, it is evident that the 12th SS expected the main enemy blow west of Caen, on its left flank. Meyer, H., P-164, pp 31-33; Meyer, H., Kriegsgeschichte, pp 134-36, 168-69.

[42]As surviving records of the 12th SS show, artillery support for the beleaguered 3rd Battalion was sorely limited due to ammunition shortages. BAMA. Anlagen zum KTB Heeresgruppe B: 12.SS Pz.Div. "HJ." Abt.Ia. Lageberichte 17.-18.6.44; Meyer, H., P-164, pp 33-34.

tinued to gnaw at the regiment's strength—its 1st Battalion alone sustaining 7 dead and 29 wounded from June 11-18.[43]

The casualties for the entire division, in fact, had begun to reach "threatening proportions." By the time Meyer assumed command, the 12th SS had already lost an alarming number of officers and NCOs, including many company commanders and platoon leaders. Infantry losses had been particularly crippling, with some companies reduced to a combat strength of 40-50 men by June 20th. On the 16th, Kurt Meyer had reported the division's total casualties and the status of its armored fighting vehicles (AFVs) to Army Group B:[44]

Personnel Losses:

403 dead (17 officers)
847 wounded (29 officers)
163 missing (5 officers)
  6 sick
1419 Total

AFVs Fit For Action:

 52 Panzer IVs
 38 Panthers
 10 105mm SP guns
  5 150mm SP guns
 23 heavy PAK
304 armored personnel carriers,
    patrol vehicles and artillery
    observation vehicles.

Despite the heavy sacrifice, which included ten percent of the division's officers, the line of the 12th SS had hitherto held firm. Meyer concluded his report on a positive note, informing his superiors that the division was still capable of holding its positions even against a major enemy attack.

*   *   *

On the "other side of the hill," Field Marshal Bernard Montgomery assessed the situation confronting his forces in mid-June with both confidence and concern. By June 18th, the Allied armies in Normandy held a firm lodgement area and had gained a clear advantage in the build-up of forces. Twenty Allied divisions now faced elements of 18 German divisions—the latter with a combat strength barely equivalent to 14. In the American sector, the 9th U.S.

---

[43]By June 24th, the combat strength (Grabenstärke) of the 1st Battalion had been reduced from some 800 men to just 489—heavy losses for a unit that occupied a quiet front sector. T-354/154/3798534. 12.SS-Panz.Div. "Hitlerjugend." I./Pz.Gren.Rgt.25. Abt.Ic. Tagesmeldung 24.6.44; KTB I./25.SS-Pz.Gren.Rgt. 14.6.-20.6.44; Meyer, H., *Kriegsgeschichte,* pp 144-46, 168.

[44]From June 17-24, the 12th SS continued to incur losses at a rate of more than 100 men per day despite the fact that its only major combat during this period was the two-day engagement at the Parc de Boislonde. Thus, by June 24th, total casualties for the division had risen to 2,550. BAMA. Anlagen zum KTB Heeresgruppe B: Generalkdo. I.SS-Pz.Korps Leibstandarte. Abt.Ia. 26.6.44.

Grenadiers resting near the front line.

Infantry Division had just captured Barneville, severing the base of the Cotentin Peninsula and isolating Cherbourg.[45] The Americans, however, had thus far
been unable to crack the German resistance north of St. Lô. In the British-
Canadian sector, XXX Corps had finally wrestled Tilly from the tenacious
Panzer Lehr (June 18th), but Caen remained firmly in German hands. The
German High Command, moreover, was now dispatching additional mobile
forces to Normandy–the 1st SS Panzer Division from Belgium and the formidable II SS Panzer Corps (9th and 10th SS Panzer Divisions) from the
eastern front.[46] Hitler had earmarked these divisions to spearhead a big offensive between Caumont and St. Lô, with the goal of driving through to Bayeux
and splitting the Allied front. The attack was scheduled for early July.[47]

Through Allied agents and Ultra intercepts, Montgomery followed the advance of the German reinforcements towards the invasion front with growing
apprehension. For the smooth development of his strategy,[48] it was essential
that he attack first, and draw them into action at Caen before the Americans
began to push southward from the base of the Cotentin Peninsula. Consequently, Montgomery planned a major enterprise for Dempsey's Second Army
with the object of enveloping Caen from the west. Code-named "Epsom," the

[45]Cherbourg would fall to the Allies on June 26th.

[46]On June 11th, Hitler had ordered the transfer of the II SS Panzer Corps from
Poland to Normandy; on June 17th, the 1st SS Panzer Division began moving from
Belgium. Schramm, *KTB OKW* (Wehrmachtführungsstab), Band IV, p 314.

[47]Hitler planned to commit a total of six Panzer Divisions--the 1st, 2nd, 9th, and
10th SS, 2nd Panzer and Panzer Lehr--to his attack. To free up the latter two formations, they were to be relieved by infantry divisions. Ibid., pp 317-18.

[48]See Chapter 8, pp 148-49.

plan was for the VIII British Corps,[49] just arriving in Normandy, to cut through the German defenses midway between Caen and Tilly, cross the Odon and the Orne, and establish its armor astride the Caen - Falaise road on the high ground between Bourguebus and Bretteville-sur-Laize. If successful, the Second Army would not only have enveloped Caen, but threatened Paris as well; that threat, Montgomery hoped, would compel the Germans to continue to commit their armored reserves on the eastern flank.[50]

To conduct its attack, VIII Corps possessed an immense force of 60,000 men and 600 tanks, with support available from 700 artillery pieces, three cruisers and a monitor.[51] Air support had also been arranged on a large scale. Standing in the immediate path of this juggernaut were two understrength battalions of the 26th SS Panzer Grenadier Regiment and the 12th SS Engineer Battalion.[52]

Operation Epsom commenced on June 26th, and it signified the beginning of the end for the 12th SS Panzer Divison.[53] At precisely 7:30 a.m., several hundred enemy cannon began to beat away, laying a devastating rolling barrage across the division's front in the sector of the VIII Corps attack. The barrage inflicted heavy casualties on the SS infantry and engineers, destroyed many of their anti-tank guns, and severed vital telephone cables that linked forward units to one another and to division headquarters in Verson. Behind the curtain of fire, the infantry of the 15th Scottish Division[54] and the Shermans of the independent 31st Tank Brigade moved into battle through tall fields of ripen-

---

[49]VIII Corps comprised the 15th Scottish Division, 43rd Wessex Division, 11th Armored Division and two independent armored brigades.

[50]Wilmont, *The Struggle for Europe,* p 320.

[51]McKee, *Last Round Against Rommel,* p 135.

[52]Well behind the front of both the 12th SS and the Panzer Lehr--between St. André-sur-Orne and Aunay-sur-Odon--stood several regiments of the III Flak Corps. Although principally intended to protect vital communications and lines of supply from air attack, the Corps could also be employed against ground targets.

[53]Epsom was preceded by a preliminary British attack, code-named "Dauntless," on June 25th. Early that morning, the 49th Infantry Division (XXX Corps), with tank support, struck the inner flanks of the 12th SS and the Panzer Lehr between Tilly-sur-Seulles and Fontenay-le-Pesnel, with the object of seizing the Rauray ridge and then exploiting southward to Noyers. Possession of the ridge, Montgomery reasoned, would secure the right flank of the VIII Corps offensive. Although the 49th Division broke through in the sector of the Panzer Lehr, the 12th SS held firm; by evening, the British infantry were still a mile short of Rauray. Despite the failure of the attack, Montgomery decided to go ahead with Epsom as planned.

Dauntless, however, was not without significant impact. To assist the hard-pressed Panzer Lehr, the 12th SS was compelled to commit both its Panther and reconnaissance battalions to the battle on the afternoon of the 25th; that evening, a jittery I SS Panzer Corps ordered the 12th SS to also dispatch its Panzer IV battalion-- presently in position behind the 26th Regiment and the engineer battalion to provide mobile anti-tank defense--to support the Panzer Lehr. Reluctantly, Kurt Meyer complied with the order; thus, when Epsom began the next morning, the 12th SS did not have any of its tanks in the threatened area. Ellis, *Victory in the West,* pp 275-77; Wilmont, *The Struggle for Europe,* p 342; Meyer, K., *Grenadiere,* pp 242-43.

[54]For the 15th Scottish, Epsom was its baptism of fire. For a detailed account of the division's operations, see Lieutenant-General H.G. Martin's *The History of the Fifteenth Scottish Division, 1939-1945* (Edinburgh and London: William Blackwood & Sons, Ldt., 1948).

ing grain. The German defenders who survived the shellfire emerged from their trenches and fought back with small arms fire and **Panzerfäuste**. As Scottish soldiers were hit and fell in the grain their comrades paused to mark their positions with a down-thrust rifle and bayonet--helmet balanced atop. Recalls one Allied observer: "It was poignant to gaze on these rifles surmounted by their tin helmets, looking like strange fungi sprouting up haphazardly through (the grainfields)." The sight was a universal one in Normandy in the summer of 1944.[55]

Four Enfield rifles mark the grave of a grenadier from the Hitler Youth Division.

Although misty, rainy weather **sharply** curtailed Allied air support,[56] the 15th Scottish rapidly overran the German main battle line along a three mile front from St. Manvieu to the area due east of Fontenay-le-Pesnel. Yet, even when overrun, small pockets of SS resisted with characteristic determination, fighting on until killed, wounded or captured. Later that morning, the commander of the engineer battalion, **SS-Sturmbannführer Müller**, got through on the telephone to division headquarters and reported the desperate situation confronting his troops. "Heavy artillery fire," he said, "has destroyed my anti-tank defense. The battalion is being overrun by British tanks. Individual strong points are still holding out in and around Cheux. Enemy tanks are attempting to crush my command bunker. Where are our tanks?" Moments

---

[55]Keegan, *Six Armies in Normandy,* pp 173-74.

[56]According to Ellis, on June 26th the "flying weather was so bad in England that the large programme of air support for the opening of Epsom had to be cancelled and, for the first time since D-Day, practically no aircraft based in England left the ground. Only 83 Group, stationed in Normandy, would be able to help VIII Corps, and though they flew over five hundred sorties their support was handicapped by low cloud and heavy ground-mist." Ellis, *Victory in the West,* p 277.

later the line went dead; all attempts by division headquarters to reach the battalion by radio were useless.[57]

Despite the rain sodden ground and furious resistance from the 12th SS, by midday, the 15th Scottish had infiltrated the villages of St. Manvieu, le Haut du Bosq and Cheux. Suicidal hand-to-hand combat ensued, and it took some time for the Scotsmen to overcome the small parties of SS who held out to the last among the ruined buildings, farmsteads and orchards.[58] In St. Manvieu, infantry of the 26th Regiment's 1st Battalion fought with fatalistic resignation; to clear some of the SS grenadiers from several stoutly defended buildings there, the British employed a weapon greatly feared by all who encountered it--flamethrower tanks. When one of the flame-spewing behemoths pressed uncomfortably close to battalion headquarters, a 24-year-old SS-Unterscharführer named Emil Dürr attacked the tank three times, finally destroying it with a magnetic hollow charge whose explosion killed him. A posthumous award of the Knight's Cross on August 23, 1944, honored the young man's sacrifice.[59]

D. Rose

Gravestone of Emil Dürr and grenadier Hans Holz.

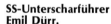

SS-Unterscharführer
Emil Dürr.

Jost W. Schneider

[57]About 9:00 a.m., enemy tanks and infantry had assaulted the command post of the 12th SS Engineer Battalion, located in an underground bunker one-half mile west of la Gaule. Throughout the day, however, Müller and his staff would successfully defend their heavily-reinforced redoubt against repeated attacks. At midnight in pouring rain, the battalion commander and nine survivors of his staff managed to escape from the bunker undetected by the enemy and make their way to German lines. T-354/154/3797709-14. 12.SS-Pz.Div. "Hitlerjugend." SS-Pz.Pi.Btl.12. Gefechtsbericht zum 26. Juni 1944; Meyer, H., P-164, p 37.

[58]In fact, isolated strongpoints of the 26th Regiment and of the engineer battalion would continue to resist in and around Cheux for several days. As late as June 28th, radio operators of the 12th SS intercepted messages from British tanks attacking remnants of the engineer battalion still holding out along the old front line. McKee, *Last Round Against Rommel,* p 138; Martin, *The History of the Fifteenth Scottish Division,* pp 35-36.

[59]The headquarters of SS-Sturmbannführer Krause's 1st Battalion was also in St. Manvieu, in a large house on the road from Cheux to Rots. Meyer, H., *Kriegsgeschichte,* pp 185-88; Schneider, *Verleihung Genehmigt!,* pp 78-79.

To prevent a catastrophic breakthrough, the 12th SS threw all available resources into the battle; even administrative and supply troops were drawn into the fighting. Gradually, the division's defenses began to stiffen. About 1:00 p.m., a regiment of the 11th British Armored Division attempted to push south from Cheux towards the Odon crossing at Gavrus but was stopped in its tracks by Panzer IVs of the 2nd Panzer Battalion. Yet the real danger of an enemy breakthrough was in the sector southeast of Cheux, towards the Odon bridges at Verson and south of Tourville; to shore up this weak point in the division's front, Kurt Meyer rushed the reconnaissance company of his former 25th Regiment into position north of Mouen. Supported by the timely arrival of a lone Tiger tank,[60] the company helped to stop an enemy thrust towards the Odon that afternoon, but in doing so was virtually annihilated. Meyer, who witnessed the formation's destruction, poignantly portrays the engagement in his memoirs:[61]

> The reconnaissance company is fighting for its life. Its positions are no longer recognizable. Furious artillery fire hurls the muddy ground into the air. Still, a single anti-tank gun stands and pumps round after round into a tank column of the 11th British Armored Division. A new barrage transforms the PAK gun into a scrap heap, and no other anti-tank weapons are operational. The company is torn apart by tank fire. The first fox holes are overrun. Some of the grenadiers attempt to eliminate the enemy tanks with Panzerfäuste but they do not succeed. The accompanying enemy infantry parries every attack on the tanks.
>
> In vain I attempt to provide the company with artillery support, but the specter of ammunition shortages has long been with us. The sporadic German artillery fire is incapable of stemming the enemy attack. The British tanks continue to wreak havoc.
>
> For the first time I feel a burning emptiness in my heart, and I curse the years of murder. For what I am now witnessing is no longer war, but naked murder.
>
> I know every one of these young grenadiers. The oldest among them is barely 18. The youths have not yet learned to live, but God knows, they understand how to die!
>
> Grinding tank tracks bring their young lives to an end. Tears run down my face and I begin to hate this war.
>
> The rain pours without interruption. Heavy clouds pass by above the tortured earth . . . Suddenly a new sound intermingles with this concert of death . . . The 88mm shell fire from a single Tiger tank forces the Shermans to an unequivocal halt. The British turn away; they suspend their attack in the direction of Mouen.

---

[60]The tank belonged to the Tiger tank battalion of the I SS Panzer Corps. Roughly six of the battalion's Tigers were now operating in the sector Verson - Grainville-sur-Odon. Meyer, H., *Kriegsgeschichte,* p 203.

[61]Meyer, K., *Grenadiere,* pp 247-48.

By evening, the 12th SS, reinforced by one company each of tanks and assault guns from the 21st Panzer Division, had brought the advance of the 15th Scottish and the 11th Armored Division to a halt well short of the Odon River.[62] More than 50 of Montgomery's tanks had been destroyed, and the war diarist at Army Group B characterized the day's fighting as a "complete defensive success" for the I SS Panzer Corps.[63] But for the 12th SS it was a Pyrrhic victory. The division had endured its greatest losses yet for a single day's combat--more than 700 soldiers killed, wounded or missing. The engineer battalion had practically ceased to exist, while the Panzer regiment had just 47 operational tanks (30 Panzer IVs and 17 Panthers) left.[64]

IWM

(Above and on facing page) Some of the first prisoners from the division taken by the British VIII Corps near Cheux.

[62]During the afternoon, two British tanks had advanced to within 200 yards of the 12th SS' headquarters in Verson, where they were destroyed by Panzerfäuste. Most of the British armor, however, had been stopped in the vicinity of Cheux. Ibid., p 248.

[63]BAMA. RH 19IX/84. KTB Heeresgruppe B. 27.6.1944.

[64]BAMA. Anlagen zum KTB Heeresgruppe B. 12.SS-Pz.Div. "Hitlerjugend." Abt. 1a. Lagebericht für den 26.6.1944; Meyer, H., *Kriegsgeschichte,* p 198.

IWM

IWM

During the night the Allies temporarily suspended their attacks. The 43rd Wessex Division began to consolidate the ground already won so that the 15th Scottish could continue its advance the next morning. The 12th SS took advantage of the lull in the fighting to reform its left flank along a line stretching from the western rim of the Carpiquet airport, across the high ground southeast of Cheux (Hill 100), to Rauray and Vendes. And a line it literally was, with little depth and few heavy weapons with which to contest the seemingly endless mass of British armor. To Kurt Meyer and his staff it was all too apparent that their greatly reduced forces were far too weak to prevent by themselves an enemy breakthrough across the Odon and beyond. Still, the grave responsibilities of the division were abundantly clear: to fight for time and to give ground as grudgingly as possible pending the arrival of the II SS Panzer Corps and other mobile reserves at the battlefront.[65]

Shortly after dawn, June 27th, VIII Corps resumed its offensive, attacking southward from Cheux with tanks and infantry. Like a solitary bulwark, four surviving tanks of SS-Hauptsturmführer Siegel's 8th Panzer Company held firm on the northern bank of a small stream, the Rau de Salbey; by late morning, they had repulsed four separate enemy attempts to break through to Grainville-sur-Odon.[66] Southeast of Cheux, however, another prong of the VIII Corps attack made better progress, overwhelming the thin line of the 12th SS Reconnaissance Battalion north of Colleville.[67] Buttressed by the tanks of the 23rd Hussars (11th Armored Division), a battalion of the 15th Scottish (2nd Battalion The Argyll and Sutherland Highlanders) captured Colleville after house-to-house fighting. Encountering light opposition, the Argylls pushed on and seized the villages of Mondrainville and Tourville in swift succession. After a brief pause to reorganize, the Scotsmen captured intact the bridge over the Odon near Tourmauville, and, by 8:00 p.m., had formed a small bridgehead on the south bank. Shortly thereafter, the 23rd Hussars crossed the river and advanced to the lower (northern) slopes of Hill 112--the dominating terrain feature southeast of Baron that would be the scene of much bitter fighting in the days to come.[68]

Through intercepted British radio communications, the headquarters of the 12th SS was soon aware that the enemy had crossed the Odon. The monitoring

---

[65]Meyer, K., *Grenadiere*, p 246.

[66]Siegel's Panzer IVs fired so fast that their ventilators could hardly cope with the fuming gases; from Siegel's own account, it is clear that his small force destroyed a large number of British tanks. Siegel, however, suffered second and third degree burns on his hands and face when his tank was hit and burst into flames. Following a stay in a military hospital, he would return to the division, and would take command of the Panzer regiment's 2nd Battalion after its commander, Sturmbannführer Prinz, was killed in action on August 14th. On August 23, 1944, Siegel was awarded the Knight's Cross. Schneider, *Verleihung Genehmigt!*, p 359; Hans Siegel, "Einsatz der 8.Pz.-Kp. Pz.-Rgt.12 am 26.6. und 27.6.1944 im Raum zwischen Rauray und Cheux - Bericht des damaligen Kompaniechefs, Hans Siegel, ausgezeichnet De. 1963;" Fragebogen, Hans Siegel.

[67]During the night of June 26-27, the 12th SS had shifted its reconnaissance battalion from the Rauray sector to a covering position southeast of Cheux, where the line of the 12th SS remained dangerously thin.

[68]Ellis, *Victory in the West*, p 280.

of enemy radio traffic also revealed that the British had discovered the location of the headquarters of the 12th SS, and were perhaps planning to attack it.[69] In response to the threat, all available men from the division staff occupied a covering position near Fontaine-Etoupefour. In the interim, the 12th SS Panzer Regiment had received instructions to secure both Hill 112 and Fontaine, and to block an enemy advance to the Orne; following the arrival of the first Panzers in Fontaine, Meyer shifted his headquarters from Verson to Louvigny, a village on the Orne directly southwest of Caen and farther back from the battlefront.[70]

In the many small and disjointed actions that had marked the day, the 12th SS once more incurred heavy losses in men and materiel. The division had again given ground, yet its defenses had not collapsed; rather, it had managed to temporarily seal off the VIII Corps breakthrough in the vicinity of Hill 112. On the division's extreme left flank, the remaining infantry of the 26th SS Panzer Grenadier Regiment's 3rd Battalion, finally expelled from Rauray, occupied new positions directly north of Brettevillette.[71]

The next morning, June 28th, the bulk of the 11th Armored Division was across the Odon; probing southward through the wooded terrain near Baron, the British tanks resumed their attack on Hill 112. Yet they did not get far, for throughout the morning and afternoon the available armor of the 12th SS counterattacked the much larger enemy force repeatedly and with punishing effect.[72] And although Wünsche's Panthers and Panzer IVs were themselves unable to capture Hill 112, the enemy was hard pressed just to retain his hold on the northern rim of the hill; by the end of the day, the 11th Armored had gained no additional ground. The 15th Scottish, however, secured a second bridgehead over Odon when the Argyll and Sutherland Highlanders, moving west along the thickly timbered banks of the river, captured Gavrus and the nearby crossings that evening.[73]

Only now were considerable German reinforcements beginning to reach the killing ground west and southwest of Caen; during the day, portions of six Panzer divisions (1st SS, 2nd SS, 2nd, 12th SS, 21st, and Panzer Lehr) were committed to action against the narrow corridor that Montgomery's forces

---

[69]Apparently a British unit (23rd Hussars?) had radioed the following query, intercepted by the 12th SS, to its superiors: "Do you still attach importance to the rapid Operation Verson?" Although the 12th SS did not intercept a reply, Meyer decided to move his headquarters from Verson. In any case, such a move was overdue, for on both June 26th and 27th, long-range Allied artillery had repeatedly bombarded division headquarters. Meyer, H., P-164, p 42.

[70]Ibid., p 42.

[71]The 12th SS was now desperately low on infantry--an unpleasant state of affairs acknowledged in the war diary of Army Group B. BAMA. KTB Heeresgruppe B. 27.6.1944.

[72]According to Hubert Meyer, no more than 30 tanks of the Panzer regiment participated in the attacks around Hill 112. In contrast, the 11th Armored Division had 165 operational Sherman and Stuart tanks in the Baron bridgehead by evening, June 28th. Meyer, H., Kriegsgeschichte, pp 217, 221.

[73]Ellis, Victory in the West, pp 281-82; Martin, The History of the Fifteenth Scottish Division, pp 42-43.

had driven through the original main battle line of the 12th SS.[74] After three days of fighting, this corridor was more than five miles deep but barely two miles wide.[75]

By the morning of the 28th, the enemy penetration south of Cheux had evoked considerable consternation at Seventh Army headquarters. To restore the situation, General Dollmann, the Seventh Army commander, decided to commit the entire II SS Panzer Corps[76] against this penetration. Once again reactivated, Geyr von Schweppenburg and his Panzer Group West staff[77] were placed in charge of the operation, which was to go in early the next day. Having ordered the counterattack, Dollmann was beyond caring about its outcome; deeply despondent over the loss of Cherbourg (June 26th), for which Hitler had ordered a court-martial inquiry, and the worsening military situation in general, he committed suicide. SS-Obergruppenführer Paul Hausser, hitherto commander of the II SS Panzer Corps, succeeded Dollmann as Seventh Army commander.

General der Artillerie Friedrich Dollmann.

[74]During the night of June 27-28, a battlegroup from the 2nd SS Panzer Division "Das Reich" had relieved the forces of the 12th SS--elements of the 26th SS Panzer Grenadier Regiment and of the Panzer regiment--fighting in the sector west of Mondrainville. It was this relief that enabled the 12th SS to concentrate most of its armor about Hill 112.

[75]Ellis, *Victory in the West*, p 282.

[76]The Corps' 9th and 10th SS Panzer Divisions were now arriving at the battlefront. See Wilhelm Tieke, *Im Feuersturm letzter Kriegsjahre. II. SS-Panzerkorps mit 9. und 10. SS-Divisionen "Hohenstaufen" und "Frundsberg"* (Osnabrück: Munin Verlag GmbH, 1975), pp 123-24.

[77]With the return of Geyr and his headquarters, the Germans reorganized their command structure in Normandy. Panzer Group West was subordinated directly to Army Group B, and, at 5:00 p.m. on the 28th, took command of all forces between the Seine and the Drome--the LXXXVI Army Corps and the I SS, II SS and XLVII Panzer Corps. Seventh Army remained responsible for the II Parachute and LXXXIV Army Corps, which were fighting west of the Drome. BAMA. KTB Panzer-Armeeoberkommando 5. 28.6.1944.

Rommel and SS-Obergruppenführer und General der Waffen SS Hausser, shortly after Hausser was made Seventh Army commander.

June 29th "broke bright and clear," and the Mustangs, Spitfires, and Typhoons of the Allied tactical air forces were out in considerable strength.[78] Harried by fighter-bombers and vigorous artillery fire, the II SS Panzer Corps was unable to complete its preparations in timely fashion and had no choice but to postpone its attack (scheduled for 6:00 a.m.) until the afternoon.[79] Meanwhile, the 11th Armored Division had gained complete possession of Hill 112. According to the war diary of Army Group B, the Panzer Corps finally counterattacked at 2:30 p.m.—its two Panzer divisions advancing astride the Odon, across the line Bougy - Noyers, and striking the western flank of the enemy salient:[80]

> During the battle which raged from copse to hedgerow throughout the evening half a dozen tanks penetrated almost to Cheux, but the Scottish battalions stood firm and the German infantry which sought to follow the armor was

---

[78]Poor weather had limited Allied air activity throughout the first three days of the Epsom offensive. On the 29th, however, their tactical air forces alone flew some 1,000 sorties, striking German troop concentrations and disrupting the movement of supplies. Ellis, *Victory in the West*, pp 283-84.

[79]Tieke, *Im Feuersturm letzter Kriegsjahre*, p 124.

[80]The quote is from Wilmont, *The Struggle for Europe*, p 345; BAMA. KTB Heeresgruppe B. 29.6.1944.

driven back. Before dark the SS troops had been routed and the lonely tanks had been destroyed. Throughout the night the British gunners continued to shell the woods and villages in which the Germans were attempting to reassemble for a fresh move.

Supported by elements of the I SS Panzer Corps, the II SS Panzer Corps resumed its offensive early the next day. Again the attack made some initial progress, and in a pincer movement tanks and infantry of the 10th and 12th SS Panzer Divisions had recaptured the now thoroughly battered Hill 112 by midday.[81] That afternoon, however, the Germans acknowledged defeat, and broke off their offensive "in the face of intensive enemy artillery fire and supporting fire of unprecedented ferocity from naval units."[82]

Following the failure of his counterstroke, Geyr submitted a candid report to Seventh Army headquarters (June 30th); in it, he recommended that German forces evacuate the part of Caen north and west of the Orne and withdraw to a new front line following the river as far as Bully (about six miles south of Caen) and thence through Avenay and Villers-Bocage to the area around Caumont. He also proposed that elements of the 12th SS, 21st Panzer, and Panzer Lehr be rapidly pulled from the line and replenished, in preparation for a "renewed transition to offensive strikes" outside the most effective range of the lethal naval gun fire. Geyr's report was forwarded to Army Group B and OB West for further consideration.[83]

In sympathy with Geyr's memorandum, Rundstedt passed it on to the High Command at Berchtesgaden with a cover letter of his own, requesting a free hand to pull back from the Caen bridgehead. Hitler's response to his generals' proposals was swift and unequivocal: he flatly forbade any withdrawal from Caen. The present positions, he decreed on July 1st, were to be held; all further enemy breakthroughs prevented by tenacious defense or limited counterthrusts.[84] Having laid down the law, the Führer summarily relieved both Geyr and Rundstedt of their commands.[85]

Following the defeat of the SS Panzer divisions, Montgomery did not resume the Epsom offensive. For the moment, he was content to consolidate

---

[81]The 12th SS committed its 2nd Panzer Battalion and infantry from the 26th Regiment's 3rd Battalion to the attack on Hill 112. The capture of the hill was facilitated by the fact that the 11th Armored had just withdrawn its tanks into reserve north of the Odon on orders from the Second British Army. Meyer, H., *Kriegsgeschichte*, p 227; Tieke, *Im Feuersturm letzter Kriegsjahre*, p 130.

[82]On the evening of the 29th, Geyr had informed Rommel's headquarters that the magnitude of the enemy artillery fire equalled the terrific bombardments on the western front in 1918. BAMA. KTB Heeresgruppe B. 29.6.1944; Wilmont, *The Struggle for Europe*, pp 345-46.

[83]A copy of Geyr's report exists among the records of the Seventh Army. BAMA. AOK 7/57350/2.

[84]BAMA. KTB Panzer-Armeeoberkommando 5. 1.7.1944.

[85]Field Marshal Günther v. Kluge replaced Rundstedt as OB West on July 2nd; the next day, General Heinrich Eberbach assumed command of Panzer Group West. According to David Irving, Rommel was only spared a similar fate because he had not wavered in his resolve to hold firm at Caen. Irving, *The Trail of the Fox*, pp 400-401.

his grasp on the bulging salient his forces had gained southwest of Caen. Clearly, the results of Epsom were mixed, for Montgomery had failed to reach the Orne and to complete the envelopment of Caen--a failure largely attributable to the furious resistance displayed by the 12th SS from June 26-28. Conversely, the British Field Marshal had pinned the German armored reserves in battle where he wanted them, at Caen--accentuating the maldistribution of German forces in Normandy.[86] Montgomery's timely thrust also destroyed whatever chances the Germans may have had of launching a counteroffensive from the Caumont - St. Lô sector, for the Panzer divisions were now too reduced in strength to be capable of major offensive action. The 12th SS alone suffered 1,052 casualties from June 26-30--a frightening diminution of its combat strength.[87] After Epsom, the complete destruction of the division--indeed, the total collapse of the German front in Normandy--was but a question of time.[88]

*   *   *

In July and August 1944, the gradual, albeit inexorable amputation of the 12th SS Panzer Division continued. Following three weeks of relative inactivity, the 3rd Canadian Infantry Division launched Operation "Windsor" on July 4th, attacking the village of Carpiquet and the adjacent airfield. Defending the village and the airfield facilities were some 200 infantry of the 26th SS Panzer Grenadier Regiment's 1st Battalion. A tremendous artillery barrage heralded the attack and caused severe German casualties; many of the survivors had to dig themselves and their weapons out of the ruins before they could fight back. With the help of flamethrower tanks, the Canadian infantry rapidly penetrated Carpiquet, and despite heavy losses captured the village along with the northernmost airfield hangers. Canadian attempts to seize the hangars south of the airfield, however, floundered in the face of determined opposition.[89]

Following the loss of Carpiquet, the 12th SS prepared its forces to meet the inevitable frontal assault on Caen. The division's only reserves of infantry were the remnants of the 26th Regiment's 3rd Battalion and the divisional escort company; both formations went into position about Caen, behind the line of the 25th SS Panzer Grenadier Regiment. To furnish mobile anti-tank

---

[86]At the end of June, seven-and-one-half of the eight Panzer divisions in Normandy were fighting opposite the Second British Army. Wilmont, *The Struggle for Europe*, p 348.

[87]The losses of the 12th SS broke down as follows: 164 dead, 437 wounded, and 451 missing. The great majority of these casualties occurred on June 26th and 27th. Ironically, the tank strength of the division had improved slightly by June 30th, when it reported 51 tanks (25 Panzer IVs and 26 Panthers) ready for action. Meyer, *Kriegsgeschichte*, p 229; Public Record Office. Ultra Signal XL771.

[88]According to a report from Army Group B, total German personnel losses in Normandy as of July 7, 1944 were more than 80,000, including 1,830 officers. As replacements, the Army Group had received only 10,671 men. BAMA. Wochenmeldung Heeresgruppe B. 3.7.-9.7.44.

[89]Strongly posted in fortifications constructed by the Luftwaffe prior to the Normandy invasion, the SS grenadiers defending the southernmost hangars would hold their positions until July 9th. Stacey, *The Victory Campaign*, pp 155, 162.

defense, the remaining armor was distributed across the entire front of the division.[90] Kurt Meyer, to be closer to the battlefield, moved his headquarters from Louvigny to the Abbaye aux Dames in Caen.

Bernhard Krause (bottom left), commander of the 1st Bn., 26th SS-Panzer Grenadier Regiment, positioning his troops in Verson, near Caen.

[90]The right flank of the 12th SS, virtually static since the 7th of June, still stretched in an arc from the Caen - Luc-sur-Mer rail line westward to Franqueville. After Epsom, the reconstituted left flank of the division extended from Carpiquet southward to Eterville. To provide sorely needed infantry, a Panzer grenadier regiment from the 1st SS Panzer Division had been temporarily subordinated to the 12th SS; one of its battalions was in position west of Bretteville-sur-Odon. Meyer, H., *Kriegsgeschichte*, pp 238-39, 250.

On the evening of July 7th, 467 Lancaster and Halifax bombers from R.A.F. Bomber Command dumped 2,560 tons of bombs on the northern outskirts of Caen in an effort to disrupt German communications through the city.[91] The next morning, Montgomery commenced Operation "Charnwood"--a frontal assault on Caen conducted by the I British Corps.[92] Hundreds of artillery pieces, as well as naval and tactical air forces, supported the offensive. On the eastern flank of I Corps, the 3rd British Infantry Division easily overran the inexperienced and poorly equipped 16th Luftwaffe Field Division,[93] and by dark had reached the northern fringe of the city. In the center and on the western flank, the 25th SS Panzer Grenadier Regiment fought with greater tenacity, but it too was largely overwhelmed by the sheer weight of the enemy attack. During the day's fighting, I Corps infantry secured most of the fortified villages covering Caen, and surrounded remnants of the 25th Regiment's 2nd

Woscidlo

Grenadiers, just inside the entrance to the Abbey Ardenne, contemplate the coming battle.

[91]The Allied aerial strike, meant to cut off the German troops defending Caen from reinforcements and supplies, did not disturb the main battle line of the 12th SS. And although numerous bombs fell in the assembly areas of the 2nd Panzer Battalion, the 3rd Battalion 26th Regiment and the divisional escort company, these formations incurred only minor losses in equipment and/or personnel. Meyer, H., *Kriegsgeschichte*, p 253; Fragebogen, Willy Kretzschmar.

[92]The I British Corps comprised the 3rd British Infantry Division, the newly available 59th (Staffordshire) Division, and the 3rd Canadian Infantry Division. Each infantry division was supported by tanks.

[93]The 16th Luftwaffe Field Division had taken over the sector of the 21st Panzer Division (northeast of Caen) only three days before.

and 3rd Battalions in the ruins of Galmanche and Buron, respectively. Counterattacking with a company of Panther tanks and a handful of grenadiers, the 12th SS managed to bring the advance of the 3rd Canadian Infantry Division to a temporary standstill before the walls of the Abbey Ardenne–its ruined buildings surrounded by knocked-out German and Canadian tanks that burned luridly through the night.[94]

A 150mm heavy infantry gun is moved to the courtyard of the Abbey Ardenne.

Despite the Führerbefehl (Hitler order) to hold firm at Caen at all cost, Kurt Meyer now resolved to abandon the portion of the city north and west of the Orne and to pull back his troops and heavy weapons behind the river barrier. Failure to do so at once, he realized, would only result in the complete encirclement and destruction of his remaining forces.[95]

Under cover of darkness, the 12th SS began to evacuate the Caen bridgehead; elements of both the encircled 2nd and 3rd Battalions were able to break through enemy lines and to make good their escape. Shortly after midnight, Meyer visited the exhausted grenadiers of the 25th Regiment's 1st Battalion:[96]

> I find the survivors of the battalion in a bunker on the edge of the city. The battle-weary soldiers have fallen into a deep sleep. Officers have taken over guard duty. Stragglers stumble into the bunker and collapse where they can find an unoccupied spot. What luck that the Canadians and British haven't followed up their attack! The soldiers of the 12th SS Panzer Division are at the end of their physical strength. They have fought without relief for four weeks in the forwardmost line and have endured the powerful hammerblows of the Materialschlacht.

---

[94]Stacey, *The Victory Campaign,* pp 160-61.
[95]Meyer's decision also meant pulling back from the shell-torn Carpiquet airfield. See Meyer, K., *Grenadiere,* pp 264-69.
[96]Ibid., pp 268-69.

With fresh, radiant faces they had marched into battle, but today smeared steel helmets hide their sunken eyes, which all too often have peered into the hereafter. The men offer a picture of profound human suffering, but they cannot rest for long, for they must defend the (south) bank of the Orne. Waldmüller receives the new order and rouses his troops from their leaden sleep. Each grenadier must be awakened individually. Drowsily, they stagger out of the bunker and hang their ammunition around their necks. The heavy machine gun belts drag the half-awakened grenadiers forward.

SS-Sturmbannführer Waldmüller, commander of the 1st Bn., 25th Rgt., in his command post in front of Cambes shortly before the Allied offensive against Caen on July 8-9, 1944.

Throughout the night and early morning hours of July 9th, the spent soldiers of the 25th SS Panzer Grenadier Regiment made their way through the rubble of Caen to positions along the south bank of the Orne.[97] The enemy did not contest the withdrawal. The new line of the 12th SS Panzer extended from the city's industrial quarters (Vaucelles) to the confluence of the Orne with the Odon. Following up the German retreat, British and Canadian forces advanced into Caen, meeting only desultory resistance. Thus, 33 days later than

---

[97] A veteran of the 25th Regiment's 1st Battalion remembered the withdrawal thusly: "We retired through the destroyed city. The sight was hardly uplifting, because dead civilians lay everywhere . . . Many of the bodies were swollen up from the heat. It simply defied all description. Herds of livestock had stumbled into our minefields, and we relieved them from their suffering." Letter to author from Frank Kucklack, June 25, 1981.

prescribed in Montgomery's original plan, the city (at least the greater part of it) was finally in Allied hands.[98] It had been a victory dearly bought, the Canadians alone having suffered 1194 casualties, including 330 dead, on July 8-9.[99] The 12th SS had sacrificed nearly 600 more of its soldiers in the final battle for Caen; losses in materiel had also been substantial, the division losing at least 20 more tanks, five or six 105mm field howitzers, two 88mm Flak, and the majority of its anti-tank guns.[100]

On July 11th, the 12th SS Hitlerjugend handed over the Caen sector to the 1st SS Panzer Division Leibstandarte and withdrew into reserve north of Falaise (area Sassy - Condé - Garcelles - Potigny - Bons). In the brief lull that followed, the 12th SS received no replacements in personnel or materiel.[101] Its troops, however, were able to rest, to perform much needed

[98]The industrial quarters of Caen (south of the Orne), however, would remain in German hands through July 18th, denying Montgomery "the through routes he needed so that Second Army could maintain its threat to Paris." Wilmont, *The Struggle for Europe*, p 351.

[99]Stacey, *The Victory Campaign*, p 163.

[100]As of July 11th, the 12th SS Panzer Division had lost an aggregate of 4,485 men since the beginning of the campaign; that same day it had 19 Panzer IVs and 18 Panthers ready for action. Only four of the division's original **complement** of 28 75mm PAK were still operational. BAMA. RH 19IV/44. KTB OB West. 12.7.44; BAMA. KTB Heeresgruppe B. 9.7.44. Meyer, H., *Kriegsgeschichte*, p 270.

[101]During the latter stages of the Normandy battle the 12th SS did receive some personnel replacements. These replacements, however, were insignificant in number.

This German youth fell during the fierce fighting around Caen on July 9, 1944.

Woscidlo

Three graves of the division's dead near Caen.

Max Wünsche awards this SS-Oberscharführer with the Iron Cross 2nd Class for shooting down five enemy aircraft with his Flak gun near Caen.

Woscidlo

Members of the 3rd Battalion, 25th Regiment, relax in Buron during a respite in the fighting.

maintenance on weapons and vehicles, and to bring forward munitions, fuel and other supplies. Cadre personnel (Stämme) from both Panzer grenadier regiments, the Panzer regiment and the reconnaissance battalion returned to their original billeting areas in Normandy (i.e., their quarters before the invasion) to begin rebuilding their shattered units. The division's remaining combat strength was organized principally into two battlegroups.[102]

On July 17th, Kurt Meyer visited the headquarters of the I SS Panzer Corps in Urville (southeast of Bretteville-sur-Laize) for a conference. Also present at the conference was the Corps commander, SS-Obergruppenführer Sepp Dietrich, and the commander of Army Group B, Field Marshal Rommel. During the meeting, Rommel expressed his admiration for the fighting qualities of the 12th SS Panzer; he then asked its commander for an appreciation of the situation at the front. Meyer stated that a major British assault was imminent south of Caen–a danger, no doubt, to which the Field Marshal was fully alert. Meyer concluded his report with a reference to the paralyzing effect of Allied air power and a plea to Rommel for Luftwaffe support, eliciting a brusk response from his superior:[103]

> Who do you think you're talking to? Do you think I drive with my eyes closed through the country? I have written report after report. Already in Africa I pointed out the devastating effect of the enemy fighter-bombers, but the gentlemen (i.e., OKW) know everything better. My reports are simply no longer taken seriously. Something has to happen. The war in the West must be ended!

Field Marshal Günther v. Kluge, the new commander of Army Group B.

---

[102]Battlegroup Wünsche was composed of some 30 tanks, infantry and self-propelled artillery; Battlegroup Waldmüller consisted of a reinforced (verstärkt) infantry battalion. During the remainder of the campaign, the battlegroups of the 12th SS would be reorganized as the situation required.

[103]Meyer, K., *Grenadiere*, pp 272-73.

The conference was the final act of Rommel's brilliant military career. Departing Panzer Group headquarters that afternoon, he was seriously wounded in a British fighter-bomber attack near a village that bore the name Ste. Foy-de-Montgomery.[104] The Commander-in-Chief West, Field Marshal von Kluge, now took command of Army Group B as well.

The anticipated enemy offensive, Operation "Goodwood," began the next day, when the tanks of the VIII British Corps attacked south from the old airborne bridgehead east of the Orne.[105] On July 19th, the 12th SS was back in action. Relieving the 21st Panzer Division in the sector Emiéville - Frénouville, the teenagers of the Hitler Youth Division thwarted all attempts by the British Guards Armored Division to crack through to Vimont. By July 20th, the depth

An entrenched 75mm anti-tank gun north of Caen.

and strength of the German defenses, which included large numbers of artillery, Nebelwerfer and 88mm guns, had checked the VIII Corps attack well short of a strategic breakthrough. The next two weeks, the 12th SS remained in the line at Vimont; although not attacked during this period, the SS grenadiers suffered heavily from the enemy artillery fire that swept their front. Relieved by the 272nd Infantry Division on August 3-4, the 12th SS again moved into reserve north of Falaise, this time in the area Vieux-Fumé - Maizières - St. Sylvain - Bray-la-Campagne, where it formed the operational reserve (Eingreifreserve) of the I SS Panzer Corps.[106]

By early August 1944, a redeployment of the Panzer divisions in Normandy had significantly weakened the German defenses south and southeast of Caen. These defenses, though still intact, were now held by several inadequately equipped and largely immobile Wehrmacht infantry divisions.[107] The 12th SS,

---

[104]Implicated in the German resistance movement against Hitler, Rommel was forced by the Führer to commit suicide on October 14, 1944.

[105]For the "Goodwood" operation, Montgomery had grouped the British 7th, 11th and Guards Armored Divisions under VIII Corps command.

[106]Wilmont, *The Struggle for Europe*, pp 356-62; Meyer, K., *Grenadiere*, p 276; Meyer, H., *Kriegsgeschichte*, p 287.

[107]These were the 272nd Infantry Division (LXXXVI Army Corps) and the 89th and 271st Infantry Divisions (I SS Panzer Corps).

Sepp Dietrich near the Normandy Front, late July 1944.

in fact, was the only German mobile formation still deployed east of the Orne, the rest of the German armor having been shifted west of the river to contest threatening enemy breakthroughs and to carry out Hitler's ill-fated Mortain offensive.[108]

Against this backdrop, the achievements of the fighting remnant of the Hitler Youth Division in its final battles of the Normandy campaign appear all the more remarkable. Once more displaying its tenacious combat technique, the division played a decisive role in halting two separate offensives ("Totalize" and "Tractable") of the First Canadian Army[109] between Caen and Falaise. In essence, the 12th SS Panzer had become an elite fire brigade, hurled repeatedly into breaches in the line to seal off breakthroughs of greatly superior enemy forces and to restore the shattered main battle line.

Shortly before midnight, August 7th, the Canadian Army launched Operation "Totalize" in an effort to push through to Falaise. In the wake of an aerial bombardment laid down by 1020 Lancaster and Halifax bombers, its infantry and armor attacked in overwhelming strength and easily steamrolled the positions of the German 89th Infantry Division astride the Caen - Falaise road (Route Nationale 158); by midday, August 8th, a spectacular Allied breakthrough appeared imminent. Steps to block such an exploitation, however, had already been taken, and primarily by one man: the commander of the 12th SS, SS-Oberführer Kurt Meyer.[110] Driving up the Caen - Falaise road that morning to reconnoiter, Meyer had suddenly encountered groups of Wehrmacht infantry streaming towards the rear in total disorder. Like a mythic teutonic warrior, he posted himself in the highway, challenged the panic-stricken stragglers and drove them back towards the front, organizing their defense in the vicinity of Cintheaux.[111]

Through stinging counterstrokes, the 12th SS, bolstered by a handful of Tiger tanks, was able to bring the enemy advance to a halt on August 10th

---

[108]On August 7-8, the Germans counterattacked at Mortain with four Panzer divisions (1st SS, 2nd SS, 2nd and 116th) in an effort to push through to the coast at Avranches and to cut off the American forces that had broken through the front of the Seventh Army. The offensive, however, was crushed by the Thunderbolts and Typhoons of the Allied tactical air forces. Wilmont, *The Struggle for Europe,* pp 401-404.

[109]Commanded by Lieutenant-General H.D.G. Crerar, the First Canadian Army consisted of the I British and the II Canadian Corps, and had taken over the sector of the Allied front east of the Orne in late July.

[110]Meyer had been promoted to SS-Oberführer on August 1, 1944. His promotion to SS-Brigadeführer followed on September 1st. SS Personalakten, Kurt Meyer.

[111]In Kurt Meyer's interrogation report there is the following entry concerning this extraordinary incident: "At the same time as Meyer was up on the [Route Nationale 158] alone, groups of the 89th Infantry Division, scattered in panic by the bombing, were making their way down the road as quickly as possible. Meyer, on perceiving this serious situation, calmly lit a cigar, stood in the middle of the road [apparently while exposed to enemy fire] and in a loud voice asked them if they were going to leave him alone to cope with the Allied attack when it came. One look at this young commander was enough and the men turned around and immediately started to take up defensive positions." PAC. Special Interrogation Report. Kurt Meyer, pp 6-7; Meyer, K., *Grenadiere,* pp 281-82.

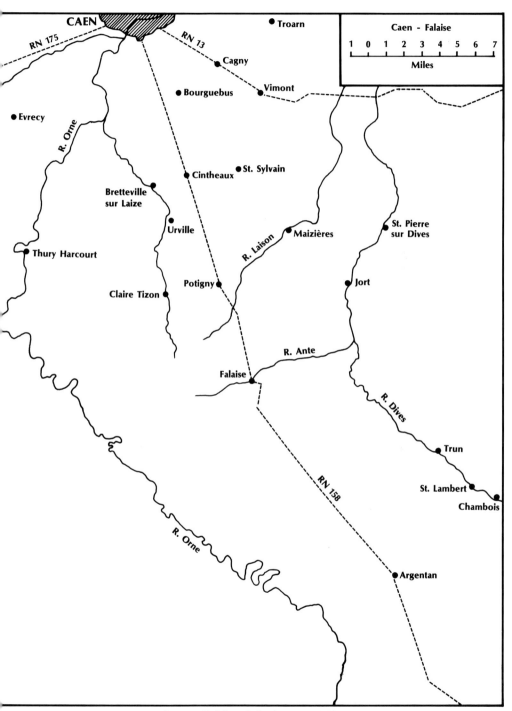

Caen - Falaise: July-August, 1944

seven miles short of Falaise, and to establish a new defensive front on the high ground north of the Laison River and above Potigny.[112] By August 15th, more fighting had reduced the division to a combat strength of some 500 infantry and 15 tanks.[113] Throughout the 15th, this rump of a fighting force succeeded in checking another Canadian breakthrough (Operation "Tractable") on the last ridge before Falaise, north of the Ante. There the survivors of the Hitler Youth Division were still holding firm the next day, when elements of the 2nd Canadian Infantry Division broke into Falaise from the west. In a final gesture of defiance, 50-60 SS grenadiers fought to the last man behind the thick walls of the city's Ecole Supérieure.[114]

While the 12th SS strained every nerve to hold intact the front south of Caen, the fate of the two German armies[115] defending Normandy was being decided by developments farther west. In late July, the First U.S. Army had finally cracked the positions of the German Seventh Army about St. Lô.[116] Exploiting the gap, General Patton's recently activated Third U.S. Army had then raced on into Brittany, south towards the Loire, and east towards the Seine, meeting only scattered German resistance. On August 8th, Patton's easternmost spearhead was in Le Mans; turning north towards the British-Canadian forces advancing on Falaise, the XV U.S. Corps had an armored division on either flank of Argentan by the evening of the 13th, threatening the remnants of 19 German divisions with encirclement. Indeed, with the Americans situated around Argentan, the gap separating the northern and southern pincers of the Allied trap was barely 20 miles wide.[117]

From August 17-19, the 12th SS conducted a successful delaying action southeast of Falaise towards the Dives, helping to hold open the northern flank of the Falaise - Argentan pocket long enough to permit thousands of German troops to make good their escape.[118] During this period the fighters

---

[112]According to the war diary of Army Group B, the 12th SS destroyed 192 enemy tanks during Operation "Totalize." Although the figure is most likely inflated, the division did eliminate a large number of enemy tanks on August 8-9. BAMA. RH 19IX/87. KTB Heeresgruppe B. 10.8.44.

[113]The 12th SS also possessed a handful of tank destroyers and the remainder of its artillery and Flak. The division's order of battle on August 12, 1944 is provided in Appendix 5. BAMA. KTB Heeresgruppe B. 15.8.44.

[114]Not until the early morning of August 18th did the Canadians, with the help of mortars and PAK, manage to crush all resistance at the Ecole Supérieure. Only two of the SS grenadiers--chosen by lot because no one had wanted to leave--escaped; they returned as messengers to the 12th SS and reported the fate of their comrades to Kurt Meyer. Meyer, H., *Kriegsgeschichte*, p 334; Meyer, K., *Grenadiere*, p 303.

[115]These were the Seventh Army and the Fifth Panzer Army (hitherto Panzer Group West).

[116]The overall success of Montgomery's **strategic** design is evident from the fact that, on the eve of the American breakout (Operation "Cobra"), only two Panzer divisions were deployed on the front of the First U.S. Army. In contrast, seven Panzer divisions (five-and-one-half of which were east of the Orne) and four heavy tank battalions were facing the Second British Army. Wilmont, *The Struggle for Europe*, p 364.

[117]Ibid., pp 404, 417.

[118]Not until August 16th, with the pocket nearly closed, did Hitler order a general withdrawal across the Orne and the Dives. BAMA. RH 19IV/45. KTB OB West. 16.8.44.

and fighter-bombers of the Allied Second Tactical Air Force averaged some 1,200 sorties per day, pouring rockets and machine gun fire into the masses of German troops and vehicles that jammed the roadways leading away from the pocket, and transforming the German withdrawal from Normandy into an utter rout.[119] On the evening of August 19th, the Allied pincers joined at Chambois; the pocket was closed.[120]

Trapped inside the encirclement ring, the survivors of the 12th SS attempted to break out across the Dives between Trun and Chambois on August 20-21.[121] Moving by vehicle or on foot along the hedgerows and sunken lanes, some contrived to slip through the enemy ring to safety; others were killed and hundreds captured.[122] Kurt Meyer and a small party that included his operations

One of many division members who fell in the Falaise pocket.

---

[119]Hilary St. George Saunders, *The Fight is Won. The Royal Air Force 1939-45* (London: Her Majesty's Stationery Office, 1954), p 137.

[120]According to Wilmont, the Germans lost 10,000 dead and 50,000 prisoners in the Falaise - Argentan pocket. Wilmont, *The Struggle for Europe*, pp 423-24.

[121]Only part of what remained of the division was actually trapped within the Falaise pocket. Elements withdrawn for refitting following the capture of Caen in July had not returned to the front, and hence were outside of the pocket when it closed. Also outside the encirclement ring were the division's supply troops and replacement battalion.

[122]One of those taken prisoner was Max Wünsche (the commander of the 12th SS Panzer Regiment), who had been wounded. Captured on August 24th, Wünsche was at first placed in a wire cage partly submerged in water. The next day, his captors transported him some 25 miles to an Allied field headquarters. To his astonishment, Wünsche suddenly found himself in the presence of Field Marshal Bernard Montgomery. Conversing with a subordinate, Montgomery, who no doubt had had his fill of the Hitler Youth Division, made abundantly clear what he thought of the Waffen SS: "We will treat German prisoners in accordance with the Geneva Convention, but not the SS. We will treat them for what they are--political vermin, political dirt." Meyer, H., *Kriegsgeschichte*, p 353; Interview, Hubert Meyer, December 9, 1979.

IWM

IWM

Wounded and dazed members of the Hitler Youth division as prisoners-of-war.

officer, Hubert Meyer, made good their escape on foot, crossing the Dives near St. Lambert on the 20th. That afternoon, the division commander and his operations officer reported to the headquarters of the I SS Panzer Corps, which had given them up for dead.[123]

The battle of Normandy was over. The 12th SS Panzer Division had anchored the eastern flank of the German front since June 7th, and its overall losses were correspondingly high. As of August 22nd, the 12th SS had lost approximately 8,000 dead, wounded or missing (40 percent of its personnel), including the great majority of its infantry. The division had also sacrificed almost all of its armored fighting vehicles, armored personnel carriers and artillery. Shorn of most of its infantry and heavy weapons, the Hitler Youth Division had become a mere shadow of the magnificent formation that had moved so confidently into battle some ten weeks before.[124]

*   *   *   *   *

---

[123]For Kurt Meyer's own account of his dramatic escape from the pocket see *Grenadiere*, pp 303-310.

[124]Although the 12th SS was now of little combat value, it still had some 12,500 personnel--not 500, as is often asserted in the post-war literature. The division had entered the invasion battle with an aggregate personnel strength (i.e., combat, supply and administrative troops) of 20,540. Meyer, H., *Kriegsgeschichte*, p 355.

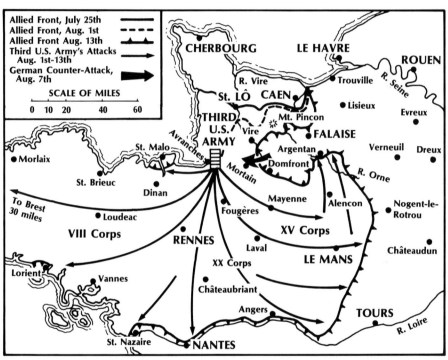

Allied Front, July 25th
Allied Front, Aug. 1st
Allied Front Aug. 13th
Third U.S. Army's Attacks
  Aug. 1st-13th
German Counter-Attack,
  Aug. 7th

SCALE OF MILES
0   10   20   40   60

CHERBOURG   LE HAVRE
                                          ROUEN
R. Vire   Trouville   R. Seine
St. LÔ   CAEN
THIRD   Lisieux   Evreux
U.S.   Mt. Pincon
ARMY   Vire   FALAISE
Avranches   Verneuil   Dreux
St. Malo   Argentan
Morlaix   Domfront   R. Orne
          Mortain
St. Brieuc   Nogent-le-
       Dinan   Mayenne   Alencon   Rotrou
To Brest
30 miles   Loudeac   Fougères   Châteaudun
VIII Corps   XV Corps
            RENNES   Laval
                                LE MANS
Lorient   XX Corps
     Vannes   Châteaubriant
                   Angers   TOURS
St. Nazaire   R. Loire
          NANTES

The Exploitation from Avranches.

Chapter 11
IN SEARCH OF AN HISTORICAL PERSPECTIVE

From the Hitler Youth has emerged a movement of young tank busters.

(Reich Youth Leader Artur Axmann
on March 28, 1945)

Following its virtual destruction in Normandy, the 12th SS Panzer Division fought a series of minor holding actions as it withdrew from France and into Belgium. By mid-September 1944, the division was back in Germany to rest and refit. Although personnel replacements included some young volunteers, the division also received large numbers of Luftwaffe ground personnel, Navy personnel, and recuperated veterans from military hospitals. On November

IWM

These survivors of the Hitler Youth division, who had crossed the Seine in late August, were captured in the Ardennes on September 2, 1944, by American troops who had cut across northeast France after liberating Paris.

15th, SS-Standartenführer Hugo Kraas, a regimental commander in the 1st SS Leibstandarte, became the last commander of the 12th SS.[1]

SS-Standartenführer Hugo Kraas.

Kurt Meyer wears the uniform of an army colonel at the time of his capture.

---

[1]Following the capture of Kurt Meyer in early September, Hubert Meyer assumed interim command of the division. Shortly before his capture, Kurt Meyer had become the 91st German soldier during the Second World War to receive the Swords to the Oak Leaves of the Knight's Cross. SS Personalakten, Kurt Meyer.

A soldier of the 6th U.S. Armored Division searches captured members of the Hitler Youth Division, Bastogne, January 7, 1945.

Bearing little resemblance to its former elite character, the division returned to action in mid-December, when it took part in Hitler's Ardennes offensive as a component of the 6th Panzer Army; New Year's Day, 1945, found the 12th SS forming part of the German encirclement ring around the village of Bastogne. Following the failure of the Ardennes offensive, the division withdrew once again and assembled west of Cologne in late January. In February 1945, the 12th SS was transferred to Hungary, where, under the command of Army Group South, it participated (March 6-18) in the abortive offensive east of Lake Balaton aimed at the recapture of Budapest. During the final weeks of the war, the division was swept along in the general retreat of Axis forces in southeastern Europe. Driven back into Austria by the victorious Red Army, the division crossed the American-Russian demarcation line at the River Enns on May 8, 1945, and capitulated to forces of the American Seventh Army. Proud and defiant to the end, the survivors of the 12th SS refused to comply with an American order to drape their vehicles with a white flag as a token of surrender.[2]

*　　*　　*

In assessing the historical significance of the 12th SS Panzer Division, it is important to note that Hitler Youths were found in other military formations in the final phase of the war. The establishment of the Volkssturm in October 1944 officially introduced compulsory military service in home guard units for

---

[2]Surrendering to the Americans were 9,870 soldiers of the 12th SS, including 328 officers and 1,698 NCOs. Most of these men had been released from captivity by the end of 1948. Meyer, H., *Kriegsgeschichte,* pp 554, 557; Meyer, K., *Grenadiere,* p 341.

Woscidlo

The division in Hungary, February 1945.

every male from the ages of 16 to 60. In practice, the recruits were often both younger as well as older. To the final moment,[3]

> Germany's youth was exhorted to mount and assist on the defense of the Reich against the 'Bolshevik hordes' and the 'Anglo-American gangsters.' And more often than not they followed the call. 'They had been fed with heroes' legends ever since they could remember. For them the 'Appell to the last Einsatz' ('call to the last battle') was no phrase but appealed to their innermost feelings. They felt that the hour had come, the moment in which they counted, in which they would no longer be pushed aside because they were too young. They could be found everywhere; they shovelled day and night on the Ostwall or on the Westwall. They fed the refugees, they helped the wounded. In the air raids they fought the flames and helped to rescue the sick and the injured. And finally they confronted the Russians with the Panzerfaust.'

Major recorded encounters involving Hitler Youths in action against the Russians took place in Breslau and Berlin. In Breslau, encircled by Soviet forces since March 1945, the local HJ leader formed a regiment of Hitler Youths to assist in the city's defense. Well equipped and led by experienced Wehrmacht NCOs, the youths succeeded repeatedly in retrieving vital positions from the enemy; they fought on until the city's capitulation on May 9th. Upon Reich Youth Leader Artur Axmann's personal order of April 23, 1945, battalions of Hitler Youth were raised to defend the Pichelsdorf bridges that spanned the Havel River in Berlin to keep the way open for Wenck's phantom army, Hitler's final hope of relief:[4]

> As the Armee Wenck in the form in which Hitler imagined it did not exist, the Hitler Youth fought in vain . . . They were sacrificed in front of the bridges and they were sacrificed outside Hitler's bunker. On his last public appearance in the garden of the Reich's Chancellory Hitler on his 56th birthday awarded decorations to some of the defenders of Berlin, including the Iron Cross second class to several 12-year-old Hitler Youths, who were simply thrown into the cauldron of destruction. The boys of the Hitler Youth Division had at least received sound military training; those coming after them had little preparation other than the myth of Langemarck and the legends of 'the heroes of the National Socialist movement.' They were frightened little boys caught between the heroic clap-trap with which their imagination had been fed and the bloody brutality of war.

As a military formation composed of Hitler Youths, the 12th SS Panzer Division deserves special attention for several reasons: its symbolic significance,

---

[3]Koch, *The Hitler Youth*, p 249.
[4]Ibid., pp 249-50.

its eliteness (at least as originally constituted), and its extraordinary exploits upon the field of battle. Established after the defeat at Stalingrad, the division was a product of Germany's transition to a total war effort, which sought to harness all human and material resources of the Reich to the purpose of waging a struggle for existence. In this context, the division's creators envisioned it as a symbol of the willingness of German youth to make the ultimate sacrifice for Führer and Fatherland in a politico-military milieu of growing crisis. For the teenagers of the 12th SS, the transition to soldiering was eased by the years of systematic indoctrination within the Hitler Youth organization. From the moment they had first entered the HJ at age ten, the boys had been told that they as individuals were nothing; that service to the state was everything.

The Hitler Youth Division became a first-class formation of the Waffen SS-- its special nature underscored by intimate ties to the super-elite Leibstandarte SS Adolf Hitler Division. These ties were symbolized by the divisional insignia of the 12th SS: a skeleton key, the emblem of the LAH (derived from the name of its first commander, Sepp Dietrich--"Dietrich" meaning key in German), running diagonally through the center of a single Gothic letter "S." Cadre personnel transferred from the Leibstandarte to the 12th SS provided the latter with an experienced nucleus and ensured that it would be imbued with the fighting qualities and élan of its sister division.

**1st SS-Panzer Division
"LSSAH"**

**12th SS-Panzer Division
"Hitler Youth"**

Despite realistic combat training and excellent equipment, nothing could adequately prepare the youngsters of the 12th SS for the terrible realities of the Normandy battle. In Normandy, the Germans experienced the purest, most violent expression of the Materialschlacht--the "force majeure" of Anglo-American ground, sea and air forces on a scale unprecedented in any other campaign of the Second World War.[5] The exigencies of Montgomery's strategy, moreover, which demanded the exertion of constant pressure in the Caen sector, meant that the fighting there was waged with particular intensity. Yet the 12th SS fought with a skill and a pugnacity unexcelled by any unit of the Wehrmacht or Waffen SS deployed at the invasion front; its success in

---

[5]According to veterans of the 12th SS who had also fought in Russia, the concentrations of enemy firepower in Normandy (where Allied air and naval units played such a major role) exceeded even those experienced on the eastern front.

slowing the advance of the First Canadian Army towards Falaise in August 1944 ranks among the finest achievements of the German armed forces in the Second World War. Time and again during the Normandy campaign, small numbers of the division's tanks and infantry were able to temporarily check the attacks of much larger enemy ground forces enjoying complete command of the air. The reasons for the defensive victories of the 12th SS were many, and include the qualitative superiority of many of its weapons (the Machine Gun 42 and the Panther tank, for example), as well as the exemplary motivation and discipline of its personnel. Also contributing to its success was the superior tactical concept that shaped so many German operations during the Second World War. The operations of the 12th SS in Normandy exemplified the successful execution of "mission tactics" (Auftragstaktik)–defined by one historian as "the necessity for subordinate commanders to act independently within a general framework, responding to specific conditions and exploiting specific opportunities without reference to higher headquarters."[6] In contrast, British and Canadian armored units attacked with less vigor, adhered rigidly to operational plans, and were not quick to take independent action; because of the methodical nature of enemy mobile operations, the 12th SS was often given time to recover from a temporary reversal and to strike back effectively.[7]

Despite the brilliant combat record of the division, its murder of more than 100 Canadian prisoners-of-war during the opening days of the Normandy fighting will forever sully its escutcheon. The accomplishments of the 12th SS, moreover, must not obscure the fact that it could only delay, not defeat, the forces arrayed against it, and that it was ultimately crushed. For as the Anglo-Americans convincingly demonstrated through their Normandy victory, there is a point where a quantitative superiority becomes a qualitative one. Perhaps this Allied victory holds a disturbing lesson for contemporary NATO commanders, who with limited resources plan the conventional defense of Europe's central front against a potential adversary possessing an alarming numerical edge, albeit an ostensible technical inferiority.

But the purpose of this book is not to examine the finer points of tactics, rather it is to record the fate of a group of young persons, who, "at the critical age when they were just beginning to feel the pulse of life, were set face to face with death."[8] In its broadest, most tragic perspective, the fate of the Hitler Youth Division mirrored the fate of the German nation during the tumultuous 12-year tenure of the Third Reich. An entire nation, unlike a deranged potentate in a Shakespearean play, cannot decide to turn evil; on the

---

[6]Dennis E. Showalter, "The Bundeswehr of the Federal Republic of Germany," In: *The Defense of Western Europe,* edited by Lewis H. Gann (London & Sidney: Croom Helm Ltd., 1987), p 236.

[7]In his memoirs, Kurt Meyer was often critical of British and Canadian armored tactics during the Normandy campaign. See for example, *Grenadiere,* p 285.

[8]The words are Erich Maria Remarque's--written in a letter to a British general in which Remarque explained his reason for writing his classic war novel *All Quiet on the Western Front.*

contrary, what is most disturbing about the Nazi period is how adroitly the National Socialist leadership was able to harness the considerable moral and physical energies of a decent and capable people to the pursuit of largely criminal objectives. To reach their nefarious goals, the Nazis did not hesitate to exploit the trust and idealism of Germany's younger generation. Steeped in traditions of public service and self-sacrifice, the boys of the 12th SS Panzer Division "Hitler Youth" were plunged into the abyss of blood and darkness that is modern total war. Too young to fear death, yet old enough to face it and die, they were "worthy of a better cause than that which the man whose name they once bore had to offer."[9]

*　*　*　*　*

[9]Koch, *The Hitler Youth,* p 252.

Appendix 1
HITLER YOUTH RANKS

(Note: Hitler Youth ranks changed frequently. Those given below were the greatly simplified ones in use in 1943.)

Reichsjugendführer: Artur Axmann

Hitler Youth (HJ) (ages 14-18)	Jungvolk (DJV) (ages 10-14)
Stabsführer	--
Obergebietsführer	--
Gebietsführer	--
Oberbannführer	--
Bannführer	Jungbannführer
Stammführer	Unterbannführer
Gefolgschaftsführer	Fähnleinführer
Scharführer	Jungzugführer
Kameradschaftsführer	Jungenschaftsführer
Hitlerjunge	Pimpf

Appendix 2
DIENSTGRADÜBERSICHT/COMPARATIVE RANKS

Waffen SS	U.S. Army
Reichsführer SS	--
SS-Oberstgruppenführer und Generaloberst der W-SS	General
SS-Obergruppenführer und General der W-SS	Lieutenant-General
SS-Gruppenführer und Generalleutnant der W-SS	Major-General
SS-Brigadeführer und Generalmajor der W-SS	Brigadier-General
SS-Oberführer	--
SS-Standartenführer	Colonel
SS-Obersturmbannführer	Lieutenant-Colonel
SS-Sturmbannführer	Major
SS-Hauptsturmführer	Captain
SS-Obersturmführer	First Lieutenant
SS-Untersturmführer	Second Lieutenant

Appendix 3
HIGH RANKING OFFICERS TRANSFERRED FROM THE LEIBSTANDARTE TO THE 12TH SS PANZER DIVISION "HITLER YOUTH"

To division command:

SS-Oberführer Fritz Witt,[1] division commander

To the divisonal staff: (Divisionsstab)

SS-Sturmbannführer Hubert Meyer, Chief of Operations (Ia)
SS-Hauptsturmführer Fritz Buchsein, Second General Staff Officer (Ib)
SS-Hauptsturmführer Heinrich Springer, Division Adjutant (IIa)

To the 12th SS Panzer Regiment:

SS-Sturmbannführer Max Wünsche, regiment commander
SS-Hauptsturmführer Arnold Jürgensen, battalion commander
SS-Hauptsturmführer Heinz Prinz, battalion commander

To the 25th SS Panzer Grenadier Regiment:

SS-Obersturmbannführer Kurt Meyer, regiment commander
SS-Hauptsturmführer Hans Scappini, battalion commander

To the 26th SS Panzer Grenadier Regiment:

SS-Obersturmbannführer Wilhelm Mohnke, regiment commander
SS-Hauptsturmführer Bernhard Krause, battalion commander
SS-Sturmbannführer Bernhard Siebken, battalion commander
SS-Hauptsturmführer Gerhard Bremer,[2] battalion commander

To the 12th SS Reconnaissance Battalion: (Aufklärungsabteilung)

SS-Hauptsturmführer Erich Olboeter,[3] battalion commander

To the 12th SS Artillery Regiment:

SS-Sturmbannführer Fritz Schröder, regiment commander
SS-Hauptsturmführer Erich Urbanits, battalion commander
SS-Hauptsturmführer Karl Bartling, battalion commander

To the 12th SS Flak Battalion: (Flakabteilung)

SS-Hauptsturmführer Rudolf Fend, battalion commander

To the 12th SS Tank Destroyer Battalion: (Panzerjägerabteilung)

SS-Hauptsturmführer Jakob Hanreich, battalion commander

To the 12th SS Rocket Projector Battalion: (Werferabteilung)

SS-Hauptsturmführer Willy Müller, battalion commander

---

[1] All ranks are those at the time of transfer to the 12th SS.
[2] Bremer later took command of the division's reconnaissance battalion.
[3] Olboeter took the battalion command in the 26th Regiment vacated by Bremer.

To the medical battalion: (Sanitätsabteilung)
SS-Sturmbannführer Dr. med. Rolf Schulz

To the divisional supply troops: (Divisionsnachschubtruppen)
SS-Hauptsturmführer Rolf Kolitz

To the maintenance battalion: (Instandsetzungsabteilung)
SS-Hauptsturmführer Artur Manthey

Appendix 4
ORDER OF BATTLE: 12TH SS PANZER DIVISION
(June 6, 1944)

I. Divisionsstab:

Divisionskommandeur, Brig.Fhr. Fritz Witt
4. Ordonnanzoffizier (04), Ustuf. Hausrath

i. Führungsabteilung (Ia):

1. Gen.St.Offz. (Ia), Stubaf. Hubert Meyer
1. Ord. Offz. (01), Ostuf. Meitzel
3. Gen.St.Offz. (Ic), Ostuf. Doldi
3. Ord. Offz. (03), Ustuf. Trommer
Div. Kartenstelle, Uscha. Kriegge
Leiter d. Nachrichtend. (LdN), Ostuf. v. Brandis
Feldgend. Komp., Ostuf. Buschhausen
Divisionsbegleitkompanie, Ostuf. Guntrum–consisting of 1.(Schützen) Zug; 2.(s.M.G.) Zug; 3.(Pak) Zug; 4.(Flak) Zug; 5.(le.I.G.) Zug; 6.(Kradschützen) Zug

ii. Quartiermeisterabteilung (Ib):

2. Gen.St.Offz., Stubaf. Buchsein
2. Ord. Offz. (02), Ustuf. Lübbe
WaMun., Ostuf. Sporer
Abt. IVa, Div. Intendant, Stubaf. Dr. Kos
Abt. IVb, Div. Arzt, Ostubaf. Dr. Schulz
Div. Zahnartz, Hstuf. Dr. Rogge
Abt. V, Div. Ing., Stubaf. Manthey

II. SS-Panzerregiment 12: (177 tanks)

Rgt.-Kommandeur, Ostubaf, Wünsche
Adjutant, Hstuf. Isecke

i. I. Abteilung (63 Panzer V "Panther" tanks)

Abteilung Kdr., Stubaf. Jürgensen

1. Kompanie, Hstuf. Berlin
2. Kompanie, Ostuf. Gaede
3. Kompanie, Ostuf. v. Ribbentrop

4. Kompanie, Hstuf. Pfeiffer
Werkstattkp., Ustuf. R. Maier

ii. II. Abteilung: (94 Panzer IV tanks; one armored Flakzug composed of 4 20mm "Vierlingsflak," each mounted on the chassis of a Panzer IV)

Abteilung Kdr., Stubaf. Prinz

5. Kompanie, Ostuf. Bando
6. Kompanie, Hstuf. Ruckdeschel
7. Kompanie, Hstuf. Bräcker
8. Kompanie, Ostuf. Siegel
9. Kompanie, Hstuf. Buettner[1]
Werkstattzug, Ostuf. D. Müller

III. SS-Panzerjägerabteilung 12: (28 Panzerjäger IV; 12 75mm Pak 40)[2]

Abteilung Kdr., Stubaf. Hanreich

1. Kompanie, Ostuf. Hurdelbrink (14 Panzerjäger IV)
2. Kompanie, Ostuf. Wachter (14 Panzerjäger IV)
3. Kompanie, Hstuf. Wöst (12 75mm Pak 40)

IV. SS-Panzergrenadierregiment 25: (mot.)

Rgt. Kdr., Staf. Kurt Meyer
Adjutant, Ostuf. Schümann

13. (s.I.G.) Kompanie, Oblt. Kaminski (6 s.I.G.)
14. (Flak) Kompanie, ? (12 20mm Flak)
15. (Aufkl.) Kompanie, Hstuf. v. Büttner
16. (Pionier) Kompanie, Ustuf. Werner

i. I. Bataillon: (mot.)

Btl. Kdr., Stubaf. Waldmüller

1. Kompanie, Oblt. F.
2. Kompanie, Ostuf. Knössel
3. Kompanie, Hstuf. Peinemann
4. Kompanie, Ostuf. Wilke[3]

ii. II. Bataillon: (mot.)

Btl. Kdr., Stubaf. Scappini

---

[1] It is unclear why the Panzer regiment had a 9th Panzer Company, which certainly was not in the prescribed order of battle for an SS Panzer divison. Perhaps the regiment received the extra company via Wünsche's connections to the German High Command (i.e., Hitler). Wünsche had served as an orderly to Hitler in the late 1930s.

[2] The tank destroyer battalion (Panzerjägerabteilung) had yet to be equipped with its command vehicles (Befehlspanzer) and, as a result, was not operational on June 6, 1944. Sometime after the invasion its 3rd Company would also be furnished with Panzerjäger IV tank destroyers, in place of its 75mm Pak 40s. This battalion would not reach the front until July - August 1944.

[3] The highest numbered company in each Panzer grenadier battalion was the heavy company of the battalion. Each heavy company was outfitted with 6 81mm (8cm) mortars, 3 75mm Pak, and 3 light artillery pieces.

5. Kompanie, Hstuf. Kreilein
6. Kompanie, Hstuf. Dr. Thirey
7. Kompanie, Hstuf. Schrott
8. Kompanie, Hstuf. Breinlich

iii. III. Bataillon: (mot.)

Btl. Kdr., Ostubaf. Milius

9. Kompanie, Oblt. Fritsch
10. Kompanie, Oblt. Dietrich
11. Kompanie, Ostuf. Stahl
12. Kompanie, Oblt. Wörner

V. SS-Panzergrenadierregiment 26: (mot./gep.)

Rgt. Kdr., Ostubaf. Mohnke
Adjutant, Hstuf. Kaiser

13. (s.I.G.) Kompanie, Ostuf. Polanski (6 s.I.G.)
14. (Flak) Kompanie, Hstuf. Stolze (12 20mm Flak)
15. (Aufkl.) Kompanie, Oblt. Bayer
16. (Pionier) Kompanie, Ostuf. Trompke

i. I. Bataillon: (mot.)

Btl. Kdr., Stubaf. Krause

1. Kompanie, Hstuf. Eggert
2. Kompanie, Ostuf. Gröschel
3. Kompanie, Ostuf. Düvel
4. Kompanie, Ostuf. Hartung

ii. II. Bataillon: (mot.)

Btl. Kdr., Stubaf. Siebken

5. Kompanie, Ostuf. Gotthard
6. Kompanie, Ostuf. Schmolke
7. Kompanie, Lt. Henne
8. Kompanie, Hstuf. Fasching

iii. III. Bataillon: (gep.)[4]

Btl. Kdr., Stubaf. Olboeter

9. Kompanie, Oblt. Göbel
10. Kompanie, Oblt. Pallas
11. Kompanie, Ostuf. Hauser
12. Kompanie, Ostuf. Riede

---

[4]This was the only battalion among the division's two Panzer grenadier regiments equipped with armored personnel carriers (Schützenpanzerwagen, or SPW), hence the designation "gep." (i.e., "gepanzert," or armored). The five remaining infantry battalions of the 12th SS possessed ordinary German or Italian trucks for the purpose of troop transport.

VI. SS-Panzeraufklärungsabteilung 12:

Abteilung Kdr., Stubaf. Bremer
Adjutant, Ostuf. Buchheim

1. (Pz.Späh) Kompanie, Ostuf. Hansmann (4-und 8 Rad Pz.Späh-Wg.)
2. (Pz.Späh) Kompanie, Ostuf. Hauck ("Kätzchen" Halbketten-Pz. Späh-Wg.)
3. (Aufkl.) Kompanie, Ostuf. Keue (mittl. Pz. Aufkl.Kp., gep.)
4. (Aufkl.) Kompanie, Ostuf. Beiersdor (same as 3. Kompanie)
5. (schw.) Kompanie, Hstuf. v. Reitzenstein

VII. SS-Panzerartillerieregiment 12: (52 light and medium artillery pieces)

Rgt. Kdr., Ostubaf. Schröder
Adjutant, ?

i. I. Abteilung: (12 l.F.H., sf.; 6 s.F.H., sf.)

Abt. Kdr., Stubaf. Urbanitz

1. Batterie, Hstuf. Gille (6 105mm l.F.H. "Wespen" on Pz.II chassis)
2. Batterie. Ostuf. Timmerbeil (same as 1. Batterie)
3. Batterie, Ostuf. Heller (6 150mm s.F.H. "Hummel" on Pz.III/IV chassis)

ii. II. Abteilung: (18 l.F.H., mot.)

Abt. Kdr., Stubaf. Schöps

4. Batterie, Oblt. Haller (6 l.F.H.)
5. Batterie, Hstuf. Kurzbein (6 l.F.H.)
6. Batterie, Ustuf. Kilchling (6 l.F.H.)

iii. III. Abteilung: (12 s.F.H., mot.; 4 105mm Kanonen, mot.)

Abt. Kdr., Stubaf. Bartling

7. Batterie, Ostuf. Etterich (4 s.F.H.)
8. Batterie, Ustuf. Peschel (4 s.F.H.)
9. Batterie, Ostuf. Balschuweit (4 s.F.H.)
10. Batterie, Hstuf. Heidrich (4 105mm Kanonen)

VIII. SS-Werferabteilung 12: (24 150mm "Nebelwerfer," mot., one 280mm/-320mm Batterie, mot.)[5]

Abt. Kdr., Stubaf. W. Müller
Adjutant, Ostuf. Lämmerhirt

1. Batterie, Hstuf. Macke
2. Batterie, Hstuf. Ziesenitz
3. Batterie, Ostuf. Bay
4. Batterie, Ostuf. Dr. Erhart

IX. SS-Flakabteilung 12: (12 88mm Flak, mot.; 9 37mm Flak)

Abt. Kdr., Stubaf. Fend
Adjutant, Ustuf. Kolb

---

[5]The rocket projector battalion (Werferabteilung) was not operational on June 6th. At that time it was still without its prime movers (Zugmittel).

1. Batterie, Hstuf. Ritzel (88mm Flak)
2. Batterie, Ostuf. Riedel (88mm Flak)
3. Batterie, Hstuf. Dr. Weygand (88mm Flak)
4. Batterie, Ostuf. Ritscher (37mm Flak)

X. SS-Panzerpionierbataillon 12: (mot./gep.)

Btl. Kdr., Stubaf. S. Müller
Adjutant, Ustuf. Betz

1. Kompanie (gep.), Oblt. Toll
2. Kompanie, Ostuf. Kuret (mot.)
3. Kompanie, Hstuf. Tiedke (mot.)
4. Kompanie, Ostuf. Bischof (schw.)
Brückenkolonne B, Ustuf. Richter[6]

XI. SS-Panzernachrichtenabteilung 12:

Abt. Kdr., Stubaf. Pandel
Adjutant, ?

1. (Fe) Kompanie, Ostuf. Dinglinger
2. (Fu) Kompanie, Hstuf. Krüger

XII. SS-Panzernachschubtruppen 12:

Abt. Kdr., Stubaf. Kolitz
Adjutant, Ustuf. Schlüter

1. Kraftf. Kompanie, Oblt. Weiss
2. Kraftf. Kompanie, Lt. Schäfer
3. Kraftf. Kompanie, Ustuf. Tiefengruber
4. Kraftf. Kompanie, Oblt. Müller
5. Kraftf. Kompanie, Ustuf. Bald
6. Kraftf. Kompanie, Ostuf. Althoff
Nachschubkompanie, Ostuf. Siedler

XIII. SS-Panzerinstandsetzungsabteilung 12:

Abt. Kdr., Stubaf. Manthey (also Divisionsingenieur, Va)
Adjutant, Ostuf. Kohlhagen

1. Werkst. Kompanie, Hstuf. Magunna
2. Werkst. Kompanie, Hstuf. Sprick
3. Werkst. Kompanie, Ostuf. Trinkhaus
4. Werkst. Kompanie (Waffen), Hstuf. Klein
5. (Ersatzteil) Kompanie, Hstuf. Löll

---

[6]The Brückenkolonne B was destroyed on D-Day by Allied fighter-bombers.

(The author has attempted to compile as complete an order of battle for the division as possible; minor errors of detail may exist. Sources include, Meyer, H., *Kriegsgeschichte,* Anlagen 17, 19; Record Group 238: Records of Proceedings. Exhibit N. T-1: Miscellaneous Organizational Data and Plans; BAMA. Tagebuch Divisions-Begleit-Kompanie; BAMA Zustandsbericht, 12. SS Pz. Div., 1.6.1944; interviews with former division members.)

XIV. SS-Wirtschaftsbataillon 12:

Btl. Kdr., Stubaf. Dr. Kos
Adjutant, Ustuf. Paschke
Bäckereikompanie, Ostuf. Schacksmeier
Schlächtereikompanie, Hstuf. Dr. Metsch
Div. Verpflegungsamt, Ostuf. Pischel
Feldpostamt, Leiter, Hstuf. Schlebusch

XV. SS-Sanitätsabteilung 12:

Abt. Kdr., Ostubaf. Dr. R. Schulz
Adjutant, Ustuf. Baierlein
1. Sanitätskompanie, Stubaf. Dr. Kirschner
    1. Hauptverbandsplatz-Zug, Hstuf. Dr. Triendl
    2. Hauptverbandsplatz-Zug, Hstuf. Dr. App
2. Sanitätskompanie, Hstuf. Dr. Vieweg
    1. Hauptverbandsplatz-Zug, Hstuf. Dr. Diensbach
    2. Hauptverbandsplatz-Zug, Stabsarzt Dr. Oborny
Krankenkraftwagenkompanie, Ostuf. F. Müller

XVI. SS-Feldersatzbataillon 12:

Btl. Kdr., Hstuf. Urabl
Adjutant, ?

Appendix 5[1]
ORDER OF BATTLE: 12TH SS PANZER DIVISION
(August 12, 1944)

Führungsstaffel des Divisionsstabes
Divisionsbegleitkompanie (in platoon strength)
Stab SS-Panzerregiment 12
I./SS-Panzerregiment 12 (with 7 Panthers)
II./SS-Panzerregiment 12 (with 17 Panzer IVs)

I./SS-Panzergrenadierregiment 25 (ca. two companies in strength)
I./SS-Panzergrenadierregiment 26 (ca. two companies in strength)
III./SS-Panzergrenadierregiment 26 (gep.)(ca. two companies in strength)

SS-Panzerartillerieregiment 12 (without two batteries of light field howitzers from 2nd Battalion destroyed in battle)

SS-Werferabteilung 12 (with three batteries)

---

[1]This Order of Battle comprises those elements of the 12th SS still fighting in Normandy. It does not include components of the division already withdrawn from the front for replenishment.

SS-Flakabteilung 12:
  one battery 88mm Flak
  one battery 37mm Flak, self-propelled
  one company 20mm Flak, self-propelled (14./26)

SS-Panzerjägerabteilung 12 (with two companies Panzerjäger IV)

Aufklärungsgruppe Wienecke (from SS-Panzeraufklärungsabteilung 12)

Funkführungsstaffel and elements of the Fernsprechkompanie of the SS-Panzernachrichtenabteilung 12

Appendix 6
PERSONNEL STRENGTH: 12TH SS PANZER DIVISION
(October 1, 1943 - April 13, 1945)

Date	Officers	NCOs	Men	Total
Oct. 1, 1943	183	808	11,481	12,472
Nov. 1, 1943	231	1,068	12,722	14,021
Jan. 1, 1944	373	1,547	17,901	19,821
Feb. 1, 1944	398	1,711	14,990	17,099
Mar. 1, 1944	430	1,870	13,839	16,139
June. 1, 1944	520	2,383	17,637	20,540
Nov. 1, 1944	309	2,553	18,349	21,211
Dec. 8, 1944	484	3,174	19,586	23,244
Dec. 31, 1944	439	2,647	16,571	19,657
March 1, 1945	457	2,538	14,428	17,423
April 13, 1945	281	1,401	6,049	7,731

Appendix 7
KNIGHT'S CROSS HOLDERS IN THE
12th SS PANZER DIVISION "HITLER YOUTH"

RK-Ritterkreuz (Knight's Cross)   EL-Eichenlaub (Oak Leaves)
Schw.-Schwerter (Oak Leaves and Swords)

Beck, SS-Hauptsturmführer d. Res. Wilhelm

RK: March 28, 1943 as SS-Ostuf. and CO of 2nd Company, 1st SS-Pz. Rgt., SS-Pz. Gren. Div. "LSSAH," Russia.

Bremer, SS-Sturmbannführer Gerhard

EL: November 25, 1944 (No. 668) as SS-Stubaf. and CO of 12th SS-Pz. Recon. Bn., 12th SS-Pz.Div. "Hitler Youth," Western Front.

RK: October 30, 1941 as SS-Ostuf. and CO of 1st Motorcycle Co., SS-Division Leibstandarte-SS "Adolf Hitler," Russia.

Wilhelm Beck.

Gerhard Bremer.

Damsch, SS-Hauptsturmführer Werner
   RK: April 17, 1945 as SS-Hastuf. in the 12th SS-Pz. Div. "Hitler Youth,"
   Southeast Front.

Dürr, SS-Unterscharführer Emil
   RK: August 23, 1944 (posthumous) as SS-Uscha. in 4th Co. (heavy), 26th SS-
   Pz. Gren. Rgt., 12th SS-Pz. Div. "Hitler Youth," Normandy.

Jost W. Schneider

Emil Dürr.

Eckstein, SS-Unterscharführer Fritz
   RK: November 18, 1944 as SS-Rottenführer and gunner in 1st Company,
   12th SS-Anti-tank Bn., 12th SS-Div. "Hitler Youth," Western Front.

(Left to right) Fritz Eckstein, Fritz Kraemer, Sepp Dietrich, Bernhard Krause and Hugo Kraas. Eckstein and Krause have just been awarded their Knight's Crosses (November 1944). Note that both men are wearing the "Hitlerjugend" divisional sleeveband on their lower left sleeves (introduced in "Verordnungsblatt der Waffen-SS," February 15, 1944, Nr. 4. Z. 64).

Machine-embroidered "Hitlerjugend" sleeveband for enlisted ranks.

Machine-woven "Hitlerjugend" sleeveband for enlisted ranks.

Hurdelbrink, SS-Obersturmführer Georg

> RK: October 16, 1944 as SS-Ostuf. and CO of 1st Company, 12th SS Anti-Tank Battalion, 12th SS-Pz. Div. "Hitler Youth," Normandy.

Jürgensen, SS-Sturmbannführer Arnold

> RK: October 16, 1944 as SS-Stubaf. and CO of 1st Battalion, 12th SS-Pz. Rgt., 12th SS-Pz. Div. "Hitler Youth," Western Front.

Arnold Jürgensen, Georg Hurdelbrink and Rudolf Roy have just been awarded the Knight's Cross (October 1944). Hubert Meyer is at far left.

Kraas, SS-Brigadeführer und Generalmajor der Waffen-SS Hugo

RK: March 28, 1943 at SS-Stubaf. and CO of 1st Bn., 2nd SS-Pz. Gren. Rgt., SS-Pz. Gren. Div. "LSSAH," Eastern Front.

EL: January 24, 1944 (No. 375) as SS-Ostubaf. and CO of 2nd SS-Pz. Gren. Rgt., 1st SS-Pz. Div. "LSSAH," Eastern Front. (Last command: CO of 12th SS-Pz. Div. "Hitler Youth.")

Krause, SS-Obersturmbannführer Bernhard

RK: November 18, 1944 as SS-Stubaf. and CO of 26th SS-Pz. Gren. Rgt., 12th SS-Pz. Div. "Hitler Youth," Normandy.

Meyer, SS-Brigadeführer und Generalmajor der Waffen-SS Kurt

Schw: August 27, 1944 (No. 91) as SS-Oberfhr. and CO of 12th SS-Pz. Div. "Hitler Youth," Normandy.

EL: May 23, 1943 (No. 195) as SS-Ostubaf. and CO of 1st SS-Pz. Recon. Bn., SS-Pz. Gren. Div. "LSSAH," Russia.

RK: May 18, 1941 as SS-Ostubaf. and CO of 1st SS-Pz. Recon. Bn., SS-Leibstandarte "Adolf Hitler," Greece.

Kurt Meyer.

Wilhelm Mohnke.   **Siegfried Müller.**   **Erich Olboeter.**

Mohnke, SS-Brigadeführer und Generalmajor der Waffen-SS Wilhelm

RK: July 11, 1944 as SS-Ostubaf. and CO of 26th SS-Pz. Gren. Rgt., 12th SS-Pz. Div. "Hitler Youth," Normandy.

Müller, SS-Obersturmbannführer Siegfried

RK: December 19, 1944 as SS-Stubaf. and CO of 25th SS-Pz. Gren. Rgt., 12th SS-Pz. Div. "Hitler Youth," Western Front.

Olboeter, SS-Sturmbannführer Erich

RK: July 27, 1944 as SS-Stubaf. and CO of 3rd Bn., 26th SS-Pz. Gren. Rgt., 12th SS-Pz. Div. "Hitler Youth," Normandy.

Prinz, SS-Sturmbannführer Karl-Heinz

RK: July 11, 1944 as SS-Stubaf. and CO of 2nd Bn., 12th SS-Pz. Rgt., 12th SS-Pz. Div. "Hitler Youth," Normandy.

Sepp Dietrich awards Karl-Heinz Prinz with the Knight's Cross. Max Wünsche is in the background.

Ribbentrop, SS-Hauptsturmführer Rudolf von

    RK: July 15, 1943 as SS-Ostuf. and CO of 6th Company, 1st SS-Pz. Rgt., 1st SS-Pz. Div. "LSSAH," Russia.

Roy, SS-Oberscharführer Rudolf

    RK: October 10, 1944 as SS-Oscha. and tank commander in 1st Co., 12th SS-Pz. Rgt., 12th SS-Pz. Div. "Hitler Youth", Western Front.

Rudolf, SS-Oberscharführer Richard

    RK: November 18, 1944 as SS-Oscha. and platoon leader, 12th SS-Pz. Rgt., 12th SS-Pz. Div. "Hitler Youth," Western Front.

Siegel, SS-Hauptsturmführer Hans

    RK: August 23, 1944 as SS-Hastuf. and CO of 8th Company, 12th SS-Pz. Rgt., 12th SS-Pz. Div. "Hitler Youth," Normandy.

Rudolf von Ribbentrop.   **Richard Rudolf.**   **Hans Siegel.**

Springer, SS-Sturmbannführer Heinrich

    RK: January 12, 1942 as SS-Hastuf. and CO of 3rd Company, SS-Inf. Rgt. (mot), SS-Div. "LSSAH," Russia.

Heinrich Springer.

Toll, Hauptmann d. Res. Otto

RK: June 10, 1941 as Lt. d. Res. and platoon leader of the 200th Army Eng. Bn.

Waldmüller, SS-Obersturmbannführer Hans

RK: August 27, 1944 as SS-Stubaf. and CO of 1st Bn., 25th SS-Pz. Gren. Rgt., 12th SS-Pz. Div. "Hitler Youth," Normandy.

Witt, SS-Brigadeführer und Generalmajor der Waffen-SS Fritz

EL: March 1, 1943 as SS-Standartenführer and CO of 1st SS-Pz. Gren. Rgt., SS-Pz. Gren. Div. "LSSAH," Russia.

RK: September 4, 1940 as SS-Stubaf. and CO of 1st Bn., SS-Standarte "Deutschland," SS-Verfügungsdivision, French campaign.

Wünsche, SS-Obersturmbannführer Max

EL: August 11, 1944 (No. 548) as SS-Ostubaf. and CO of 12th SS-Pz. Rgt., 12th SS-Pz. Div. "Hitler Youth," Normandy.

RK: February 28, 1943 as SS-Stubaf. and CO of 1st Bn., 1st SS-Pz. Rgt., SS-Pz. Gren. Div. "LSSAH," Russia.

Jost W. Schneider

| Hans Waldmüller. | Fritz Witt. | Max Wünsche |

Appendix 8
ORDER OF BATTLE: 3RD CANADIAN INFANTRY DIVISION (June 1944)

3rd Canadian Infantry Division
Major-General R.F.L. Keller, commander

7th Brigade	8th Brigade
The Royal Winnipeg Rifles	The Queen's Own Rifles
1st Battalion The Regina Rifle Regiment	of Canada
	Le Régiment de la Chaudière
1st Battalion The Canadian Scottish Regiment	The North Shore (New Brunswick) Regiment

9th Brigade

The Highland Light Infantry of Canada
The Stormont, Dundas and Glengarry Highlanders
The North Nova Scotia Highlanders

Divisional Troops

7th Reconnaissance Regiment
(17th Duke of York's Royal
Canadian Hussars)
3rd Canadian Divisional Engineers
3rd Canadian Divisional Signals

12th, 13th and 14th Field,
3rd Anti-Tank and 4th
Light Anti-Aircraft
Regiments R.C.A.
The Cameron Highlanders of
Ottawa (Machine Gun)

Appendix 9
THE WEHRMACHT IN THE WEST
(June 6, 1944)

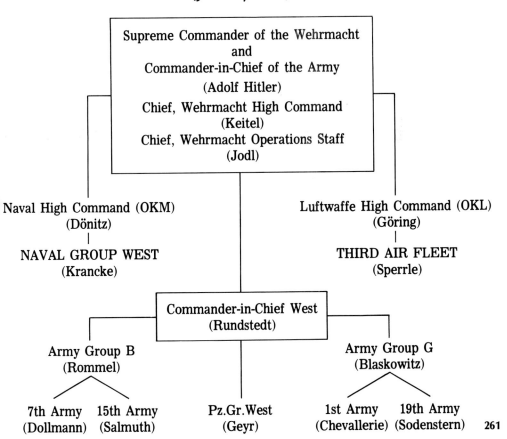

Supreme Commander of the Wehrmacht
and
Commander-in-Chief of the Army
(Adolf Hitler)
Chief, Wehrmacht High Command
(Keitel)
Chief, Wehrmacht Operations Staff
(Jodl)

Naval High Command (OKM)
(Dönitz)

NAVAL GROUP WEST
(Krancke)

Luftwaffe High Command (OKL)
(Göring)

THIRD AIR FLEET
(Sperrle)

Commander-in-Chief West
(Rundstedt)

Army Group B
(Rommel)

Army Group G
(Blaskowitz)

7th Army   15th Army
(Dollmann) (Salmuth)

Pz.Gr.West
(Geyr)

1st Army   19th Army
(Chevallerie) (Sodenstern)   261

Appendix 10
ALLIED SUPREME COMMAND FOR OPERATION 'OVERLORD'
(June 6, 1944)

<u>SHAEF</u>

Supreme Commander
(General Dwight D. Eisenhower)

Allied Naval Expeditionary Force (Admiral Ramsay)[1]	21st Army Group (Field Marshal Montgomery)[2]	Allied Expeditionary Air Force (Air Chief Marshal Leigh-Mallory)[3]

Eighth U.S. Air Force[4]
(Lieutenant-General James Doolittle)

R.A.F. Bomber Command
(Air Chief Marshal Sir Arthur Harris)

---

[1]Under the command of Admiral Sir Bertram Ramsay (R.N.) were the Western and Eastern Task Forces.

[2]Under Montgomery's command were the First U.S. and the Second British Armies.

[3]Air Chief Marshal Sir Trafford Leigh-Mallory commanded the Ninth U.S. Air Force and the Second Tactical Air Force.

[4]There was no single command for all the Allied air forces. The strategic bombers, although ultimately responsible to the Combined Chiefs of Staff, were placed under Eisenhower's operational control for Overlord.

BIBLIOGRAPHY

I. Unpublished Materials:

a. United States National Archives (Washington, D.C.)

Miscellaneous German Records Collection. Microcopy T-84. Roll 281. Kriegstagebuch Heeresgruppe B.

Records of the Reichsführer SS. Microcopy T-175. Rolls 18, 70, 108, 111.

Records of the German Field Commands, Armies. Microcopy T-312. Rolls 1568, 1569: Armeeoberkommando 7.

Miscellaneous Records 12th SS Panzer Division. Microcopy T-354. Rolls 153, 154, 155, 156.

Record Group 218: Supplementary Report of the SHAEF Court of Inquiry re: Shooting of Allied Prisoners of War by 12. SS Panzer Division (Hitler-Jugend) in Normandy, France, 7-21 June, 1944.

Record Group 238: Records of Proceedings (revised) of the Trial by Canadian Military Court of SS Brigadeführer Kurt Meyer.

b. Public Archives of Canada (Ottawa)

War Diaries: (Battalions, 3rd Canadian Infantry Division)
1st Battalion The Canadian Scottish Regiment
The North Nova Scotia Highlanders
The Queen's Own Rifles of Canada
1st Battalion The Regina Rifles Regiment
The Royal Winnipeg Rifles

War Diary, 3rd Canadian Infantry Division

War Diary, 2nd Canadian Armored Brigade

War Diary, 27th Canadian Armored Regiment

Special Interrogation Report, Brigadeführer Kurt Meyer. HQ Cdn. Forces in the Netherlands, 24 August 1945.

Spencer, Captain R.A. "Topographic Notes--French Battlefields. July-August 1946.

c. Public Record Office (London)

Collection of Ultra Signals concerning Normandy campaign, 1944.

War Diary, Sherwood Rangers Yeomanry (tank regiment)

War Diary, 24th Lancers (tank regiment)

Battle Logs: (British battleships)
H.M.S. "Rodney"
H.M.S. "Nelson"
H.M.S. "Warspite"

d. Berlin Documentation Center (West Berlin)

SS Personalakten for leading personalities in 12th SS Panzer Division, including Fritz Witt, Kurt Meyer, Hubert Meyer, Max Wünsche, Wilhelm Mohnke, etc.

e. Bundesarchiv-Militärarchiv (BAMA) (Freiburg)

RH 10/321. Materielle und Personelle Lage, 12. SS Panzer Division.

RH 19IV/43-44. Kriegstagebuch OB West. 5.6.-31.7.44.

RH 19IV/134. Telefonkladde, Meyer-Detring (Ic OB West),

RH 19IX/3 (fol. 1-78). Verluste, Iststärkemeldungen, Zustandsberichte der Panzerdivisionen.

RH 19IX/8. Wochenmeldungen Heeresgruppe B. 15.5.-21.8.44.

RH 19IX/84-88. Kriegstagebuch Heeresgruppe B. 16.6.-31.8.44.

RS 3-12/1. Tagebuch Divisions-Begleit-Kompanie der 12.SS-Pz. Div. "H.J." 1943-1945.

RS 3-12/34. Rgt. Kriegstagebuch Nr. 1 von 1.5.-5.7.44 des I./SS Pz.Gren.Rgt. 25.

63181/1. KTB Panzer-Armeeoberkommando 5 (Panzergruppe West).

f. Foreign Military Studies (U.S. National Archives and Militärgeschichtliches Forschungsamt, Freiburg).

Bittrich, Wilhelm. "Bearbeitung für die Invasionskämpfe in der Normandie vom 29.6.-24.7.44." B-747.

Buttlar-Brandenfels, Horst. "OB West: Command Relationships." Annex Five: OKW Interpretation of the Normandy Landing at Noon on 6 June 1944." B-672.

Feuchtinger, Edgar. "History of the 21st Panzer Division from the Time of its Formation until the Beginning of the Invasion." B-441.

Geyr von Schweppenburg, Freiherr Leo. "Geschichte der Panzergruppe West." B-466.

Kraemer, Fritz. "I. SS Panzer Korps im Westen." C-024.

Lüttwitz, Heinrich von. "2. Panzer Division in Normandie." B-257.

Meyer, Hubert. "Der Einsatz der 12. SS-Panzerdivision 'Hitlerjugend' während der Invasionskämpfe in Frankreich von Juni bis September 1944." P-164.

Pickert, Wolfgang. "III. Flak Korps." B-597.

Richter, Wilhelm. "Kampf der 716. Infanterie Division in der Normandie vom 6.6.-23.6.1944." B-621.

Ruge, Friedrich. "Rommel and the Atlantic Wall." A-982.

Speidel, Dr. Hans. "Gedanken Rommels über Abwehr und Operationen im Westen." B-720.

Staubwasser, Anton. "Das Feindbild beim O.dHg.B. 6.6.-24.7.44. B-782.

Staudinger, Walter. "Artillerie in Normandie." B-832.

Zimmermann, Bodo. "OB West: Atlantic Wall to Siegfried Line, A Study in Command." B-308.

g. manuscripts

Rempel, Gerhard. The Misguided Generation: Hitler Youth and SS: 1933-1945 (unpublished doctoral dissertation, University of Wisconsin, 1971).

II. Published Materials:

a. books

A History of the First Hussars Regiment 1856-1945 (London: Hunter Printing, 1951).

Barnard, Lieutenant-Colonel W.T. The Queen's Own Rifles of Canada 1860-1960 (Ontario: Ontario Publishing Company Limited, 1960).

Bennett, Ralph. Ultra in the West--The Normandy Campaign, 1944-45 (London: Hutchinson & Co., Ltd., 1979).

Bowyer, Michael J.F. 2 Group R.A.F.--A Complete History, 1936-1945 (London: Faber and Faber).

Brandenburg, Hans-Christian. Die Geschichte der Hitlerjugend. Wege und Irrwege einer Generation (Köln: Verlag Wissenschaft und Politik, 1968).

Buchheim, Hans, et. al. Anatomy of the SS State (New York: Walker and Company, 1968).

Davidson, Eugene. The Trial of the Germans (New York: Macmillan, 1966).

Die 3. Kompanie. SS-Panzer-Regiment 12, 12.SS-Panzerdivision "Hitlerjugend" (Kompanie-Kameradschaft, Eigenverlag, 1978).

Ellis, L.F. Victory in the West. United Kingdom Military Services. Sir James Butler, Ed. (London: Her Majesty's Stationery Office, 1962).

Foster, Tony. Meeting of Generals (Toronto: Methuen, 1986).

Greiner, Helmuth; Schramm, Percy Ernst. Kriegstagebuch des Oberkommandos der Wehrmacht (Wehrmachtführungsstab)1940-1945. Bd. IV: 1. Januar 1944 - 22. Mai 1945 (Frankfurt am Main: Bernard & Graefe Verlag für Wehrwesen, 1961).

Halder, Generaloberst Franz. Kriegstagebuch. Tägliche Aufzeichnungen des Chefs des Generalstabes des Heeres 1939-42. Bd. III (Stuttgart: W. Kohlhammer Verlag, 1964).

Handbook on German Military Forces. War Department Technical Manual TM-E 30-451 (United States Government Printing Office, 1945).

Hauck, Walter. L'Affaire D'Ascq. Acte d'Accusation, Tribunal Militaire Permanent Metz. Expose des Faits (Paris: 1949).

Hayn, Friedrich. Die Invasion. Von Cotentin bis Falaise. Wehrmacht im Kampf series. Bd. II (Heidelberg: Kurt Vowinckel Verlag, 1954).

Heiber, Helmut (ed.). Hitlers Lagebesprechungen. Die Protokollfragmente seiner militärischen Konferenzen, 1942-1945 (Stuttgart: Deutsche Verlags-Anstalt, 1962).

Höhne, Heinz. The Order of the Death's Head. The Story of Hitler's SS (New York: Ballentine Books, 1966).

Hillgruber, Andreas. Deutsche Grossmacht-und Weltpolitik im 19. und 20. Jahrhundert (Dusseldorf: Droste Verlag, 1977).

Hubatsch, Walther (ed.). Hitlers Weisungen für die Kriegführung 1939-1945 (Frankfurt am Main: Bernard & Graefe Verlag für Wehrwesen, 1962).

Irving, David. The Trail of the Fox (New York: E.P. Dutton, 1977).

Keegan, John. Six Armies in Normandy (New York: The Viking Press, 1982).

Klietmann, Dr. K.G. Die Waffen-SS - eine Dokumentation (Osnabrück: Verlag "Der Freiwillige," 1965).

Klönne, Dr. Arno. Hitlerjugend. Die Jugend und ihre Organisation im Dritten Reich (Hannover: Norddeutsche Verlagsanstalt, 1956).

Klose, Werner, Generation im Gleichschritt (Hamburg: Gerhard Stalling Verlag, 1964).

Koch, H.W. The Hitler Youth. Origins and Development 1922-45 (London: MacDonald and Jane's, 1975).

Krätschmer, Ernst-Günther. Ritterkreuzträger der Waffen-SS (Göttingen: Plesse Verlag, 1957).

Kurowski, Franz. Die Panzer Lehr Division. Die grösste deutsche Panzer Division und ihre Aufgabe: die Invasion zerschlagen - die Ardennenschlacht entscheiden (Bad Nauheim: Podzun Verlag, 1964).

Lehmann, Rudolf. Die Leibstandarte. 3 Bd. (Osnabrück: Munin Verlag GmbH, 1977-82).

Lewin, Ronald. Montgomery as Military Commander (London: B.T. Batsford, Ltd., 1971).

MacDonald, B.J.S. The Trial of Kurt Meyer (Clarke, Irwin and Company, Ltd., 1954).

Martin, Lieutenant-General H.G. The History of the Fifteenth Scottish Division, 1939-1945 (Edinburgh and London: William Blackwood & Sons, 1948).

McKee, Alexander. Last Round Against Rommel: Battle of the Normandy Beachhead (New York: The New American Library, Inc., 1966).

Meyer, Hubert. Kriegsgeschichte der 12.SS-Panzerdivision "Hitlerjugend." 2 Bd. (Osnabrück: Munin Verlag GmbH, 1982).

Meyer, Kurt. Grenadiere (München-Lochhausen: Schild Verlag, 1956).

Montgomery, Field Marshal Viscount. The Memoirs of Field-Marshal The Viscount Montgomery of Alamein, K.G. (New York: The World Publishing Company, 1958).

Müller-Hillebrand, Burkhart. Das Heer 1933-1945. Entwicklung des organisatorischen Aufbaues. Bd. III: Der Zweifrontenkrieg (Frankfurt am Main: Verlag E.S. Mittler und Sohn, 1969).

Ritgen, Helmut. Die Geschichte der Panzer-Lehr-Division im Westen, 1944-1945 (Stuttgart: Motorbuch Verlag, 1979).

Saunders, Hilary St. George. The Fight is Won. The Royal Air Force 1939-1945 (London: Her Majesty's Stationery Office, 1954).

Scarfe, Norman. Assault Division. A History of the 3rd Division from the Invasion of Normandy to the Surrender of Germany (London: 1947).

Scheibert, Horst; Elfrath, Ulrich. Panzer in Russland. Die deutschen gepanzerten Verbände im Russland-Feldzug 1941-1944 (Dorheim: Podzun Verlag, 1971).

Schneider, Jost W. Verleihung Genehmigt! Eine Bild-und Dokumentargeschichte der Waffen-SS und Polizei, 1940-1945 (San Jose: Bender Publishing, 1977).

Stacey, Colonel C.P. The Victory Campaign, The Operations in North-West Europe. 1944-1945. Official History of the Canadian Army in the Second World War: Volume III (Ottawa: The Queen's Printer and Controller of Stationery, 1960).

Stachura, Peter. The German Youth Movement 1900-1945: An Interpretive and Documentary History (New York; St. Martin's Press, 1981).

Stein, George H. The Waffen SS. Hitler's Elite Guard at War 1939-1945 (Ithaca, New York: Cornell University Press, 1966).

Tessin, Georg. Verbände und Truppen der deutschen Wehrmacht und Waffen-SS im Zweiten Weltkrieg 1939-1945. 2. Band (Osnabrück: Biblio Verlag, 1975).

Tieke, Wilhelm. Im Feuersturm letzter Kriegsjahre (Osnabrück: Munin Verlag GmbH, 1975).

Thompson, Kenneth. H.M.S. "Rodney" at War (London: Hollis and Carter, 1946).

Vokes, Major-General Chris (with John P. Maclean). Vokes, My Story (Ottawa: Gallery Books).

Wegner, Bernd. Hitlers Politische Soldaten: Die Waffen-SS 1933-1945 (Paderborn: Ferdinand Schoningh, 1982).

Weingartner, James J. Hitler's Guard. The Story of the Leibstandarte SS Adolf Hitler. 1933-1945 (London: Southern Illinois University Press, 1974).

Wilmont, Chester. The Struggle for Europe (New York: Harper and Row, 1952).

b. articles

Guderian, Heinz G. (Jr.). "Noch einmal: Zu: Friedrich Ruge, Rommel und die Invasion." In: Europäische Wehrkunde 2/80.

Jaggi, Major O. "Die Auswirkungen der allierten Luftüberlegenheit auf die deutsche Abwehr." In: Allgemeine Schweizerische Militärzeitschrift. Jg.124. H.5. 1958.

Meitzel, Bernhard-Georg. "Caen-Falaise." In: The Canadian Army Journal. Vol. 4. April-June, 1950.

Showalter, Dennis E. "The Bundeswehr of the Federal Republic of Germany." In: The Defense of Western Europe. Edited by Lewis H. Gann (London & Sydney: Croom Helm Ltd., 1987).

Weingartner, James, J. "Sepp Dietrich, Heinrich Himmler, and the Leibstandarte SS Adolf Hitler, 1933-1938." In: Journal of Central European History. Vol. 1. Number 3. September 1968.

III. Correspondence and Interviews

a. German

Berner, Heinz	6./II./12.SS Pz.Rgt.
Besuden, Hermann	12.SS Pz.Div.
Beyer, Kurt	7./II./25.SS Pz.Gren.Rgt.
Damsch, Werner	Leibstandarte Adolf Hitler
Dettmann, Hans	4./I./25.SS Pz.Gren.Rgt.
Fischer, Wilhelm	3./I./12.SS Pz.Rgt.
Gotha, Günther	3./I./12.SS Pz.Rgt.
Grabher-Meyer, Rudolf	4./I./25.SS Pz.Gren.Rgt.
Gurowski, Günther	4./I./25.SS Pz.Gren.Rgt.
Haase, Ernst	9./II./12.SS Pz.Rgt.
Harder, Hans	12.SS Pz.Div.
Hartmann, Hans	5./II./12.SS Pz.Art.Rgt.
Heindl, Leopold	3./I./12.SS Pz.Rgt.
Josupeit, Werner	8./II./2.SS Pz.Gren.Rgt. (LAH)
Kändler, Dr. Willi	5./II./12.SS Pz.Rgt.
Klein, Rudolf	Nachschubtruppe, 12.SS Pz.Div.
Korte, Heinz	3./I./12.SS Pz.Rgt.
Kretzschmar, Willy	5./II./12.SS Pz.Rgt.
Kucklach, Frank	4./I./25.SS Pz.Gren.Rgt.
Lincke, Wolfgang	Panzeraufklärungszug, 12.SS Pz.Rgt.
Meyer, Hubert	Ia, 12.SS Pz.Div.
Morawetz, Alois	3./I./12.SS Pz.Rgt.
Müller, Heinz	9./II./12.SS Pz.Rgt.
Poch, Hellmuth	I-Staffel/I./12.SS Pz.Rgt.
Sallach, Helmut	7./II./26.SS Pz.Gren.Rgt.
Siegel, Hans	8./II./12.SS Pz.Rgt.
Springer, Heinrich	Div.Stab.12.SS Pz.Div.
Stark, Karl	5./II./12.SS Pz.Rgt.
Witt, Peter	(son of Fritz Witt)

b. Allied

Adair, Alex	Queen's Own Rifles of Canada
Bolt, Vincent	3rd Anti-Tank Regiment
Brabant, Larry	Royal Winnipeg Rifles

[1]All Allied correspondents served with units of the 3rd Canadian Infantry Division or with the 6th Canadian Armored Regiment (2nd Canadian Armored Brigade); the one exception is Mr. Webb.

Daigle, Joseph	North Shore (New Brunswick) Regiment
Dodds, A.O.	6th Canadian Armored Regiment
Lacouvee, George	3rd Anti-Tank Regiment
Paisley, J.W.	6th Canadian Armored Regiment
Raymond, Dixon	Cameron Highlanders of Ottawa
Shearer, John	12th Field Regiment, RCA
Webb, Sydney	7th Battalion Duke of Wellington's Regiment (49th British Infantry Division)

INDEX OF NAMES

Hausser, SS-Obergruppenführer Paul, 218
Hein, HJ-Oberbannführer Gerhard, 21
Herff, SS-Obergruppenführer Maximilian von, 27, 30
Heydrich, SS-Obergruppenführer Reinhard, 48
Himmler, Reichsführer SS Heinrich, 12, 24-26, 30, 33-35, 38, 44, 46-47, 59
Hitler, Adolf, 11-12, 14-15, 17-18, 21, 26-27, 32-34, 38, 41-47, 49, 51, 53, 55-56, 58-59, 71-72, 75, 86-89, 94, 110-111, 196-97, 209, 220, 242
Hube, General Hans, 80

Jesionek, SS-Sturmmann Jan, 181-82
Jodl, General Alfred, 109, 111
Jürs, SS-Brigadeführer, 26
Jüttner, SS-Obergruppenführer Hans, 27, 31, 35, 38, 60

Keitel, Field Marshal Wilhelm, 19
Kleist, Colonel-General Ewald von, 50, 53, 55
Kluge, Field Marshal Günther von, 229-30
Kraas, SS-Standartenführer Hugo, 239
Krause, SS-Sturmbannführer Bernhard, 156
Kugler, SS-Obersturmführer Karl, 61

Lachèvre, Daniel, 191
Lüdemann, Captain, 172, 175

MacDonald, Lieutenant-Colonel, B.J.S., 190, 192
Manstein, General Erich von, 55
Marcks, General Erich, 84, 103-104, 110-111, 122
Meitzel, SS-Obersturmführer Bernhard-Georg, 124, 163
Meyer, SS-Sturmbannführer Hubert, 80, 84-85, 100, 108, 168, 176, 236
Meyer, SS-Brigadeführer Kurt, 48-53, 71-73, 76, 101, 111, 117, 119-24, 127-30, 133-34, 137-39, 141, 143-46, 150-51, 162-68, 170-73, 181-82, 185-92, 198, 205, 207-208, 213, 216-17, 222, 224, 229, 232, 235
Milius, SS-Obersturmbannführer Karl-Heinz, 134, 137-38, 183, 185
Möckel, Helmut, 24-27
Mohnke, SS-Obersturmbannführer Wilhelm, 71, 74, 130, 146, 152-53, 156, 158, 162, 167-68, 177, 185-86, 200
Montgomery, Field Marshal Bernard, 148-49, 169, 208-10, 214, 220-21, 223, 226
Morawetz, SS-Unterscharführer Alois, 172-73
Müller, SS-Sturmbannführer Siegfried, 177, 186, 211

Olboeter, SS-Sturmbannführer Erich, 158

Patton, General George S., 197, 234
Paulus, Field Marshal Friedrich, 11
Pemsel, Major-General Max, 101, 104, 110

*   *   *